W. E. Gladstone

Rome and the Newest Fashions in Religion

W. E. Gladstone

Rome and the Newest Fashions in Religion

ISBN/EAN: 9783743324800

Manufactured in Europe, USA, Canada, Australia, Japa

Cover: Foto ©ninafisch / pixelio.de

Manufactured and distributed by brebook publishing software (www.brebook.com)

W. E. Gladstone

Rome and the Newest Fashions in Religion

ROME

AND

THE NEWEST FASHIONS IN RELIGION.

THREE TRACTS.

THE VATICAN DECREES.—VATICANISM.—
SPEECHES OF THE POPE.

BY THE
RIGHT HON. W. E. GLADSTONE, M.P.

COLLECTED EDITION, WITH A PREFACE.

LONDON:
JOHN MURRAY, ALBEMARLE STREET.
1875.

LONDON: PRINTED BY WILLIAM CLOWES AND SONS, STAMFORD STREET
AND CHARING CROSS.

PREFACE.

If there has ever been, and if there still be, a question reaching far into the future, it is the question of Church Power, and of its monstrous exaggeration into Papal Power, such as it has now for the first time been accepted by the Latin Church in its corporate capacity; amidst the cold indifference or half-suppressed, ineffectual, murmurs of a multitude of its members, the brave and wise resistance of a portion as yet far smaller, and the apathy, amazement, or indignation of the world.

The vast moment and practical character of the subject form my excuse for republishing together the two Tracts respectively entitled 'A Political Expostulation' and 'Vaticanism,' and for adding to them, with the proper sanction, an article from the 'Quarterly Review' of January on the Speeches of Pope Pius IX. It has not been agreeable to deal so pointedly, as in this article, with any personal performances of the very aged and so widely venerated Pontiff. But those performances have been such as to open a new, strange and startling chapter of the general subject, and they require accordingly the searching notice of the world.

The interest attaching to the discussion has led to reprinting the Tracts in America and Australia, and to their translation into various languages. I regret, however, to find that, even at a moment when Ultramontanism bitterly complains of suffering restraint in certain countries, it has been thought worth while, where some, I hope untruly, suppose that system possesses an influence over the existing civil authority, to restrain the circulation of these not very formidable works. The gentleman who translated 'The Vatican Decrees' into French, apprises me that, on the part of the Government of France, the Duc de Decazes has refused to allow the free sale of the Translation at the railway bookstalls, on the public highways, and in the kiosks. I hope that no similar restraint will be placed on the circulation of the recent translation into French of Monsignor Nardi's Italian answer to my work.

Upon surveying the immediate field of contest, I am thankful to record that many noble protests against a portentous mischief have been called forth. There has also been exhibited, in bad logic but in good faith, much halting at points situate between certain premisses and the undeniably just conclusion from them. Some degree of public attention has, I trust, been drawn not only to the tendency, but to the design, of Vaticanism to disturb civil society; and to proceed, when it may be requisite and practicable, to the issue of blood for the accomplishment of its aims. It has also been shown distinctly to the world, that a pretended Article of the Christian

Faith, namely the Decree of 1870 on Infallibility, may be denied with impunity in the Roman Church. The theological position of that church, brought about by its own suicidal acts, has been sketched with great learning and ability, in the work entitled 'Results of the Expostulation, by Umbra Oxoniensis.' And Italy, which holds a position of the utmost importance in relation to this subject, appears to become increasingly aware that she cannot wisely treat the questions of Church and religion by the method of simple neglect.

The adverse comments on 'Vaticanism' have not been such as seem to call on me for specific notice. I shall, however, take advantage of this preface to offer a few corroborative remarks and statements.

I. The intention of those, who rule the ostensible rulers of the Roman Church, to disturb civil society will doubtless be developed in a variety of forms, as circumstances and seasons may serve, but at present it is nowhere more conspicuous than in regard to the law of marriage. In this intricate subject many doubtful questions may arise; but there can be no doubt as to the shameful outrages on morality and decency which are commended in the works of Perrone, and of which we have recently had within our own borders a signal example. I will very briefly sketch the leading facts of the case I refer to, but without indicating names, dates, or places, as they are not required for my purpose.

More than thirty years ago, X, a male British

subject, was married to Y, in a foreign country, but under the provisions of an Act of Parliament, by the chaplain of the British Legation, in the house and in the presence of the British Minister. Both professed the religion of the English Church. They lived together for more than a quarter of a century; and a family, the issue of the marriage, grew up to maturity.

In the later years of this union the husband formed an adulterous connection with a foreign woman. After a period of much patience on the part of the wife, a separation took place. In a short time, he joined the Church of Rome; and, about four years ago, under the authority of certain Roman Ecclesiastics, and in an English Roman Catholic chapel, he went through the form of marriage with his partner in guilt. He was subsequently informed by a higher functionary, that he must obtain a judgment from Rome. He made application accordingly; and the judgment given was that the original marriage was null, and that the second so-called marriage, so far as appeared,* was valid.

In the meantime, the injured wife had applied to a court for the judicial establishment of her position. She was duly declared to be the lawful wife, and the bigamous husband admitted that she was such according to British law.

Within the jurisdiction of that law, he had taken his paramour to his paternal estate in ——shire,

---

* "*Dummodo nullum aliud obstet canonicum impedimentum.*"

and had designated and caused her to be addressed there as his lawful wife, to the great scandal of the neighbours, who were well acquainted with the true wife. He likewise entered his spurious offspring, born since the pretended marriage, as legitimate; and a witness of position and character on the spot asserts that the woman received visits, and the most marked and open countenance, at the husband's seat, from Roman Catholic Priests and Sisters of Charity.

There is not in this statement one word beyond dry fact. It might have been much enlarged; but it is indeed a statement of which no epithets could heighten the significance. The Judgment from Rome, to which I have referred, has lately been published textually in a leading German paper. And notice was taken in a London print, a considerable time back, of the judicial proceeding I have mentioned, which included the main facts; but simply as a piece of law intelligence. Except in two articles of the 'Saturday Review,' this gross outrage, which is also a heavy crime, has not been thought worthy of notice by the Newspaper Press. But that to which it is my duty to point is, that the act has had the full countenance and approval of the highest authorities of the Papal Church.

If there be those who doubt the allegations I have made, I have only to state that Cardinal Manning is sufficiently cognisant of the case, and will best know whether he can contradict them. Other Roman Prelates are, I believe, in the same condition; but I do not wish unnecessarily to localise or identify the narrative.

To such a statement as this it is but a feeble postscript to add, that in July 1874 the same Roman authority, acting on behalf of the Pope, and in a rescript addressed to the Archbishop of Munich, authorised a person therein named to proceed to a new marriage after a divorce from a first wife previously obtained; not, of course, because the divorce was valid, but because the original marriage, being a Protestant marriage at Munich, was void. I might refer to other cases; not as parallel to that which I have given at some length, but simply as auxiliary proofs of the intention of the Roman Church, wherever she thinks it may be safely ventured, to trample the law under foot. Even from so remote a quarter as one of the South Sea Islands, we are informed by Mr. Herbert Meade* of the complaint of a Baptist missionary, that his married converts are tempted to become Romish proselytes, by the promise to give them fresh wives if they then desire it.

And yet a London newspaper, deemed to be in the first ranks of enlightened civilisation, has, within the last few weeks, written as follows on the discussions respecting Vaticanism :—

"Such discussions are not unsuited to beguile a vacant hour; it is only when they are forced upon us as involving issues of vital moment, and requiring the immediate attention of the statesman and of every Englishman who desires to save his

---

* 'A Ride through New Zealand,' &c., p. 201. Murray, 1870.

country from ruin, that we deprecate the mistaken zeal which exalts them to a factitious importance."

The matter thus relegated into the category of insignificance, and reserved for a vacant hour, amounts to no more than I will now describe. The Latin Church has probably a hundred and eighty millions of nominal adherents; a clergy counted by hundreds of thousands; a thousand Bishops, and the Pope at their head. Nearly the entire hierarchical power in this great communion, together with a faction everywhere spread, and everywhere active, among its laity, are now deliberately set upon a design distinguished by the following characteristics. Internally, it aims at the total destruction of right. Not of right as opposed to wrong, but of right as opposed to arbitrary will. Such right there shall be none, if the conspiracy succeeds, in the Bishops against the Pope, in the clergy against the Bishops or the Pope, in the laity against any of the three. Externally, it maintains the right and duty of the spiritualty, thus organised, to override at will, in respect of right and wrong, the entire action of the civil power; and likewise to employ force, as and when it may think fit, for the fulfilment of its purposes. Nowhere, perhaps, has the design been so succinctly described as in the remarkable work entitled *Otto Mesi a Roma* (p. 194): it is a design to establish "absolutism of the Church, and absolutism in the Church."

II. To what has been written in the pages I now reprint, with respect to the intention of proceeding to blood upon the first suitable occasion, I will only add the very explicit declaration of Archbishop (now Cardinal) Manning, at the meeting of the League of Saint Sebastian, on the 20th of January, 1874 :—

"Now, when the nations of Europe have revolted, and when they have dethroned, as far as men can dethrone, the Vicar of Jesus Christ, and when they have made the usurpation of the Holy City a part of international law—when all this has been done, there is only one solution of the difficulty—a solution I fear impending, and that is the terrible scourge of continental war: a war, which will exceed the horrors of any of the wars of the first Empire. I do not see how this can be averted. And it is my firm conviction that, in spite of all obstacles, the Vicar of Jesus Christ will be put again in his own rightful place." *

This speech was delivered some months before the attention of the British public had been specially invited to the plans of the Conspiracy. The idea of force is not new. It took effect in the French occupation of Rome from 1849 to 1866, and of Civita Vecchia at a still later time. At present, and for the moment, we have words of a milder tone; and invitations to Italy to destroy that national unity, which she has wrought out with so much suffering, and after so many generations of depression. At the proper time, the more outspoken and more sanguinary strain will of course be resumed.

III. It has long been customary to quote the case of Maryland, in proof that, more than two centuries ago, the Roman Catholic Church, where power was in its hands, could use it for the purposes of tolera-

* League of St. Sebastian. Report of the Council, 1874, p. 24.

tion. Archbishop Manning has repeated the boast, and with very large exaggeration.

I have already shown,* from Bancroft's History, that in the case of Maryland there was no question of a merciful use of power towards others, but simply of a wise and defensive prudence with respect to themselves: that is to say, so far as the tolerant legislation of the colony was the work of Roman Catholics. But it does not appear to have been their work. By the fourth article of the Charter, we find that no church could be consecrated there except according to the laws of the Church at home. The tenth article guaranteed to the colonists generally "all privileges, franchises, and liberties of this our kingdom of England."† It was in 1649 that the Maryland Act of Toleration was passed; which, however, prescribed the punishment of death for any one who denied the Trinity. Of the small legislative body which passed it, two-thirds appear to have been Protestant, the recorded numbers being sixteen and eight respectively.‡ The colony was open to the immigration of Puritans and all Protestants, and any permanent and successful oppression by a handful of Roman Catholics was altogether impossible. But the Colonial Act seems to have been an echo of the order of the House of Commons at home, on the 27th of

---

* 'Vaticanism,' p. 128.

† 'Maryland Toleration.' By Rev. Ethan Allen. Baltimore, 1855, pp. 12, 13.

‡ 'Maryland not a Roman Catholic Colony.' By E. D. N. Minneapolis, 1875, p. 7.

October, 1645, that the inhabitants of the Summer Islands, and such others as shall join themselves to them, " shall without any molestation or trouble have and enjoy the liberty of their consciences in matters of God's worship; and of a British Ordinance* of 1647. The writer, whom I quote,† ascribes the Resolution of the Commons to the entreaties of the friends of Williams, the Independent, of Rhode Island, and of Copeland, a learned Episcopal divine, who shared his views of toleration.

Upon the whole, then, the picture of Maryland legislation is a gratifying one; but the historic theory which assigns the credit of it to the Roman Church has little foundation in fact.

W. E. G.

London, *July* 7, 1875.

---

* An Ordinance, not in Scobell's collection, is mentioned in Rushworth, vol. vii., pp. 834, 840, 841. I cannot say whether this is the Ordinance intended by the American writer. Probably not, for it excepts Papists and Churchmen, and it does not name the plantations.

† 'Maryland not a Roman Catholic Colony.' By E. D. N. Minneapolis, 1875, p. 4. See also Thornton's Historical Relation of New England to the English Commonwealth, 1874, p. 22.

THE VATICAN DECREES

IN THEIR BEARING ON

CIVIL ALLEGIANCE:

A POLITICAL EXPOSTULATION.

Published Nov. 7, 1874.

CONTENTS.

I. THE OCCASION AND SCOPE OF THIS TRACT xvii
   Four Propositions. Are they True?

II. THE FIRST AND FOURTH PROPOSITIONS .. xxiv
   1. "That Rome has substituted for the proud boast of 'semper eadem' a policy of violence and change in faith."
   4. "That she has equally repudiated modern thought and ancient history."

III. THE SECOND PROPOSITION xxvii
   "That she has refurbished, and paraded anew, every rusty tool she was thought to have disused."

IV. THE THIRD PROPOSITION xxxii
   "That Rome requires a convert, who now joins her, to forfeit his moral and mental freedom, and to place his loyalty and civil duty at the mercy of another."

V. BEING TRUE, ARE THE PROPOSITIONS MATERIAL? lvii

VI. BEING TRUE AND MATERIAL, WERE THE PROPOSITIONS PROPER TO BE SET FORTH BY THE PRESENT WRITER? .. lxvi

VII. ON THE HOME POLICY OF THE FUTURE .. lxxi

APPENDICES lxxvii

THE VATICAN DECREES

IN THEIR BEARING ON

CIVIL ALLEGIANCE.

I. THE OCCASION AND SCOPE OF THIS TRACT.

IN the prosecution of a purpose not polemical but pacific, I have been led to employ words which belong, more or less, to the region of religious controversy; and which, though they were themselves few, seem to require, from the various feelings they have aroused, that I should carefully define, elucidate, and defend them. The task is not of a kind agreeable to me; but I proceed to perform it.

Among the causes, which have tended to disturb and perplex the public mind in the consideration of our own religious difficulties, one has been a certain alarm at the aggressive activity and imagined growth of the Roman Church in this country. All are aware of our susceptibility on this side; and it was not, I think, improper for one who desires to remove everything that can interfere with a calm and judicial temper, and who believes the alarm to be groundless, to state, pointedly though briefly, some reasons for that belief.

Accordingly I did not scruple to use the following language, in a paper inserted in the number of the 'Contemporary Review' for the month of October. I was speaking of "the question whether a handful of the clergy are or are not engaged in an utterly hopeless and visionary effort to Romanise the Church and people of England."

"At no time since the bloody reign of Mary has such a scheme been possible. But if it had been possible in the seventeenth or eighteenth centuries, it would still have become impossible in the nineteenth: when Rome has substituted for the proud boast of *semper eadem* a policy of violence and change in faith; when she has refurbished, and paraded anew, every rusty tool she was fondly thought to have disused; when no one can become her convert without renouncing his moral and mental freedom, and placing his civil loyalty and duty at the mercy of another; and when she has equally repudiated modern thought and ancient history."[*]

Had I been, when I wrote this passage, as I now am, addressing myself in considerable measure to my Roman Catholic fellow-countrymen, I should have striven to avoid the seeming roughness of some of these expressions; but as the question is now about their substance, from which I am not in any particular disposed to recede, any attempt to recast their general form would probably mislead. I proceed, then, to deal with them on their merits.

---

[*] 'Contemporary Review,' Oct. 1874, p. 674.

More than one friend of mine, among those who have been led to join the Roman Catholic communion, has made this passage the subject, more or less, of expostulation. Now, in my opinion, the assertions which it makes are, as coming from a layman who has spent most and the best years of his life in the observation and practice of politics, not aggressive but defensive.

It is neither the abettors of the Papal Chair, nor any one who, however far from being an abettor of the Papal Chair, actually writes from a Papal point of view, that has a right to remonstrate with the world at large; but it is the world at large, on the contrary, that has the fullest right to remonstrate, first with His Holiness, secondly with those who share his proceedings, thirdly even with such as passively allow and accept them.

I therefore, as one of the world at large, propose to expostulate in my turn. I shall strive to show to such of my Roman Catholic fellow-subjects as may kindly give me a hearing that, after the singular steps which the authorities of their Church have in these last years thought fit to take, the people of this country, who fully believe in their loyalty, are entitled, on purely civil grounds, to expect from them some declaration or manifestation of opinion, in reply to that ecclesiastical party in their Church who have laid down, in their name, principles adverse to the purity and integrity of civil allegiance.

Undoubtedly my allegations are of great breadth. Such broad allegations require a broad and a deep foundation. The first question which they raise is, Are they, as to the material part of them, true? But even their truth might not suffice to show that their publication was opportune. The second question, then, which they raise is, Are they, for any practical purpose, material? And there is yet a third, though a minor, question, which arises out of the propositions in connection with their authorship, Were they suitable to be set forth by the present writer?

To these three questions I will now set myself to reply. And the matter of my reply will, as I conceive, constitute and convey an appeal to the understandings of my Roman Catholic fellow-countrymen, which I trust that, at the least, some among them may deem not altogether unworthy of their consideration.

From the language used by some of the organs of Roman Catholic opinion, it is, I am afraid, plain that in some quarters they have given deep offence. Displeasure, indignation, even fury, might be said to mark the language which in the heat of the moment has been expressed here and there. They have been hastily treated as an attack made upon Roman Catholics generally, nay, as an insult offered them. It is obvious to reply, that of Roman Catholics generally they state nothing. Together with a reference to " converts," of which I shall say more, they constitute generally a free and strong animadversion on the conduct of the Papal Chair, and of its advisers and abettors. If I am told that he who animadverts upon these assails thereby, or insults, Roman Catholics at large, who do not choose their ecclesiastical rulers, and are not recognised as having any voice in the government of their Church, I cannot be bound by or accept a proposition which seems to me to be so little in accordance with reason.

Before all things, however, I should desire it to be understood that, in the remarks now offered, I desire to eschew not only religious bigotry, but likewise theological controversy. Indeed, with theology, except in its civil bearing, with theology as such, I have here nothing whatever to do. But it is the peculiarity of Roman theology that, by thrusting itself into the temporal domain, it naturally, and even necessarily, comes to be a frequent theme of political discussion. To quiet-minded Roman Catholics, it must be a subject of infinite annoyance, that their religion is, on this ground more than any other, the subject of criticism; more than any other, the occasion of conflicts with the State and of civil disquietude. I feel sincerely how much hardship their case entails. But this hardship is brought upon them altogether by the conduct of the authorities of their own Church. Why did theology enter so largely into the debates of Parliament on Roman Catholic Emancipation? Certainly not because our statesmen and debaters of fifty years ago had an abstract love of such controversies, but because it was extensively believed that the Pope of Rome had been and was a trespasser upon ground which belonged to the civil authority, and that he affected to determine by spiritual prerogative questions of the civil sphere. This fact, if fact it be, and not the truth or falsehood, the reasonableness or unreasonableness, of any article of purely religious belief, is the whole and sole cause of the mischief. To this fact, and to this fact alone, my language is referable: but for this fact, it would have been neither my duty nor my desire to use it. All other Christian bodies are content with freedom in their own religious domain. Orientals, Lutherans, Calvinists, Presbyterians, Episcopalians, Nonconformists, one and all, in the present day, contentedly and thankfully accept the benefits of civil order; never pretend that the State is not its own master; make no religious claims to temporal possessions or advantages; and, consequently, never are in perilous collision with the State. Nay more, even so I believe it is with the mass of Roman Catholics individually. But not so with the leaders of their Church, or with those who take pride in following the leaders. Indeed, this has been made matter of boast :—

"There is not another Church so called" (than the Roman), "nor any community professing to be a Church, which does not submit, or obey, or hold its peace, when the civil governors of the world command."—'The Present Crisis of the Holy See,' by H. E. Manning, D.D. London, 1861, p. 75.

The Rome of the Middle Ages claimed universal monarchy. The modern Church of Rome has abandoned nothing, retracted nothing. Is that all? Far from it. By condemning (as will be seen) those who, like Bishop Doyle in 1826,* charge the mediæval Popes with aggression, she unconditionally,

---

* Lords' Committee, March 18, 1826. Report, p. 190.

even if covertly, maintains what the mediæval Popes maintained. But even this is not the worst. The worst by far is that whereas, in the national Churches and communities of the Middle Ages, there was a brisk, vigorous, and constant opposition to these outrageous claims, an opposition which stoutly asserted its own orthodoxy, which always caused itself to be respected, and which even sometimes gained the upper hand; now, in this nineteenth century of ours, and while it is growing old, this same opposition has been put out of court, and judicially extinguished within the Papal Church, by the recent decrees of the Vatican. And it is impossible for persons accepting those decrees justly to complain, when such documents are subjected in good faith to a strict examination as respects their compatibility with civil right and the obedience of subjects.

In defending my language, I shall carefully mark its limits. But all defence is reassertion, which properly requires a deliberate reconsideration; and no man who thus reconsiders should scruple, if he find so much as a word that may convey a false impression, to amend it. Exactness in stating truth according to the measure of our intelligence, is an indispensable condition of justice, and of a title to be heard.

My propositions, then, as they stood, are these:—

1. That "Rome has substituted for the proud boast of *semper eadem*, a policy of violence and change in faith."

2. That she has refurbished and paraded anew

every rusty tool she was fondly thought to have disused.

3. That no one can now become her convert without renouncing his moral and mental freedom, and placing his civil loyalty and duty at the mercy of another.

4. That she ("Rome") has equally repudiated modern thought and ancient history.

II. The First and the Fourth Propositions.

Of the first and fourth of these propositions I shall dispose rather summarily, as they appear to belong to the theological domain. They refer to a fact, and they record an opinion. One fact to which they refer is this: that, in days within my memory, the constant, favourite, and imposing argument of Roman controversialists was the unbroken and absolute identity in belief of the Roman Church from the days of our Saviour until now. No one, who has at all followed the course of this literature during the last forty years, can fail to be sensible of the change in its present tenour. More and more have the assertions of continuous uniformity of doctrine receded into scarcely penetrable shadow. More and more have another series of assertions, of a living authority, ever ready to open, adopt, and shape Christian doctrine according to the times, taken their place. Without discussing the abstract compatibility of these lines of argument, I note two of the immense practical differences between them. In the first, the office claimed by the Church is principally that of a witness to facts;* in the second, principally that of a judge, if not a revealer, of doctrine. In the first, the processes which the Church undertakes are subject to a constant challenge and appeal to history; in the second, no amount of historical testimony can avail against the unmeasured power of the theory of development. Most important, most pregnant considerations, these, at least for two classes of persons: for those who think that exaggerated doctrines of Church power are among the real and serious dangers of the age; and for those who think that against all forms, both of superstition and of unbelief, one main preservative is to be found in maintaining the truth and authority of history, and the inestimable value of the historic spirit.

So much for the fact; as for the opinion, that the recent Papal decrees are at war with modern thought, and that, purporting to enlarge the necessary creed of Christendom, they involve a violent breach with history, this is a matter unfit for me to discuss, as it is a question of Divinity; but not unfit for me to have mentioned in my article; since the opinion

---

* Thus Dryden, on the Council of Nice; evidently describing the Roman Catholic view prevalent in his own time:—

> "The good old Bishops took a simpler way:
> Each asked but *what he heard his father say*,
> Or *how he was instructed in his youth;*
> And by tradition's force upheld the truth."
> *The Hind and the Panther*, Part II.

given there is the opinion of those with whom I was endeavouring to reason, namely, the great majority of the British public.

If it is thought that the word violence was open to exception, I regret I cannot give it up. The justification of the ancient definitions of the Church, which have endured the storms of 1500 years, was to be found in this, that they were not arbitrary or wilful, but that they wholly sprang from, and related to theories rampant at the time, and regarded as menacing to Christian belief. Even the Canons of the Council of Trent have in the main this amount, apart from their matter, of presumptive warrant. But the decrees of the present perilous Pontificate have been passed to favour and precipitate prevailing currents of opinion in the ecclesiastical world of Rome. The growth of what is often termed among Protestants Mariolatry, and of belief in Papal Infallibility, was notoriously advancing, but it seems not fast enough to satisfy the dominant party. To aim the deadly blows of 1854* and 1870 at the old historic, scientific, and moderate school, was surely an act of violence; and with this censure the proceeding of 1870 has actually been visited by the first living theologian now within the Roman Communion, I mean, Dr. John Henry Newman; who has used these significant words, among others: " Why should an aggressive and insolent faction be allowed to make

---

* Decree of the Immaculate Conception.

the heart of the just sad, whom the Lord hath not made sorrowful?" *

III. The Second Proposition.

I take next my second Proposition: that Rome has refurbished, and paraded anew, every rusty tool she was fondly thought to have disused.

Is this then a fact, or is it not?

I must assume that it is denied; and therefore I cannot wholly pass by the work of proof. But I will state in the fewest possible words, and with references, a few propositions, all the holders of which have been *condemned* by the See of Rome during my own generation, and especially within the last twelve or fifteen years. And, in order that I may do nothing towards importing passion into what is matter of pure argument, I will avoid citing any of the fearfully energetic epithets in which the condemnations are sometimes clothed.

1. Those who maintain the Liberty of the Press. Encyclical Letter of Pope Gregory XVI., in 1831: and of Pope Pius IX., in 1864.

2. Or the liberty of conscience and of worship. Encyclical of Pius IX., December 8, 1864.

3. Or the liberty of speech. 'Syllabus' of December 8, 1864. Prop. lxxix. Encyclical of Pope Pius IX., December 8, 1864.

4. Or who contend that Papal judgments and

---

* See the remarkable Letter of Dr. Newman to Bishop Ullathorne, in the 'Guardian' of April 6, 1870.

decrees may, without sin, be disobeyed, or differed from, unless they treat of the rules (*dogmata*) of faith or morals. Ibid.

5. Or who assign to the State the power of defining the civil rights (*jura*) and province of the Church. 'Syllabus' of Pope Pius IX., December 8, 1864. Ibid. Prop. xix.

6. Or who hold that Roman Pontiffs and Ecumenical Councils have transgressed the limits of their power, and usurped the rights of princes. Ibid. Prop. xxiii.

(*It must be borne in mind, that " Ecumenical Councils" here mean Councils of the Roman obedience, not recognised by the rest of the Church. The Councils of the early and united Church did not interfere with the jurisdiction of the civil power.*)

7. Or that the Church may not employ force. (*Ecclesia vis inferendæ potestatem non habet.*) 'Syllabus,' Prop. xxiv.

8. Or that power, not inherent in the office of the Episcopate, but granted to it by the civil authority, may be withdrawn from it at the discretion of that authority. Ibid. Prop. xxv.

9. Or that the civil immunity (*immunitas*) of the Church and its ministers, depends upon civil right. Ibid. Prop. xxx.

10. Or that in the conflict of laws civil and ecclesiastical, the civil law should prevail. Ibid. Prop. xlii.

11. Or that any method of instruction of youth, solely secular, may be approved. Ibid. Prop. xlviii.

12. Or that knowledge of things philosophical and civil, may and should decline to be guided by Divine and *Ecclesiastical* authority. Ibid. Prop. lvii.

13. Or that marriage is not in its essence a Sacrament. Ibid. Prop. lxvi.

14. Or that marriage, not sacramentally contracted,* (*si sacramentum excludatur*) has a binding force. Ibid. Prop. lxxiii.

15. Or that the abolition of the Temporal Power of the Popedom would be highly advantageous to the Church. Ibid. Prop. lxxvi. Also lxx.

16. Or that any other religion than the Roman religion may be established by a State. Ibid. Prop. lxxvii.

17. Or that in " Countries called Catholic," the free exercise of other religions may laudably be allowed. 'Syllabus,' Prop. lxxviii.

18. Or that the Roman Pontiff ought to come to terms with progress, liberalism, and modern civilization. Ibid. Prop. lxxx.†

This list is now perhaps sufficiently extended, although I have as yet not touched the decrees of 1870. But, before quitting it, I must offer three observations on what it contains.

---

* [Note inserted in 79th thousand on receiving Mr. Coleridge's Sermon : " My rendering is disputed ; and the passage is obscure.—W. E. G. Dec. 2, 1874." It will be seen from *inf.* 'Vaticanism,' pp. 26-30, that my caution was supererogatory ; the propositions here given do not require alteration. " If the sacrament be shut out" would, however, be more literal than " not sacramentally contracted."]

† For the original passages from the Encyclical and Syllabus of Pius IX., see Appendix A.

Firstly. I do not place all the Propositions in one and the same category; for there are a portion of them which, as far as I can judge, might, by the combined aid of favourable construction and vigorous explanation, be brought within bounds. And I hold that favourable construction of the terms used in controversies is the right general rule. But this can only be so, when construction is an open question. When the author of certain propositions claims, as in the case before us, a sole and unlimited power to interpret them in such manner and by such rules as he may from time to time think fit, the only defence for all others concerned is at once to judge for themselves, how much of unreason or of mischief the words, naturally understood, may contain.

Secondly. It may appear, upon a hasty perusal, that neither the infliction of penalty in life, limb, liberty, or goods, on disobedient members of the Christian Church, nor the title to depose sovereigns, and release subjects from their allegiance, with all its revolting consequences, has been here reaffirmed. In terms, there is no mention of them; but in the substance of the propositions, I grieve to say, they are beyond doubt included. For it is notorious that they have been declared and decreed by "Rome," that is to say by Popes and Papal Councils; and the stringent condemnations of the Syllabus include all those who hold that Popes and Papal Councils (declared ecumenical) have transgressed the just limits of their power, or usurped the rights of princes. What have been their opinions and decrees about persecution I need hardly say; and indeed the right to employ physical force is even here undisguisedly claimed (No. 7).

Even while I am writing, I am reminded, from an unquestionable source, of the words of Pope Pius IX. himself on the deposing power. I add only a few italics; the words appear as given in a translation, without the original:—

"The present Pontiff used these words in replying to the address from the Academia of the Catholic Religion (July 21, 1873):—

"'There are many errors regarding the Infallibility: but the most malicious of all is that which includes, in that dogma, the *right* of deposing sovereigns, and declaring the people no longer bound by the obligation of fidelity. This *right* has now and again, in critical circumstances, been exercised by the Pontiffs: but it has nothing to do with Papal Infallibility. Its origin was not the infallibility, but the authority of the Pope. This authority, in accordance with public right, which was then vigorous, and with the acquiescence of all Christian nations, who reverenced in the Pope the supreme Judge of the Christian Commonwealth, *extended so far as to pass judgment, even in civil affairs, on the acts of Princes and of Nations.*'" *

Lastly. I must observe that these are not mere opinions of the Pope himself, nor even are they opinions which he might paternally recommend to the pious consideration of the faithful. With the promulgation of his opinions is unhappily combined, in

---

* 'Civilization and the See of Rome.' By Lord Robert Montagu. Dublin, 1874. A Lecture delivered under the auspices of the Catholic Union of Ireland. I have a little misgiving about the version: but not of a nature to affect the substance. [The misgiving was justified: see *inf.* 'Speeches of Pope Pius IX.,' p. 183; but the substance is worse, not better, than the inaccurate version of Lord R. Montagu.]

the Encyclical Letter, which virtually, though not expressly, includes the whole, a command to all his spiritual children (from which command we the disobedient children are in no way excluded) to hold them.

"Itaque omnes et singulas pravas opiniones et doctrinas singillatim hisce literis commemoratas auctoritate nostrâ Apostolicâ reprobamus, proscribimus, atque damnamus; easque ab omnibus Catholicæ Ecclesiæ filiis, veluti reprobatas, proscriptas, atque damnatas omnino haberi volumus et mandamus" Encycl. Dec. 8, 1864.*

And the decrees of 1870 will presently show us, what they establish as the binding force of the *mandate* thus conveyed to the Christian world.

IV. The Third Proposition.

I now pass to the operation of these extraordinary declarations on personal and private duty.

When the cup of endurance, which had so long been filling, began, with the council of the Vatican in 1870, to overflow, the most famous and learned living theologian of the Roman Communion, Dr. von Döllinger, long the foremost champion of his Church, refused compliance, and submitted, with his temper

---

* "Therefore do We, by our Apostolic authority, repudiate, proscribe, and condemn, all and each of the evil opinions and doctrines severally mentioned in this Letter, and We will and order that they be absolutely held, by all the children of the Catholic Church, to be repudiated, proscribed, and condemned."

undisturbed and his freedom unimpaired, to the extreme and most painful penalty of excommunication. With him, many of the most learned and respected theologians of the Roman Communion in Germany underwent the same sentence. The very few, who elsewhere (I do not speak of Switzerland) suffered in like manner, deserve an admiration rising in proportion to their fewness. It seems as though Germany, from which Luther blew the mighty trumpet that even now echoes through the land, still retained her primacy in the domain of conscience, still supplied the *centuria prærogativa* of the great *comitia* of the world.

But let no man wonder or complain. Without imputing to anyone the moral murder, for such it is, of stifling conscience and conviction, I for one cannot be surprised that the fermentation, which is working through the mind of the Latin Church, has as yet (elsewhere than in Germany) but in few instances come to the surface. By the mass of mankind, it is morally impossible that questions such as these can be adequately examined; so it ever has been, and so in the main it will continue, until the principles of manufacturing machinery shall have been applied, and with analogous results, to intellectual and moral processes. Followers they are and must be, and in a certain sense ought to be. But what as to the leaders of society, the men of education and of leisure? I will try to suggest some answer in few words. A change of religious profession is under all circumstances a great and awful thing. Much more is the question, however, between conflicting, or apparently conflicting, duties arduous, when the religion of a man has been changed for him, over his head, and without the very least of his participation. Far be it then from me to make any Roman Catholic, except the great hierarchic Power, and those who have egged it on, responsible for the portentous proceedings which we have witnessed. My conviction is that, even of those who may not shake off the yoke, multitudes will vindicate at any rate their loyalty at the expense of the consistency, which perhaps in difficult matters of religion few among us perfectly maintain. But this belongs to the future; for the present, nothing could in my opinion be more unjust than to hold the members of the Roman Church in general already responsible for the recent innovations. The duty of observers, who think the claims involved in these decrees arrogant and false, and such as not even impotence real or supposed ought to shield from criticism, is frankly to state the case, and, by way of friendly challenge, to intreat their Roman Catholic fellow-countrymen to replace themselves in the position which five-and-forty years ago this nation, by the voice and action of its Parliament, declared its belief that they held.

Upon a strict re-examination of the language, as apart from the substance of my Third Proposition, I find it faulty, inasmuch as it seems to imply that a "convert" now joining the Papal Church, not only gives up certain rights and duties of freedom, but surrenders them by a conscious and deliberate act. What I have less accurately said that he renounced, I might have more accurately said that he forfeited.

To speak strictly, the claim now made upon him by the authority, which he solemnly and with the highest responsibility acknowledges, requires him to surrender his mental and moral freedom, and to place his loyalty and civil duty at the mercy of another. There may have been, and may be, persons who in their sanguine trust will not shrink from this result, and will console themselves with the notion that their loyalty and civil duty are to be committed to the custody of one much wiser than themselves. But I am sure that there are also " converts " who, when they perceive, will by word and act reject, the consequence which relentless logic draws for them. If, however, my proposition be true, there is no escape from the dilemma. Is it then true, or is it not true, that Rome requires a convert, who now joins her, to forfeit his moral and mental freedom, and to place his loyalty and civil duty at the mercy of another?

In order to place this matter in as clear a light as I can, it will be necessary to go back a little upon our recent history.

A century ago we began to relax that system of penal laws against Roman Catholics, at once pettifogging, base, and cruel, which Mr. Burke has scathed and blasted with his immortal eloquence.

When this process had reached the point, at which the question was whether they should be admitted into Parliament, there arose a great and prolonged national controversy; and some men, who at no time of their lives were narrow-minded, such as Sir Robert Peel, the Minister, resisted the concession.

The arguments in its favour were obvious and strong, and they ultimately prevailed. But the strength of the opposing party had lain in the allegation that, from the nature and claims of the Papal power, it was not possible for the consistent Roman Catholic to pay to the crown of this country an entire allegiance, and that the admission of persons, thus self-disabled, to Parliament was inconsistent with the safety of the State and nation; which had not very long before, it may be observed, emerged from a struggle for existence.

An answer to this argument was indispensable; and it was supplied mainly from two sources. The Josephine laws,* then still subsisting in the Austrian empire, and the arrangements which had been made after the peace of 1815 by Prussia and the German States with Pius VII. and Consalvi, proved that the Papal Court could submit to circumstances, and could allow material restraints even upon the exercise of its ecclesiastical prerogatives. Here, then, was a reply in the sense of the phrase *solvitur ambulando*. Much information of this class was collected for the information of Parliament and the country.† But there

---

* See the work of Count dal Pozzo on the 'Austrian Ecclesiastical Law.' London: Murray, 1827. The Leopoldine Laws in Tuscany may also be mentioned.

† See 'Report from the Select Committee appointed to report the nature and substance of the Laws and Ordinances existing in Foreign States, respecting the regulation of their Roman Catholic subjects in Ecclesiastical matters, and their intercourse with the See of Rome, or any other Foreign Ecclesiastical Jurisdiction.' Printed for the House of Commons in 1816 and 1817. Reprinted 1851.

were also measures taken to learn, from the highest Roman Catholic authorities of this country, what was the exact situation of the members of that communion with respect to some of the better known exorbitancies of Papal assumption. Did the Pope claim any temporal jurisdiction? Did he still pretend to the exercise of a power to depose kings, release subjects from their allegiance, and incite them to revolt? Was faith to be kept with heretics? Did the Church still teach the doctrines of persecution? Now, to no one of these questions could the answer really be of the smallest immediate moment to this powerful and solidly compacted kingdom. They were topics selected by way of sample; and the intention was to elicit declarations showing generally that the fangs of the mediæval Popedom had been drawn, and its claws torn away; that the Roman system, however strict in its dogma, was perfectly compatible with civil liberty, and with the institutions of a free State moulded on a different religious basis from its own.

Answers in abundance were obtained, tending to show that the doctrines of deposition and persecution, of keeping no faith with heretics, and of universal dominion, were obsolete beyond revival; that every assurance could be given respecting them, except such as required the shame of a formal retractation; that they were in effect mere bugbears, unworthy to be taken into account by a nation, which prided itself on being made up of practical men.

But it was unquestionably felt that something more

than the renunciation of these particular opinions was necessary in order to secure the full concession of civil rights to Roman Catholics. As to their individual loyalty, a State disposed to generous or candid interpretation had no reason to be uneasy. It was only with regard to requisitions, which might be made on them from another quarter, that apprehension could exist. It was reasonable that England should desire to know not only what the Pope[*] might do for himself, but to what demands, by the constitution of their Church, they were liable; and how far it was possible that such demands could touch their civil duty. The theory which placed every human being, in things spiritual and things temporal, at the feet of the Roman Pontiff, had not been an *idolum specûs*, a mere theory of the chamber. Brain-power never surpassed in the political history of the world had been devoted for centuries to the single purpose of working it into the practice of Christendom; had in the West achieved for an impossible problem a partial success; and had in the East punished the obstinate independence of the Church by that Latin conquest of Constantinople, which effectually prepared the way for the downfall of the Eastern empire, and the establishment of the Turks in Europe. What

---

[*] At that period the eminent and able Bishop Doyle did not scruple to write as follows: "We are taunted with the proceedings of Popes. What, my Lord, have we Catholics to do with the proceedings of Popes, or why should we be made accountable for them?"—'Essay on the Catholic Claims.' To Lord Liverpool, 1826, p. 111.

was really material therefore was, not whether the Papal chair laid claim to this or that particular power, but whether it laid claim to some power that included them all, and whether that claim had received such sanction from the authorities of the Latin Church, that there remained within her borders absolutely no tenable standing-ground from which war against it could be maintained. Did the Pope then claim infallibility? Or did he, either without infallibility or with it (and if with it so much the worse), claim an universal obedience from his flock? And were these claims, either or both, affirmed in his Church by authority which even the least Papal of the members of that Church must admit to be binding upon conscience?

The two first of these questions were covered by the third. And well it was that they were so covered. For to them no satisfactory answer could even then be given. The Popes had kept up, with comparatively little intermission, for well-nigh a thousand years their claim to dogmatic infallibility;* and had, at periods within the same tract of time, often enough made, and never retracted, that other claim which is theoretically less but practically larger; their claim to an obedience virtually universal from the baptised members of the Church. To the third question it was fortunately more practicable to prescribe a satisfactory reply. It was well known that,

---

* This admission, made without sufficient reflection, was retracted in 'Vaticanism,' see *inf.* p. 53.

in the days of its glory and intellectual power, the great Gallican Church had not only not admitted, but had denied Papal infallibility, and had declared that the local laws and usages of the Church could not be set aside by the will of the Pontiff. Nay, further, it was believed that in the main these had been, down to the close of the last century, the prevailing opinions of the Cisalpine Churches in communion with Rome. The Council of Constance had in act as well as word shown that the Pope's judgments, and the Pope himself, were triable by the assembled representatives of the Christian world. And the Council of Trent, notwithstanding the predominance in it of Italian and Roman influences, if it had not denied, yet had not affirmed either proposition.

All that remained was, to know what were the sentiments entertained on these vital points by the leaders and guides of Roman Catholic opinion nearest to our own doors. And here testimony was offered, which must not, and cannot, be forgotten. In part, this was the testimony of witnesses before the Committees of the two Houses in 1824 and 1825. I need quote two answers only, given by the Prelate, who more than any other represented his Church, and influenced the mind of this country in favour of concession at the time, namely, Bishop Doyle. He was asked,*

---

* Committees of both Lords and Commons sat; the former in 1825, the latter in 1824-5. The References were identical, and ran as follows: " To inquire into the state of Ireland, more particularly with reference to the circumstances which may have

" In what, and how far, does the Roman Catholic profess to obey the Pope?"

He replied:

"The Catholic professes to obey the Pope in matters which regard his religious faith: and in those matters of ecclesiastical discipline which have already been defined by the competent authorities."

And again:

"Does that justify the objection that is made to Catholics, that their allegiance is divided?"

"I do not think it does in any way. We are bound to obey the Pope in those things that I have already mentioned. But our obedience to the law, and the allegiance which we owe the sovereign, are complete, and full, and perfect, and undivided, inasmuch as they extend to all political, legal, and civil rights of the king or of his subjects. I think the allegiance due to the king, and the allegiance due to the Pope, are as distinct and as divided in their nature, as any two things can possibly be."

Such is the opinion of the dead Prelate. We shall presently hear the opinion of a living one. But the sentiments of the dead man powerfully operated on the open and trustful temper of this people to induce them to grant, at the cost of so much popular feeling and national tradition, the great and just concession of 1829. That concession, without such declarations, it would, to say the least, have been far more difficult to obtain.

Now, bodies are usually held to be bound by the

---

led to disturbances in that part of the United Kingdom." Bishop Doyle was examined March 21, 1825, and April 21, 1825, before the Lords. The two citations in the text are taken from Bishop Doyle's evidence before the Commons' Committee, March 12, 1825, p. 190.

evidence of their own selected and typical witnesses. But in this instance the colleagues of those witnesses thought fit also to speak collectively.

First let us quote from the collective "Declaration," in the year 1826, of the Vicars Apostolic, who, with Episcopal authority, governed the Roman Catholics of Great Britain:—

"The allegiance which Catholics hold to be due, and are bound to pay, to their Sovereign, and to the civil authority of the State, is perfect and undivided. . . . .

"They declare that neither the Pope, nor any other prelate or ecclesiastical person of the Roman Catholic Church . . . . has any right to interfere directly or indirectly in the Civil Government . . . . nor to oppose in any manner the performance of the civil duties which are due to the king."

Not less explicit was the Hierarchy of the Roman Communion in its "Pastoral Address to the Clergy and Laity of the Roman Catholic Church in Ireland, dated January 25, 1826. This address contains a Declaration, from which I extract the following words:—

"It is a duty which they owe to themselves, *as well as to their Protestant fellow-subjects*, whose good opinion they value, to endeavour once more to remove the false imputations that have been frequently cast upon the faith and discipline of that Church which is intrusted to their care, *that all may be enabled to know with accuracy their genuine principles.*"

In Article 11 :—

"They declare on oath their belief that it is not an article of the Catholic Faith, neither are they thereby required to believe, that the Pope is infallible."

and, after various recitals, they set forth

"After this full, explicit, and sworn declaration, we are utterly at a loss to conceive on what possible ground we could be justly charged with bearing towards our most gracious Sovereign only a divided allegiance."

Thus, besides much else that I will not stop to quote, Papal infallibility was most solemnly declared to be a matter on which each man might think as he pleased; the Pope's power to claim obedience was strictly and narrowly limited: it was expressly denied that he had any title, direct or indirect, to interfere in civil government. Of the right of the Pope to define the limits which divide the civil from the spiritual by his own authority, not one word is said by the Prelates of either country.

Since that time, all these propositions have been reversed. The Pope's infallibility, when he speaks *ex cathedrâ* on faith and morals, has been declared, with the assent of the Bishops of the Roman Church, to be an article of faith, binding on the conscience of every Christian; his claim to the obedience of his spiritual subjects has been declared in like manner without any practical limit or reserve; and his supremacy, without any reserve of civil rights, has been similarly affirmed to include everything which relates to the discipline and government of the Church throughout the world. And these doctrines, we now know on the highest authority, it is of necessity for salvation to believe.

Independently, however, of the Vatican Decrees themselves, it is necessary for all who wish to understand what has been the amount of the wonderful change now consummated in the constitution of the Latin Church, and what is the present degradation of its Episcopal order, to observe also the change, amounting to revolution, of form in the present, as compared with other Conciliary decrees. Indeed, that spirit of centralisation, the excesses of which are as fatal to vigorous life in the Church as in the State, seems now nearly to have reached the last and furthest point of possible advancement and exaltation.

When, in fact, we speak of the decrees of the Council of the Vatican, we use a phrase which will not bear strict examination. The Canons of the Council of Trent were, at least, the real Canons of a real Council: and the strain in which they are promulgated is this:—*Hæc sacrosancta, ecumenica, et generalis Tridentina Synodus, in Spiritu Sancto legitimè congregata, in eâ præsidentibus eisdem tribus apostolicis Legatis, hortatur,* or *docet,* or *statuit,* or *decernit,** and the like: and its canons, as published in Rome, are "*Canones et decreta Sacrosancti ecumenici Concilii Tridentini,*" † and so forth. But what we have now to do with is the *Constitutio Dogmatica Prima de Ecclesiâ Christi, edita in Sessione tertiâ* of the Vatican Council. It is not a constitution made by the Council, but one promulgated in the Council.‡ And who is

---

* "This most holy, ecumenical, and general Tridentine Synod, in the Holy Ghost regularly assembled, and having for Presidents the three aforesaid Apostolic Legates, exhorts, *or* teaches, *or* determines, *or* decrees."

† 'Romæ: in Collegio urbano de Propagandâ Fide.' 1833. "The Canons and Decrees of the most holy ecumenical Council of Trent."

‡ I am aware that, as some hold, this was the case with the Council of the Lateran in A.D. 1215. But, first, this has not been

it that legislates and decrees? It is *Pius Episcopus, servus servorum Dei:** and the seductive plural of his *docemus et declaramus* is simply the dignified and ceremonious " We " of Royal declarations. The document is dated *Pontificatûs nostri Anno XXV:* and the humble share of the assembled Episcopate in the transaction is represented by *sacro approbante concilio.* And now for the propositions themselves.

First comes the Pope's infallibility :—

"Docemus, et divinitus revelatum dogma esse definimus, Romanum Pontificem, cum ex Cathedrâ loquitur, id est cum, omnium Christianorum Pastoris et Doctoris munere fungens, pro supremâ suâ Apostolicâ auctoritate doctrinam de fide vel moribus ab universâ Ecclesiâ tenendam definit, per assistentiam divinam, ipsi in Beato Petro promissam, eâ infallibilitate pollere, quâ Divinus Redemptor Ecclesiam suam in definiendâ doctrinâ de fide vel moribus instructam esse voluit : ideòque ejus Romani Pontificis definitiones ex sese non autem ex consensu Ecclesiæ irreformabiles esse "†

Will it, then, be said that the infallibility of the Pope accrues only when he speaks *ex cathedrâ*? No doubt this is a very material consideration for those

---

established : secondly, the very gist of the evil we are dealing with consists in following (and enforcing) precedents from the period and practice of Pope Innocent III. [It is alleged that the form used in 1870 was that regularly employed in Councils held at Rome : pending further examination, I do not insist on the argument.]

* " Pius, Bishop, servant of the servants of God."

† 'Constitutio de Ecclesiâ,' c. iv. " We teach and define it to be a dogma divinely revealed that, when the Roman Pontiff speaks *ex cathedrâ*, that is when, in discharge of the office of Pastor and Teacher of all Christians, by virtue of his supreme Apostolic authority, he defines that a doctrine regarding faith

who have been told that the private conscience is to derive comfort and assurance from the emanations of the Papal Chair: for there is no established or accepted definition* of the phrase *ex cathedrâ*, and they have no power to obtain one, and no guide to direct them in their choice among some twelve theories† on the subject, which, it is said, are bandied to and fro among Roman theologians, except the despised and discarded agency of his private judgment. But while thus sorely tantalised, he is not one whit protected. For there is still one person, and one only, who can unquestionably declare *ex cathedrâ* what is *ex cathedrâ* and what is not, and who can declare it when and as he pleases. That person is the Pope himself. The provision is, that no document he issues shall be valid without a seal: but the seal remains under his own sole lock and key.

Again, it may be sought to plead, that the Pope

---

or morals is to be held by the Universal Church, he enjoys, by the Divine assistance promised to him in blessed Peter, that infallibility with which the Divine Redeemer willed His Church to be endowed in defining a doctrine regarding faith or morals; and that therefore such definitions of the Roman Pontiff are irreformable of themselves, and not from the consent of the Church."—*Taken from the version in 'Dogmatic Contributions.'* Dublin: O'Toole. 1870.

* That is to say no available definition: no interpretation, intended in good faith to assist the ordinary Christian in recognising these *ex cathedrâ* definitions; by which he is bound, for the salvation of his soul, as much as by the Holy Scriptures. A description, which differs from a definition, is inserted in the text of the Decree.

† See Mr. Maskell's Tract.

is, after all, only operating by sanctions which unquestionably belong to the religious domain. He does not propose to invade the country, to seize Woolwich, or burn Portsmouth. He will only, at the worst, excommunicate opponents, as he has excommunicated Dr. von Döllinger and others. Is this a good answer? After all, even in the Middle Ages, it was not by the direct action of fleets and armies of their own that the Popes contended with kings who were refractory; it was mainly by interdicts, and by the refusal, which they entailed when the Bishops were not brave enough to refuse their publication, of religious offices to the people. It was thus that England suffered under John, France under Philip Augustus, Leon under Alphonso the Noble, and every country in its turn. But the inference may be drawn that they who, while using spiritual weapons for such an end, do not employ temporal means, only fail to employ them because they have them not. A religious society, which delivers volleys of spiritual censures in order to impede the performance of civil duties, does all the mischief that is in its power to do, and brings into question, in the face of the State, its title to civil protection.

Will it be said, finally, that the Infallibility touches only matter of faith and morals? Only matter of morals! Will any of the Roman casuists kindly acquaint us what are the departments and functions of human life which do not and cannot fall within the domain of morals? If they will not tell us, we must look elsewhere. In his work entitled 'Literature and Dogma,'* Mr. Matthew Arnold quaintly informs us—as they tell us nowadays how many parts of our poor bodies are solid, and how many aqueous—that about seventy-five per cent. of all we do belongs to the department of "conduct." Conduct and morals, we may suppose, are nearly co-extensive. Three-fourths, then, of life are thus handed over. But who will guarantee to us the other fourth? Certainly not St. Paul; who says, "Whether therefore ye eat, or drink, or whatsoever ye do, do *all* to the glory of God." And "Whatsoever ye do, in word or in deed, do *all* in the name of the Lord Jesus." † No! Such a distinction would be the unworthy device of a shallow policy, vainly used to hide the daring of that wild ambition which at Rome, not from the throne but from behind the throne, prompts the movements of the Vatican. I care not to ask if there be dregs or tatters of human life, such as can escape from the description and boundary of morals. I submit that Duty is a power which rises with us in the morning, and goes to rest with us at night. It is co-extensive with the action of our intelligence. It is the shadow which cleaves to us go where we will, and which only leaves us when we leave the light of life. So then it is the supreme direction of us in respect to all Duty, which the Pontiff declares to belong to him, *sacro approbante concilio:* and this declaration he makes, not as an otiose

---

* Pages 15, 44.
† 1 Cor. x. 31 ; Col. iii. 7.

opinion of the schools, but *cunctis fidelibus credendam et tenendam.**

But we shall now see that, even if a loophole had at this point been left unclosed, the void is supplied by another provision of the Decrees. While the reach of the Infallibility is as wide as it may please the Pope, or those who may prompt the Pope, to make it, there is something wider still, and that is the claim to an absolute and entire Obedience. This Obedience is to be rendered to his orders in the cases I shall proceed to point out, without any qualifying condition, such as the *ex cathedrâ*. The sounding name of Infallibility has so fascinated the public mind, and riveted it on the Fourth Chapter of the Constitution *de Ecclesiâ*, that its near neighbour, the Third Chapter, has, at least in my opinion, received very much less than justice. Let us turn to it.

"Cujuscunque ritûs et dignitatis pastores atque fideles, tam seorsum singuli quam simul omnes, officio hierarchicæ subordinationis veræque obedientiæ obstringuntur, non solum in rebus, quæ ad fidem et mores, sed etiam in iis, quæ ad disciplinam et regimen Ecclesiæ per totum orbem diffusæ pertinent. . . . . Hæc est Catholicæ veritatis doctrina, a quâ deviare, salvâ fide atque salute, nemo potest. . . . .

"Docemus etiam et declaramus eum esse judicem supremum fidelium, et in omnibus causis ad examen ecclesiasticum spectantibus ad ipsius posse judicium recurri : Sedis vero Apostolicæ, cujus auctoritate major non est, judicium a nemine fore retractandum. Neque cuiquam de ejus licere judicare judicio." †

Even, therefore, where the judgments of the Pope do not present the credentials of infallibility, they

---

* "To be believed and held by all the faithful."
† 'Dogmatic Constitutions,' &c., c. iii.: Dublin, 1870, pp. 30–

are unappealable and irreversible : no person may pass judgment upon them; and all men, clerical and lay, dispersedly or in the aggregate, are bound truly to obey them; and from this rule of Catholic truth no man can depart, save at the peril of his salvation. Surely, it is allowable to say that this Third Chapter on universal obedience is a formidable rival to the Fourth Chapter on Infallibility. Indeed, to an observer from without, it seems to leave the dignity to the other, but to reserve the stringency and efficiency to itself. The Fourth Chapter is the titular Merovingian Monarch; the Third is the Carolingian Mayor of the Palace. The Fourth has an overawing splendour; the Third, an iron gripe. Little does it matter to me whether my superior claims infallibility, so long as he is entitled to demand and exact conformity. This,

---

32. "All, both pastors and faithful, of whatsoever rite and dignity, both individually and collectively, are bound to submit, by the duty of hierarchical subordination and true obedience, not only in matters belonging to faith and morals, but also in those that appertain to the discipline and government of the Church throughout the world. . . . This is the teaching of the Catholic Faith, from which no one can deviate without detriment to faith and salvation." *Ibid.* (But I consider the word detriment to be much too weak: for the deviation is made the subject of Anathema at the end of the chapter.) . . . "We further teach and declare, that he (the Pope) is the supreme Judge of the Faithful, and that, in all causes [appertaining to ecclesiastical jurisdiction], recourse may be had to his judgment; and that none may reopen the judgment of the Apostolic See, than whose there is no greater authority; and that it is not lawful for any one to sit in judgment on its judgment." *Ibid.* But for the words in brackets I should substitute "of ecclesiastical cognisance."

it will be observed, he demands even in cases not covered by his infallibility; cases, therefore, in which he admits it to be possible that he may be wrong, but finds it intolerable to be told so. As he must be obeyed in all his judgments though not *ex cathedrâ*, it seems a pity he could not likewise give the comforting assurance that, they are all certain to be right.

But why this ostensible reduplication, this apparent surplusage? Why did the astute contrivers of this tangled scheme conclude that they could not afford to rest content with pledging the Council to Infallibility in terms which are not only wide to a high degree, but elastic beyond all measure?

Though they must have known perfectly well that "faith and morals" carried everything, or everything worth having, in the purely individual sphere, they also knew just as well that, even where the individual was subjugated, they might and would still have to deal with the State.

In mediæval history, this distinction is not only clear, but glaring. Outside the borders of some narrow and proscribed sect, now and then emerging, we never, or scarcely ever, hear of private and personal resistance to the Pope. The manful "Protestantism" of mediæval times had its activity almost entirely in the sphere of public, national, and state rights. Too much attention, in my opinion, cannot be fastened on this point. It is the very root and kernel of the matter. Individual servitude, however abject, will not satisfy the party now dominant in the Latin Church: the State must also be a slave.

Our Saviour had recognised as distinct the two provinces of the civil rule and the Church: had nowhere intimated that the spiritual authority was to claim the disposal of physical force, and to control in its own domain the authority which is alone responsible for external peace, order, and safety among civilised communities of men. It has been alike the peculiarity, the pride, and the misfortune of the Roman Church, among Christian communities, to allow to itself an unbounded use, as far as its power would go, of earthly instruments for spiritual ends. We have seen with what ample assurances* this nation and Parliament were fed in 1826; how well and roundly the full and undivided rights of the civil power, and the separation of the two jurisdictions, were affirmed. All this had at length been undone, as far as Popes could undo it, in the Syllabus and the Encyclical. It remained to complete the undoing, through the subserviency or pliability of the Council.

And the work is now truly complete. Lest it should be said that supremacy in faith and morals, full dominion over personal belief and conduct, did not cover the collective action of men in States, a third province was opened, not indeed to the abstract assertion of Infallibility, but to the far more practical and decisive demand of absolute Obedience. And this is the proper work of the Third Chapter, to which I am endeavouring to do a tardy justice. Let us listen again to its few but pregnant words on the point:

---

* See further Appendix B.

"Non solum in rebus, quæ ad fidem et mores, sed etiam in iis, quæ ad disciplinam et regimen Ecclesiæ per totum orbem diffusæ pertinent."*

Absolute obedience, it is boldly declared, is due to the Pope, at the peril of salvation, not alone in faith, in morals, but in all things which concern the discipline and government of the Church. Thus are swept into the Papal net whole multitudes of facts, whole systems of government, prevailing, though in different degrees, in every country of the world. Even in the United States, where the severance between Church and State is supposed to be complete, a long catalogue might be drawn of subjects belonging to the domain and competency of the State, but also undeniably affecting the government of the Church; such as, by way of example, marriage, burial, education, prison discipline, blasphemy, poor-relief, incorporation, mortmain, religious endowments, vows of celibacy and obedience. In Europe the circle is far wider, the points of contact and of interlacing almost innumerable. But on all matters, respecting which any Pope may think proper to declare that they concern either faith, or morals, or the government or discipline of the Church, he claims, with the approval of a Council undoubtedly Ecumenical in the Roman sense, the absolute obedience, at the peril of salvation, of every member of his communion.

It seems not as yet to have been thought wise to

---

* "Not only in matters belonging to faith and morals, but also in those that appertain to the discipline and government of the Church throughout the world." *Ibid.*

pledge the Council in terms to the Syllabus and the Encyclical. That achievement is probably reserved for some one of its sittings yet to come. In the meantime it is well to remember, that this claim in respect of all things affecting the discipline and government of the Church, as well as faith and conduct, is lodged in open day by and in the reign of a Pontiff, who has condemned free speech, free writing, a free press, toleration of nonconformity, liberty of conscience, the study of civil and philosophical matters in independence of the ecclesiastical authority, marriage unless sacramentally contracted, and the definition by the State of the civil rights (*jura*) of the Church; who has demanded for the Church, therefore, the title to define its own civil rights, together with a divine right to civil immunities, and a right to use physical force; and who has also proudly asserted that the Popes of the Middle Ages with their councils did not invade the rights of princes: as for example, Gregory VII., of the Emperor Henry IV.; Innocent III., of Raymond of Toulouse; Paul III., in deposing Henry VIII.; or Pius V., in performing the like paternal office for Elizabeth.

I submit, then, that my fourth proposition is true: and that England is entitled to ask, and to know, in what way the obedience required by the Pope and the Council of the Vatican is to be reconciled with the integrity of civil allegiance?

It has been shown that the Head of their Church, so supported as undoubtedly to speak with its highest authority, claims from Roman Catholics a plenary obedience to whatever he may desire in relation not to faith but to morals, and not only to these, but to all that concerns the government and discipline of the Church : that, of this, much lies within the domain of the State : that, to obviate all misapprehension, the Pope demands for himself the right to determine the province of his own rights, and has so defined it in formal documents, as to warrant any and every invasion of the civil sphere ; and that this new version of the principles of the Papal Church inexorably binds its members to the admission of these exorbitant claims, without any refuge or reservation on behalf of their duty to the Crown.

Under circumstances such as these, it seems not too much to ask of them to confirm the opinion which we, as fellow-countrymen, entertain of them, by sweeping away, in such manner and terms as they may think best, the presumptive imputations which their ecclesiastical rulers at Rome, acting autocratically, appear to have brought upon their capacity to pay a solid and undivided allegiance; and to fulfil the engagement which their Bishops, as political sponsors, promised and declared for them in 1825.

It would be impertinent, as well as needless, to suggest what should be said. All that is requisite is to indicate in substance that which (if the foregoing argument be sound) is not wanted, and that which is. What is not wanted is vague and general assertion, of whatever kind, and however sincere. What is wanted, and that in the most specific form and the clearest terms, I take to be one of two things; that is to say, either—

I. A demonstration that neither in the name of faith, nor in the name of morals, nor in the name of the government or discipline of the Church, is the Pope of Rome able, by virtue of the powers asserted for him by the Vatican decree, to make any claim upon those who adhere to his communion, of such a nature as can impair the integrity of their civil allegiance; or else,

II. That, if and when such claim is made, it will even although resting on the definitions of the Vatican, be repelled and rejected; just as Bishop Doyle, when he was asked what the Roman Catholic clergy would do if the Pope intermeddled with their religion, replied frankly, "The consequence would be, that we should oppose him by every means in our power, even by the exercise of our spiritual authority." *

In the absence of explicit assurances to this effect, we should appear to be led, nay, driven, by just reasoning upon that documentary evidence, to the conclusions:—

1. That the Pope, authorised by his Council, claims for himself the domain (*a*) of faith, (*b*) of morals, (*c*) of all that concerns the government and discipline of the Church.

2. That he in like manner claims the power of determining the limits of those domains.

---

* 'Report.' March 18, 1826. p. 191.

3. That he does not sever them, by any acknowledged or intelligible line, from the domains of civil duty and allegiance.

4. That he therefore claims, and claims from the month of July 1870 onwards with plenary authority, from every convert and member of his Church, that he shall "place his loyalty and civil duty at the mercy of another:" that other being himself.

V. Being True, are the Propositions Material?

But next, if these propositions be true, are they also material? The claims cannot, as I much fear, be denied to have been made. It cannot be denied that the Bishops, who govern in things spiritual more than five millions (or nearly one-sixth) of the inhabitants of the United Kingdom, have in some cases promoted, in all cases accepted, these claims. It has been a favourite purpose of my life not to conjure up, but to conjure down, public alarms. I am not now going to pretend that either foreign foe or domestic treason can, at the bidding of the Court of Rome, disturb these peaceful shores. But though such fears may be visionary, it is more visionary still to suppose for one moment that the claims of Gregory VII., of Innocent III., and of Boniface VIII., have been disinterred, in the nineteenth century, like hideous mummies picked out of Egyptian sarcophagi, in the interests of archæology, or without a definite and practical aim. As rational beings, we must rest assured that only with a very clearly conceived and foregone purpose have these astonishing reassertions been paraded before the world. What is that purpose?

I can well believe that it is in part theological. There have always been, and there still are, no small proportion of our race, and those by no means in all respects the worst, who are sorely open to the temptation, especially in times of religious disturbance, to discharge their spiritual responsibilities by *power of attorney*. As advertising Houses find custom in proportion, not so much to the solidity of their resources as to the magniloquence of their promises and assurances, so theological boldness in the extension of such claims is sure to pay, by widening certain circles of devoted adherents, however it may repel the mass of mankind. There were two special encouragements to this enterprise at the present day: one of them the perhaps unconscious but manifest leaning of some, outside the Roman precinct, to undue exaltation of Church power; the other the reaction, which is and must be brought about in favour of superstition, by the levity of the destructive speculations so widely current, and the notable hardihood of the anti-Christian writing of the day.

But it is impossible to account sufficiently in this manner for the particular course which has been actually pursued by the Roman Court. All morbid spiritual appetites would have been amply satisfied by claims to infallibility in creed, to the prerogative of miracle, to dominion over the unseen world. In truth there was occasion, in this view, for nothing, except a liberal supply of Salmonean thunder :—

"Dum flammas Jovis, et sonitus imitatur Olympi."*

All this could have been managed by a few Tetzels, judiciously distributed over Europe. Therefore the question still remains, Why did that Court, with policy for ever in its eye, lodge such formidable demands for power of the vulgar kind in that sphere which is visible, and where hard knocks can undoubtedly be given as well as received?

It must be for some political object, of a very tangible kind, that the risks of so daring a raid upon the civil sphere have been deliberately run.

A daring raid it is. For it is most evident that the very assertion of principles which establish an exemption from allegiance, or which impair its completeness, goes, in many other countries of Europe, far more directly than with us, to the creation of political strife, and to dangers of the most material and tangible kind. The struggle, now proceeding in Germany, at once occurs to the mind as a palmary instance. I am not competent to give any opinion upon the particulars of that struggle. The institutions of Germany, and the relative estimate of State power and individual freedom, are materially different from ours. But I must say as much as this. First, it is not Prussia alone that is touched; elsewhere, too, the bone lies ready, though the contention may be delayed. In other States, in Austria particularly, there are recent laws in force, raising much the same

---

* Æn. vi. 586.

issues as the Falck laws have raised. But the Roman Court possesses in perfection one art, the art of waiting; and it is her wise maxim to fight but one enemy at a time. Secondly, if I have truly represented the claims promulgated from the Vatican, it is difficult to deny that those claims, and the power which has made them, are primarily responsible for the pains and perils, whatever they may be, of the present conflict between German and Roman enactments. And that which was once truly said of France, may now also be said with not less truth of Germany: when Germany is disquieted, Europe cannot be at rest.

I should feel less anxiety on this subject had the Supreme Pontiff frankly recognised his altered position since the events of 1870; and, in language as clear, if not as emphatic, as that in which he has proscribed modern civilisation, given to Europe the assurance that he would be no party to the re-establishment by blood and violence of the Temporal Power of the Church. It is easy to conceive that his personal benevolence, no less than his feelings as an Italian, must have inclined him individually towards a course so humane; and I should add, if I might do it without presumption, so prudent. With what appears to an English eye a lavish prodigality, successive Italian Governments have made over the ecclesiastical powers and privileges of the Monarchy, not to the Church of the country for the revival of the ancient, popular, and self-governing elements of its constitution, but to the Papal Chair, for the establishment of ecclesiastical despotism, and the suppression of the last vestiges of independence. This course, so difficult for a foreigner to appreciate, or even to justify, has been met, not by reciprocal conciliation, but by a constant fire of denunciations and complaints. When the tone of these denunciations and complaints is compared with the language of the authorised and favoured Papal organs in the press, and of the Ultramontane party (now the sole legitimate party of the Latin Church) throughout Europe, it leads many to the painful and revolting conclusion that there is a fixed purpose among the secret inspirers of Roman policy to pursue, by the road of force, upon the arrival of any favourable opportunity, the favourite project of re-erecting the terrestrial throne of the Popedom, even if it can only be re-erected on the ashes of the city, and amidst the whitening bones of the people.*

It is difficult to conceive or contemplate the effects of such an endeavour. But the existence at this day of the policy, even in bare idea, is itself a portentous evil. I do not hesitate to say that it is an incentive to general disturbance, a premium upon European wars. It is in my opinion not sanguine only, but almost ridiculous to imagine that such a project could eventually succeed; but it is difficult to over-estimate the effect which it might produce in generating and exasperating strife. It might even, to some extent, disturb and paralyse the action of such Governments as might interpose for no separate purpose of their

---

* Appendix C.

own, but only with a view to the maintenance or restoration of the general peace. If the baleful Power which is expressed by the phrase *Curia Romana*, and not at all adequately rendered in its historic force by the usual English equivalent " Court of Rome," really entertains the scheme, it doubtless counts on the support in every country of an organised and devoted party; which, when it can command the scales of political power, will promote interference, and, when it is in a minority, will work for securing neutrality. As the peace of Europe may be in jeopardy, and as the duties even of England, as one (so to speak) of its constabulary authorities, might come to be in question, it would be most interesting to know the mental attitude of our Roman Catholic fellow-countrymen in England and Ireland with reference to the subject; and it seems to be one, on which we are entitled to solicit information.

For there cannot be the smallest doubt that the temporal power of the Popedom comes within the true meaning of the words used at the Vatican to describe the subjects on which the Pope is authorised to claim, under awful sanctions, the obedience of the "faithful." It is even possible that we have here the key to the enlargement of the province of Obedience beyond the limits of Infallibility, and to the introduction of the remarkable phrase *ad disciplinam et regimen Ecclesiæ*. No impartial person can deny that the question of the temporal power very evidently concerns the discipline and government of the Church—concerns it, and most mischievously as

I should venture to think; but in the opinion, up to a late date, of many Roman Catholics, not only most beneficially, but even essentially. Let it be remembered, that such a man as the late Count Montalembert, who in his general politics was of the Liberal party, did not scruple to hold that the millions of Roman Catholics throughout the world were co-partners with the inhabitants of the States of the Church in regard to their civil government; and, as constituting the vast majority, were of course entitled to override them. It was also rather commonly held, a quarter of a century ago, that the question of the States of the Church was one with which none but Roman Catholic Powers could have anything to do. This doctrine, I must own, was to me at all times unintelligible. It is now, to say the least, hopelessly and irrecoverably obsolete.

Archbishop Manning, who is the head of the Papal Church in England, and whose ecclesiastical tone is supposed to be in the closest accordance with that of his headquarters, has not thought it too much to say that the civil order of all Christendom is the offspring of the Temporal Power, and has the Temporal Power for its keystone; that on the destruction of the Temporal Power "the laws of nations would at once fall in ruins;" that (our old friend) the deposing Power "taught subjects obedience and princes clemency."* Nay, this high

---

* 'Three Lectures on the Temporal Sovereignty of the Popes,' 1860, pp. 34, 46, 47, 58-9, 63.

authority has proceeded further; and has elevated the Temporal Power to the rank of necessary doctrine.

"The Catholic Church cannot be silent, it cannot hold its peace; it cannot cease to preach the doctrines of Revelation, not only of the Trinity and of the Incarnation, but likewise of the Seven Sacraments, and of the Infallibility of the Church of God, and of the necessity of Unity, and of the Sovereignty, both spiritual and temporal, of the Holy See." *

I never, for my own part, heard that the work containing this remarkable passage was placed in the 'Index Prohibitorum Librorum.' On the contrary, its distinguished author was elevated, on the first opportunity, to the headship of the Roman Episcopacy in England, and to the guidance of the million or thereabouts of souls in its communion. And the more recent utterances of the oracle have not descended from the high level of those already cited. They have, indeed, the recommendation of a comment, not without fair claims to authority, on the recent declarations of the Pope and the Council; and of one which goes to prove how far I am from having exaggerated or strained in the foregoing pages the meaning of those declarations. Especially does this hold good on the one point, the most vital of the whole—the title to define the border line of the two provinces, which the Archbishop not unfairly takes to be the true criterion of supremacy, as between rival powers like the Church and the State.

* 'The present Crisis of the Holy See.' By H. E. Manning, D.D. London, 1861, p. 73.

"If, then, the civil power be not competent to decide the limits of the spiritual power, and if the spiritual power can define, with a divine certainty, its own limits, it is evidently supreme. Or, in other words, the spiritual power knows, with divine certainty, the limits of its own jurisdiction: and it knows therefore the limits and the competence of the civil power. It is thereby, in matters of religion and conscience, supreme. I do not see how this can be denied without denying Christianity. And if this be so, this is the doctrine of the Bull *Unam Sanctam*,* and of the Syllabus, and of the Vatican Council. It is, in fact, Ultramontanism, for this term means neither less nor more. The Church, therefore, is separate and supreme.

"Let us then ascertain somewhat further, what is the meaning of supreme. Any power which is independent, *and can alone fix the limits of its own jurisdiction, and can thereby fix the limits of all other jurisdictions, is,* ipso facto, *supreme*.† But the Church of Jesus Christ, within the sphere of revelation, of faith and morals, is all this, or is nothing, or worse than nothing, an imposture and an usurpation—that is, it is Christ or Antichrist." ‡

But the whole pamphlet should be read by those who desire to know the true sense of the Papal declarations and Vatican decrees, as they are understood by the most favoured ecclesiastics; understood, I am bound to own, so far as I can see, in their natural, legitimate, and inevitable sense. Such readers will be assisted by the treatise in seeing clearly, and in admitting frankly that, whatever demands may hereafter, and in whatever circumstances, be made upon us, we shall be unable to advance with any

---

* On the Bull *Unam Sanctam*, "of a most odious kind;" see Bishop Doyle's Essay, already cited. He thus describes it.

† The italics are not in the original.

‡ 'Cæsarism and Ultramontanism.' By Archbishop Manning, 1874, pp. 35-6.

fairness the plea that it has been done without due notice.

There are millions upon millions of the Protestants of this country, who would agree with Archbishop Manning, if he were simply telling us that Divine truth is not to be sought from the lips of the State, nor to be sacrificed at its command. But those millions would tell him, in return, that the State, as the power which is alone responsible for the external order of the world, can alone conclusively and finally be competent to determine what is to take place in the sphere of that external order.

I have shown, then, that the Propositions, especially that which has been felt to be the chief one among them, being true, are also material; material to be generally known, and clearly understood, and well considered, on civil grounds; inasmuch as they invade, at a multitude of points, the civil sphere, and seem even to have no very remote or shadowy connection with the future peace and security of Christendom.

VI. WERE THE PROPOSITIONS PROPER TO BE SET FORTH BY THE PRESENT WRITER?

There remains yet before us only the shortest and least significant portion of the inquiry, namely, whether these things, being true, and being material to be said, were also proper to be said by me. I must ask pardon, if a tone of egotism be detected in this necessarily subordinate portion of my remarks.

For thirty years, and in a great variety of circumstances, in office and as an independent Member of Parliament, in majorities and in small minorities, and during the larger portion of the time * as the representative of a great constituency, mainly clerical, I have, with others, laboured to maintain and extend the civil rights of my Roman Catholic fellow-countrymen. The Liberal party of this country, with which I have been commonly associated, has suffered, and sometimes suffered heavily, in public favour and in influence, from the belief that it was too ardent in the pursuit of that policy; while at the same time it has always been in the worst odour with the Court of Rome, in consequence of its (I hope) unalterable attachment to Italian liberty and independence. I have sometimes been the spokesman of that party in recommendations which have tended to foster in fact the imputation I have mentioned, though not to warrant it as matter of reason. But it has existed in fact. So that while (as I think) general justice to society required that these things which I have now set forth should be written, special justice, as towards the party to which I am loyally attached, and which I may have had a share in thus placing at a disadvantage before our countrymen, made it, to say the least, becoming that I should not shrink from writing them.

In discharging that office, I have sought to perform the part not of a theological partisan, but simply of a good citizen; of one hopeful that many of his Roman

---

* From 1847 to 1865 I sat for the University of Oxford.

Catholic friends and fellow-countrymen, who are, to say the least of it, as good citizens as himself, may perceive that the case is not a frivolous case, but one that merits their attention.

I will next proceed to give the reason why, up to a recent date, I have thought it right in the main to leave to any others, who might feel it, the duty of dealing in detail with this question.

The great change, which seems to me to have been brought about in the position of Roman Catholic Christians as citizens, reached its consummation, and came into full operation in July 1870, by the proceedings or so-called decrees of the Vatican Council.

Up to that time, opinion in the Roman Church on all matters involving civil liberty, though partially and sometimes widely intimidated, was free wherever it was resolute. During the Middle Ages, heresy was often extinguished in blood, but in every Cisalpine country a principle of liberty, to a great extent, held its own, and national life refused to be put down. Nay more, these precious and inestimable gifts had not infrequently for their champions a local prelacy and clergy. The Constitutions of Clarendon, cursed from the Papal throne, had the support of the English Bishops. Stephen Langton, appointed directly, through an extraordinary stretch of power, by Innocent III., to the See of Canterbury, headed the Barons of England in extorting from the Papal minion John, the worst and basest of all our Sovereigns, that Magna Charta, which the Pope at once visited with his anathemas. In the reign of Henry VIII., it was Tunstal, Bishop of Durham, who first wrote against the Papal domination. Tunstal was followed by Gardiner; and even the recognition of the Royal Headship was voted by the clergy, not under Cranmer, but under his unsuspected predecessor Warham. Strong and domineering as was the high Papal party in those centuries, the resistance was manful. Thrice in history, it seemed as if what we may call the Constitutional party in the Church was about to triumph: first, at the epoch of the Council of Constance; secondly, when the French Episcopate was in conflict with Pope Innocent XI.; thirdly, when Clement XIV. levelled with the dust the deadliest foes that mental and moral liberty have ever known. But from July 1870, this state of things has passed away, and the death-warrant of that Constitutional party has been signed, and sealed, and promulgated in form.

Before that time arrived, although I had used expressions* sufficiently indicative as to the tendency of things in the great Latin Communion, yet I had for very many years felt it to be the first and paramount duty of the British Legislature, whatever Rome might say or do, to give to Ireland all that

---

* [For example, on May 14, 1872, in a speech at King's College: "I must own that, admitting the incapacity of my understanding to grasp fully what has occurred, the aspect of the recent Decrees at Rome appears to me too much to resemble the proclamation of a perpetual war against the progress and the movement of the human mind." Cited in the Charge of Bishop Thirlwall (of St. David's) for 1872. I might add various other references, to the same effect.]

justice could demand, in regard to matters of conscience and of civil equality, and thus to set herself right in the opinion of the civilised world. So far from seeing, what some believed they saw, a spirit of unworthy compliance in such a course, it appeared to me the only one which suited either the dignity or the duty of my country. While this debt remained unpaid, both before and after 1870, I did not think it my province to open formally a line of argument on a question of prospective rather than immediate moment, which might have prejudiced the matter of duty lying nearest our hand, and morally injured Great Britain not less than Ireland, Churchmen and Nonconformists not less than adherents of the Papal Communion, by slackening the disposition to pay the debt of justice. When Parliament had passed the Church Act of 1869 and the Land Act of 1870, there remained only, under the great head of Imperial equity, one serious question to be dealt with—that of the higher Education. I consider that the Liberal majority in the House of Commons, and the Government to which I had the honour and satisfaction to belong, formally tendered payment in full of this portion of the debt by the Irish University Bill of February 1873. Some indeed think, that it was overpaid: a question into which this is manifestly not the place to enter. But the Roman Catholic prelacy of Ireland thought fit to procure the rejection of that measure, by the direct influence which they exercised over a certain number of Irish Members of Parliament, and by the temptation which they thus offered—the bid, in effect, which (to use a homely phrase) they made, to attract the support of the Tory Opposition. Their efforts were crowned with a complete success. From that time forward I have felt that the situation was changed, and that important matters would have to be cleared by suitable explanations. The debt to Ireland had been paid: a debt to the country at large had still to be disposed of, and this has come to be the duty of the hour. So long, indeed, as I continued to be Prime Minister, I should not have considered a broad political discussion on a general question suitable to proceed from me; while neither I nor (I am certain) my colleagues would have been disposed to run the risk of stirring popular passions by a vulgar and unexplained appeal. But every difficulty, arising from the necessary limitations of an official position, has now been removed.

VII. On the Home Policy of the Future.

I could not, however, conclude these observations without anticipating and answering an inquiry they suggest. "Are they, then," it will be asked, "a recantation and a regret; and what are they meant to recommend as the policy of the future?" My reply shall be succinct and plain. Of what the Liberal party has accomplished, by word or deed, in establishing the full civil equality of Roman Catholics, I regret nothing, and I recant nothing.

It is certainly a political misfortune that, during the last thirty years, a Church so tainted in its views of civil obedience, and so unduly capable of changing its front and language after Emancipation from what it had been before, like an actor who has to perform several characters in one piece, should have acquired an extension of its hold upon the highest classes of this country. The conquests have been chiefly, as might have been expected, among women;* but the number of male converts, or captives (as I might prefer to call them), has not been inconsiderable. There is no doubt, that every one of these secessions is in the nature of a considerable moral and social severance. The breadth of this gap varies, according to varieties of individual character. But it is too commonly a wide one. Too commonly, the spirit of the neophyte is expressed by the words which have become notorious: " a Catholic first, an Englishman afterwards." Words which properly convey no more than a truism; for every Christian must seek to place his religion even before his country in his inner heart. But very far from a truism in the sense in which we have been led to construe them. We take them to mean that the "convert" intends, in case of any conflict between the Queen and the Pope, to follow the Pope, and let the Queen shift for herself; which, happily, she can well do.

Usually, in this country, a movement in the highest

---

* [It was not intended in this passage, to point to the fact that, with less of the critical, and moreover of the judicial faculty, women have quicker religious susceptibilities; but to their greater disposition, as compared with men, to lean and depend. In this indication, there is, I hope, nothing like disrespect.]

class would raise a presumption of a similar movement in the mass. It is not so here. Rumours have gone about that the proportion of members of the Papal Church to the population has increased, especially in England. But these rumours would seem to be confuted by authentic figures. The Roman Catholic Marriages, which supply a competent test, and which were 4·89 per cent. of the whole in 1854, and 4·62 per cent. in 1859, were 4·09 per cent. in 1869, and 4·02 per cent. in 1871.*

There is something at the least abnormal in such a partial growth, taking effect as it does among the wealthy and noble, while the people cannot be charmed, by any incantation, into the Roman camp. The original Gospel was supposed to be meant especially for the poor; but the gospel of the nineteenth century from Rome courts another and less modest destination. If the Pope does not control more souls among us, he certainly controls more acres.

The severance, however, of a certain number of lords of the soil from those who till it, can be borne. And so I trust will in like manner be endured the new and very real "aggression" of the principles promulgated by Papal authority, whether they are or are not loyally disclaimed. In this matter, each man is his own judge and his own guide: I can speak for myself. I am no longer able to say, as I would have said before 1870, "There is nothing in the necessary

---

* [As far as I can gather from the Report of the Registrar-General, more recently published, they were in 1872 a little over 4·01 per cent. (pp. ix., x.).]

belief of the Roman Catholic which can appear to impeach his full civil title; for, whatsoever be the follies of ecclesiastical power in his Church, his Church itself has not required of him, with binding authority, to assent to any principles inconsistent with his civil duty." That ground is now, for the present at least, cut from under my feet. What then is to be our course of policy hereafter? First let me say that, as regards the great Imperial settlement, achieved by slow degrees, which has admitted men of all creeds subsisting among us to Parliament, that I conceive to be so determined beyond all doubt or question, as to have become one of the deep foundation-stones of the existing Constitution. But inasmuch as, short of this great charter of public liberty, and independently of all that has been done, there are pending matters of comparatively minor moment which have been, or may be, subjects of discussion, not without interest attaching to them, I can suppose a question to arise in the minds of some. My own views and intentions in the future are of the smallest significance. But, if the arguments I have here offered make it my duty to declare them, I say at once the future will be exactly as the past: in the little that depends on me, I shall be guided hereafter, as heretofore, by the rule of maintaining equal civil rights irrespectively of religious differences; and shall resist all attempts to exclude the members of the Roman Church from the benefit of that rule. Indeed I may say that I have already given conclusive indications of this view, by supporting in Parliament, as a Minister, since 1870, the repeal of the Ecclesiastical Titles Act, for what I think ample reasons. Not only because the time has not yet come when we can assume the consequences of the revolutionary measures of 1870 to have been thoroughly weighed and digested by all capable men in the Roman Communion. Not only because so great a numerical proportion are, as I have before observed, necessarily incapable of mastering, and forming their personal judgment upon, the case. Quite irrespectively even of these considerations, I hold that our onward even course should not be changed by follies, the consequences of which, if the worst come to the worst, this country will have alike the power and, in case of need, the will to control. The State will, I trust, be ever careful to leave the domain of religious conscience free, and yet to keep it to its own domain ; and to allow neither private caprice nor, above all, foreign arrogance to dictate to it in the discharge of its proper office. " England expects every man to do his duty ;" and none can be so well prepared under all circumstances to exact its performance as that Liberal party, which has done the work of justice alike for Nonconformists and for Papal dissidents, and whose members have so often, for the sake of that work, hazarded their credit with the markedly Protestant constituencies of the country. Strong the State of the United Kingdom has always been in material strength; and its moral panoply is now, we may hope, pretty complete.

It is not then for the dignity of the Crown and

people of the United Kingdom to be diverted from a path which they have deliberately chosen, and which it does not rest with all the myrmidons of the Apostolic Chamber either openly to obstruct, or secretly to undermine. It is rightfully to be expected, it is greatly to be desired, that the Roman Catholics of this country should do in the Nineteenth century what their forefathers of England, except a handful of emissaries, did in the Sixteenth, when they were marshalled in resistance to the Armada, and in the Seventeenth when, in despite of the Papal Chair, they sat in the House of Lords under the Oath of Allegiance. That which we are entitled to desire, we are entitled also to expect: indeed, to say we did not expect it, would, in my judgment, be the true way of conveying an "insult" to those concerned. In this expectation we may be partially disappointed. Should those to whom I appeal, thus unhappily come to bear witness in their own persons to the decay of sound, manly, true life in their Church, it will be their loss more than ours. The inhabitants of these Islands, as a whole, are stable, though sometimes credulous and excitable; resolute, though sometimes boastful: and a strong-headed and soundhearted race will not be hindered, either by latent or by avowed dissents, due to the foreign influence of a caste, from the accomplishment of its mission in the world.

APPENDICES.

APPENDIX A.

The numbers here given correspond with those of the Eighteen Propositions given in the text, where it would have been less convenient to cite the originals.

1, 2, 3. " Ex quâ omnino falsâ socialis regiminis ideâ haud timent erroneam illam fovere opinionem, Catholicæ Ecclesiæ, animarumque saluti maxime exitialem, a rec. mem. Gregorio XVI. prædecessore Nostro *deliramentum* appellatam (eâdem Encycl. 'Mirari'), nimirum, libertatem conscientiæ et cultuum esse proprium cujuscunque hominis jus, quod lege proclamari, et asseri debet in omni recte constitutâ societate, et jus civibus inesse ad omnimodam libertatem nullâ vel ecclesiasticâ, vel civili auctoritate coarctandam, quo suos conceptus quoscumque sive voce sive typis, sive aliâ ratione palam publiceque manifestare ac declarare valeant."—*Encyclical Letter.*

4. " Atque silentio præterire non possumus eorum audaciam, qui sanam non sustinentes doctrinam 'illis Apostolicæ Sedis judiciis, et decretis, quorum objectum ad bonum generale Ecclesiæ, ejusdemque jura, ac disciplinam spectare declaratur, dummodo fidei morumque dogmata non attingat, posse assensum et obedientiam detrectari absque peccato, et absque ullâ Catholicæ professionis jacturâ.'"—*Ibid.*

5. " Ecclesia non est vera perfectaque societas plane libera, nec pollet suis propriis et constantibus juribus sibi a divino

suo Fundatore collatis, sed civilis potestatis est definire quæ sint Ecclesiæ jura, ac limites, intra quos eadem jura exercere queat."—*Syllabus* v.

6. "Romani Pontifices et Concilia œcumenica a limitibus suæ potestatis recesserunt, jura Principum usurpârunt, atque etiam in rebus fidei et morum definiendis errârunt."—*Ibid.* xxiii.

7. "Ecclesia vis inferendæ potestatem non habet, neque potestatem ullam temporalem directam vel indirectam."—*Ibid.* xxiv.

8. "Præter potestatem episcopatui inhærentem, alia est attributa temporalis potestas a civili imperio vel expressè vel tacitè concessa, revocanda propterea, cum libuerit, a civili imperio."—*Ibid.* xxv.

9. "Ecclesiæ et personarum ecclesiasticarum immunitas a jure civili ortum habuit."—*Ibid.* xxx.

10. "In conflictu legum utriusque potestatis, jus civile prævalet."—*Ibid.* xlii.

11. "Catholicis viris probari potest ea juventutis instituendæ ratio, quæ sit a Catholicâ fide et ab Ecclesiæ potestate sejuncta, quæque rerum dumtaxat, naturalium scientiam ac terrenæ socialis vitæ fines tantummodo vel saltem primarium spectet."—*Ibid.* xlviii.

12. "Philosophicarum rerum morumque scientia, itemque civiles leges possunt et debent a divinâ et ecclesiasticâ auctoritate declinare."—*Ibid.* lvii.

13, 14. "Matrimonii sacramentum non est nisi contractui accessorium ab eoque separabile, ipsumque sacramentum in unâ tantum nuptiali benedictione situm est."—*Ibid.* lxvi.

"Vi contractûs mere civilis potest inter Christianos constare veri nominis matrimonium; falsumque est, aut contractum matrimonii inter Christianos semper esse sacramentum, aut nullum esse contractum, si sacramentum excludatur."—*Ibid.* lxxiii.

15. "De temporalis regni cum spirituali compatibilitate disputant inter se Christianæ et Catholicæ Ecclesiæ filii."—*Syllabus* lxxv.

"Abrogatio civilis imperii, quo Apostolica Sedes potitur, ad Ecclesiæ libertatem felicitatemque vel maxime conduceret."—*Ibid.* lxxvi.

16. "Ætate hac nostra non amplius expedit religionem Catholicam haberi tanquam unicam status religionem, cæteris quibuscumque cultibus exclusis."—*Ibid.* lxxvii.

17. "Hinc laudabiliter in quibusdam Catholici nominis regionibus lege cautum est, ut hominibus illuc immigrantibus liceat publicum proprii cujusque cultus exercitium habere." —*Ibid.* lxxviii.

18. "Romanus Pontifex potest ac debet cum progressu, cum liberalismo et cum recenti civilitate sese reconciliare et componere."—*Ibid.* lxxx.

APPENDIX B.

I have contented myself with a minimum of citation from the documents of the period before Emancipation. Their full effect can only be gathered by such as are acquainted with, or will take the trouble to refer largely to the originals. It is worth while, however, to cite the following passage from Bishop Doyle, as it may convey, through the indignation it expresses, an idea of the amplitude of the assurances which had been (as I believe, most honestly and sincerely) given.

"There is no justice, my Lord, in thus condemning us. Such conduct on the part of our opponents creates in our bosoms a sense of wrong being done to us; it exhausts our patience, it provokes our indignation, and prevents us from reiterating our efforts to obtain a more impartial hearing. We are tempted, in such cases as these, to attribute unfair motives to those who differ from us, as we cannot conceive how men gifted with intelligence can fail to discover truths so plainly demonstrated as,

"That our faith or our allegiance is not regulated by any such doctrines as those imputed to us;

"That our duties to the Government of our country are not influenced nor affected by any Bulls or practices of Popes;

"That these duties are to be learned by us, as by every other class of His Majesty's subjects, from the Gospel, from the reason given to us by God, from that love of country which nature has implanted in our hearts, and from those constitutional maxims, which are as well understood, and as highly appreciated, by Catholics of the present day, as by their ancestors, who founded them with Alfred, or secured them at Runnymede."—*Doyle's 'Essay on the Catholic Claims,'* London, 1826, p. 38.

The same general tone, as in 1826, was maintained in the answers of the witnesses from Maynooth College before the Commission of 1855. See, for example, pp. 132, 161–4, 272–3, 275, 361, 370–5, 381–2, 394–6, 405. The Commission reported (p. 64), "We see no reason to believe that there has been any disloyalty in the teaching of the College, or any disposition to impair the obligations of an unreserved allegiance to your Majesty."

APPENDIX C.

Compare the recent and ominous forecasting of the future European policy of the British Crown, in an Article from a Romish Periodical for the current month, which has direct relation to these matters, and which has every appearance of proceeding from authority.

"Surely in any European complication, such as may any day arise, nay, such as must ere long arise, from the natural gravitation of the forces, which are for the moment kept in check and truce by the necessity of preparation for their inevitable collision, it may very well be that the future prosperity of England may be staked in the struggle, and that the side which she may take may be determined, not either by justice or interest, but *by a passionate resolve to keep up the Italian kingdom at any hazard.*"—The '*Month*' for November, 1874: 'Mr. Gladstone's Durham Letter,' p. 265.

This is a remarkable disclosure. With *whom* could England be brought into conflict by any disposition she might feel to keep up the Italian kingdom? Considered as States, both Austria and France are in complete harmony with Italy. But it is plain that Italy has some enemy; and the writers of the 'Month' appear to know who it is.

APPENDIX D.

Notice has been taken, both in this country and abroad, of the apparent inertness of public men, and of at least one British Administration, with respect to the subject of these pages. See Friedberg, 'Gränzen zwischen Staat und Kirche,' Abtheilung iii. pp. 755–6; and the Preface to the Fifth Volume of Mr. Greenwood's elaborate, able, and judicial work, entitled 'Cathedra Petri,' p. iv.

"If there be any chance of such a revival, it would become our political leaders to look more closely into the peculiarities of a system, which denies the right of the subject to freedom of thought and action upon matters most material to his civil and religious welfare. There is no mode of ascertaining the spirit and tendency of great institutions but in a careful study of their history. The writer is profoundly impressed with the conviction that our political instructors have wholly neglected this important duty: or, which is perhaps worse, left it in the hands of a class of persons whose zeal has outrun their discretion, and who have sought rather to engage the prejudices than the judgment of their hearers in the cause they have, no doubt sincerely, at heart."

VATICANISM:

AN ANSWER

TO

REPROOFS & REPLIES.

PUBLISHED FEBRUARY 1875.

ERRATA.

Page 26, note, line 3 from foot, *for* "B," *read* "C."

Page 62, line 2 from foot, add foot-note: "But see Cardinal Manning's 'Vatican Decrees,' pp. 31–2."

Page 63, line 19, *for* "1393," *read* "1398."

Page 84, line 2 from foot, *for* "yet," *read* "set."

Page 98, line 9, *for* "implicitly hereafter," *read* "explicitly hereafter."

Page 105, line 8 from foot, *for* "those," *read* "the;" line 2 from foot, *for* "more," *read* "these."

Page 117, line 11, *for* "necessity," *read* "safety."

CONTENTS.

		PAGE
I. INTRODUCTION	.. ..	5

THE REPLIES WHICH HAVE APPEARED ON THIS OCCASION. THE INSULT. EVIDENCES OF PERSONAL LOYALTY, ALL THAT COULD BE WISHED. DR. NEWMAN. HIS REMARKABLE ADMISSIONS. EVIDENCES AS TO THE CHARACTER AND TENDENCIES OF VATICANISM; MOST UNSATISFACTORY.

II. THE RUSTY TOOLS. THE SYLLABUS 19
    1. WHAT ARE ITS CONTENTS? 21
    2. WHAT IS ITS AUTHORITY? 32

III. THE VATICAN COUNCIL AND THE INFALLIBILITY OF THE POPE 37

BREACH WITH HISTORY, No. 1. FROM THE OPINIONS AND DECLARATIONS OF THE ROMAN CATHOLICS OF THE UNITED KINGDOM FOR TWO CENTURIES.

IV. THE VATICAN COUNCIL AND THE INFALLIBILITY OF THE POPE—*continued* 53

BREACH WITH HISTORY, No. 2. FROM THE HISTORY OF THE COUNCIL OF CONSTANCE. GALLICANISM.

V. THE VATICAN COUNCIL AND OBEDIENCE TO THE POPE 65

VI. REVIVED CLAIMS OF THE POPE 70
    1. TO THE DEPOSING POWER 70
    2. TO THE USE OF FORCE 75

CONTENTS.

	PAGE
VII. WARRANT OF ALLEGIANCE ACCORDING TO THE VATICAN	79
1. ITS ALLEGED SUPERIORITY	79
2. ITS REAL FLAWS	82
3. ALLEGED NON-INTERFERENCE OF THE POPES FOR TWO HUNDRED YEARS	88
VIII. ON THE INTRINSIC NATURE AND CONDITIONS OF THE PAPAL INFALLIBILITY DECREED IN THE VATICAN COUNCIL	92
IX. CONCLUSION	109
APPENDICES	121

VATICANISM.

I. INTRODUCTION.

THE number and quality of the antagonists, who have been drawn into the field on the occasion offered by my tract on the Vatican Decrees,* and the interest in the subject which has been manifested by the public of this and of many other countries, appear to show that it was not inopportune. The only special claim to attention with which I could invest it was this, that for thirty years I had striven hard, together with others, to secure a full measure of civil justice for my Roman Catholic fellow-countrymen, and that I still retained the convictions by which these efforts had been prompted. Knowing well the general indisposition of the English mind, amidst the pressing demands of our crowded daily life, to touch any subject comparatively abstract and remote, I was not surprised when many journals of great influence, reflecting this indisposition, condemned the publication of the Tract, and inspired Roman authorities among us with the vain conception that the discussion was not practical

---

* Appendix A.

or significant.* In Rome itself, a different view was taken; and the veiled prophets behind the throne, by whom the Latin Church is governed, brought about its condemnation as blasphemous, without perusal, from the lips of the Holy Father.† The object, probably, was at once to prevent or neutralise avowals of sympathy from Roman Catholic quarters. It may have been with a like aim that a number of Prelates at once entered, though by no means with one voice, into the lists. At length the great name of Dr. Newman was announced, and he too has replied to me, and explained himself, in a work to which I shall presently refer. Even apart from the *spolia opima* of this transcendent champion, I do not undervalue the ability, accomplishments, and discipline of that division of the Roman Army, which confronts our Church and nation. Besides its supply from indigenous sources, it has been strangely but very largely recruited from the ranks of the English Church, and her breasts have, for thirty years, been pierced mainly by the children whom they had fed.

In these replies, of which the large majority adopt without reserve the Ultramontane hypothesis, it is most commonly alleged that I have insulted the Roman Catholics of these kingdoms. Dr. Newman, averse to the use of harsh words, still announces (p. 3) that "heavy

---

* For example: "The various organs of the press, with the shrewd political sense for which they are conspicuous, without any possible collusion, extinguished its political import in a single morning."— Bishop Vaughan's 'Pastoral Letter,' p. 5.

† The declaration of *non avenu*, which, after a brief interval, followed the announcement of the condemnation, appeared upon some subsequent discussion to be negatived by the evidence. But such declarations are, I conceive, well understood in Rome to depend, like an English "*not at home*," upon convenience.

charges have been made against the Catholics of England." Bishop Clifford, in a pastoral letter of which I gladly acknowledge the equitable, restrained, and Christian spirit, says I have proclaimed that since the Vatican Decrees were published "it is no longer possible for English Catholics to pay to their temporal sovereign a full and undivided allegiance" (p. 5).

I am obliged to assert that not one of the writers against me has apprehended or stated with accuracy my principal charge. Except a prospective reference to "converts," the subject (to speak technically) of all my propositions is the word "Rome"; and with reference to these "converts," I speak of what they suffer, not of what they do. It is an entire, and even a gross, error to treat all affirmations about Rome as equivalent to affirmations about British subjects of the Roman communion. They may adopt the acts of Rome : the question was and is, whether they do. I have done nothing to leave this question open to doubt; for I have paraphrased my monosyllable "Rome" by the words "the Papal Chair, and its advisers and abettors" (p. 9). Unable as I am to attenuate the charges, on the contrary bound rather to plead guilty to the fault of having understated them, I am on that account the more anxious that their aim shall be clearly understood. First, then, I must again speak plainly, and I fear hardly, of that system, political rather than religious, which in Germany is well termed Vaticanism. It would be affectation to exclude from my language and meaning its contrivers and conscious promoters. But here in my mind, as well as in my page, anything approaching to censure stops. The Vatican Decrees do, in the strictest sense, establish for the Pope a supreme command over loyalty and civil duty. To the vast majority of Roman Catholics they are, and in all likelihood will long in their carefully enveloped meaning remain, practically unknown. Of that small minority, who have spoken or fitted themselves to speak, a portion reject them. Another portion receive them with an express reserve, to me perfectly satisfactory, against all their civil consequences. Another portion seem to suspend their judgment until it is determined what is a free Council, what is moral unanimity, what are declarations *ex cathedrâ*, whether there has been a decisive and binding promulgation so as to create a law, and whether the claim for an undue obedience need be considered until some act of undue obedience is asked. A very large class, as it seems to me, think they receive these Decrees, and do not. They are involved in inconsistency, and that inconsistency is dangerous. So I presume they would tell me that when I recite in the Creed the words, "I believe in the Holy Catholic Church," I am involved in inconsistency, and my inconsistency is dangerous. To treat this as a "heavy charge" is surely inaccurate; to call it an insult is (forgive the word) preposterous.

Not even against men who voted under pressure, against their better mind, for these deplorable Decrees, nay, not even against those who resisted them and now enforce them, is it for me to utter a word of censure. The just appreciation of their difficulties, the judgment of their conduct, lies in a region far too high for me. To assail the system is the Alpha and Omega of my desire; and it is to me matter of regret that I am not able to handle it as it deserves without reflecting upon the persons, be they who they may, that have brought it into the world; have sedulously fed it in its weakness; have reared it up to its baleful maturity; have forced it upon those, who now force it upon others; are obtaining for it from day to day fresh command over the pulpit, the press, the confessional, the teacher's chair, the bishop's throne; so that every father of a family, and every teacher in the Latin communion, shall, as he dies, be replaced by some one more deeply imbued with the new colour, until at the last, in that moiety of the whole Christian family, nothing shall remain except an Asian monarchy; nothing, but one giddy height of despotism, and one dead level of religious subserviency.

But even of the most responsible abettors of that system I desire once for all to say, that I do not presume in any way to impeach their sincerity; and that, as far as I am acquainted with their personal characters, I should think it great presumption to place myself in comparison or competition with any of them.

So much for insult. Much has also been said of my ignorance and incapacity in theology;* a province which I had entered only at the points where it crossed the border of the civil domain. Censures of this kind have great weight, when they follow upon demonstration given of errors committed by the person who is the object of them; but they can have very little, when they are used as substitutes for such a demonstration. In the absence of such proof, they can rank no higher, than as a mere artifice of controversy. I have endeavoured to couch all my positive

---

* For example:—By Archbishop Manning, pp. 13, 177. Bishop Ullathorne, Letter, p. 10. 'Exposition Unravelled,' p. 68. Bishop Vaughan, p. 37. 'Month,' December, 1874, p. 497. Monk of St. Augustine's, p. 10. With these legitimate reproaches is oddly combined on the part of the Archbishop, and, apparently, of Bishop Ullathorne, a supposition that Dr. Döllinger was in some manner concerned in my tract on the Vatican Decrees. See Appendix B.

statements in language of moderation, and not one among them that appertains to the main line of argument has been shaken. As to the use of rhetoric, another matter of complaint, I certainly neither complain of strong language used against me, nor do I think that it can properly be avoided, when the matters of fact, carefully ascertained and stated, are such that it assists towards a comprehension of their character and consequences. At the same time, in the use of such language earnestness should not be allowed to degenerate into dogmatism, and to qualify is far more pleasant than to employ it.

With so much of preface, I proceed to execute my twofold duty. One of its branches is to state in what degree I conceive the immediate purpose of my Expostulation to have been served; and the other, to examine whether the allegations of antagonists have dislodged my arguments from their main positions, or, on the contrary, have confirmed them; and to re-state, nay, even to enlarge, those positions accordingly.

In considering the nature of the declarations on civil duty which have been elicited, it will not be thought unnatural if I begin with the words of one to whom age and fame combine in assigning the most conspicuous place —I mean Dr. Newman.

Of this most remarkable man I must pause to speak a word. In my opinion, his secession from the Church of England has never yet been estimated among us at anything like the full amount of its calamitous importance. It has been said that the world does not know its greatest men; neither, I will add, is it aware of the power and weight carried by the words and by the acts of those among its greatest men, whom it does know. The Ecclesiastical historian will perhaps hereafter judge that this secession was a much greater event even than the partial secession of John Wesley, the only case of personal loss suffered by the Church of England, since the Reformation, which can be at all compared with it in magnitude. I do not refer to its effect upon the mere balance of schools or parties in the Church; that is an inferior question. I refer to its effect upon the state of positive belief, and the attitude and capacities of the religious mind of England. Of this, thirty years ago, he had the leadership; an office and power from which none but himself could eject him.

" Quis desiderio sit pudor aut modus
Tam cari capitis?"

It has been his extraordinary, perhaps unexampled case, at a critical period, first to give to the religious thought of his time and country the most powerful impulse which for a long time it had received from any individual; and then to be the main though, without doubt, involuntary cause of disorganising it in a manner as remarkable, and breaking up its forces into a multitude of not only severed but conflicting bands.

My duty calls me to deal freely with his Letter to the Duke of Norfolk. But in doing so, I can never lose the recollection of the perhaps ill-appreciated greatness of his early life and works. I do not presume to intrude into the sanctuary of his present thoughts; but, by reason of that life and those works, it seems to me that there is something we must look upon with an affection, like that of Americans for those Englishmen who lived and wrought before the colonisation, or the severance, of their country. Nay, it may not be presumptuous to say we have a possessory right in the better half of him. All he produces is and must be most notable. But has he outrun, has he overtaken the greatness of the 'History of the Arians' and of the ' Parochial Sermons,' those indestructible classics of English theology?

And again, I thankfully record the admissions, which such integrity, combined with such acuteness, has not been able to withhold. They are of the greatest importance to the vindication of my argument. In my reading of his work, we have his authority for the following statements. That Roman Catholics are bound to be "as loyal as other subjects of the State;" and that Rome is not to give to the civil power " trouble or alarm " (p. 7). That the assurances given by the Roman Catholic Bishops in 1825-6 have not been strictly fulfilled (pp. 12-14). That Roman Catholics cannot wonder that statesmen should feel themselves aggrieved (p. 17). That Popes are sometimes in the wrong, and sometimes to be resisted, even in matters affecting the government and welfare of the Church (pp. 33, 34). That the Deposing power is defensible only upon condition of " the common consent of peoples" (p. 37). That if England supported Italy against any violent attempt to restore the Pope to his throne, Roman Catholics could offer no opposition but such as the constitution of the country allows (p. 49). That a soldier or sailor employed in a war which (in his private judgment, be it observed) he did not think unjust, ought not to retire from the prosecution of that war on the command of the Pope (p. 52). That conscience is the aboriginal vicar of Christ (p. 57): *ein tüchtiges Wort!* and Dr. Newman, at an ideal public dinner, will drink to conscience first, and the Pope afterwards (p. 66). That one of the great dangers of the Roman Catholic Church is to be found in the exaggerated language and proceedings allowed among its own members (pp. 4, 80, 94, 125), and that there is much *malaria* in the court of Rome. That a definition by a general Council, which the Pope approves, is not absolutely binding thereby, but requires a moral unanimity, and a subsequent reception by the Church (pp. 96-8). That antecedently to the theological definitions of 1854 and 1870, an opponent might have "fairly said" "it might appear that there were no sufficient historical grounds in behalf of either of them ;" and that the confutation of such an opponent is now to be sought only in "the fact of the definition being made" (p. 107). I shall indulge in none of the taunts, which Dr. Newman anticipates, on the want of correspondence between him and other Apologists; and I shall leave it to theologians to examine the bearing of these admissions on the scheme of Vaticanism, and on other parts of his own work. It is enough for me to record that, even if they stood alone, they would suffice to justify the publication which has given "occasion" for them; and that on the point of Dr. Newman's practical reservation of his command over his own "loyalty and civil duty," they are entirely satisfactory. As regards this latter point, the Pastoral of Bishop Clifford is also everything that can be wished. Among laymen who declare they accept the Decrees of 1870, I must specially make the same avowal as to my esteemed friend Mr. De Lisle ; and again, as to Mr. Stores Smith, who regards me with "silent and intense contempt," but who does not scruple to write as follows :—

"If this country decide to go to war, for any cause whatsoever, I will hold my own opinion as to the justice or policy of that war, but I will do all that in me lies to bring victory to the British standard. If there be any Parliamentary or Municipal election, and any Priest or Bishop, backed by Archbishop and the Pope, advise me to take a certain line of action, and I conceive that the opposite course is necessary for the general weal of my fellow-countrymen, I shall take the opposite."*

When it is considered that Dr. Newman is like the sun in the intellectual hemisphere of Anglo-Romanism, and that, besides those acceptors of the Decrees who write in the same sense, various Roman Catholics of weight and distinction, well known to represent the views of many more, have held equally outspoken and perhaps more consistent language, I cannot but say that the immediate purpose of my appeal has been attained, in so far that the loyalty of our Roman Catholic fellow-subjects in the mass remains evidently untainted and secure.

It would be unjust to Archbishop Manning, on whose opinions, in many points, I shall again have to animadvert, were I not to say that his declarations † also materially assist in leading me to this conclusion; an avowal I am the more bound to make, because I think the premisses from which he draws them are such as, if I were myself to accept them, would certainly much impair the guarantees for my performing, under all circumstances, the duties of a good subject.

This means that the poison, which circulates from Rome, has not actually been taken into the system. Unhappily, what I may term the minority among the Apologists do not represent the *ecclesia docens*; the silent diffusion of its influence in the lay atmosphere; the true current and aim of thought in the Papal Church, now given up to Vaticanism *de jure*, and likely, according to all human probability, to come from year to year more under its power. And here again the ulterior purpose of my Tract has been

---

* Letter in 'Halifax Courier' of December 5, 1874.
† Archbishop Manning, 'Vatican Decrees,' pp. 136-40.

thus far attained. It was this. To provide that if, together with the ancient and loyal traditions of the body, we have now imported among us a scheme adverse to the principles of human freedom and in its essence unfaithful to civil duty, the character of that scheme should be fully considered and understood. It is high time that the chasm should be made visible, severing it, and all who knowingly and thoroughly embrace it, from the principles which we had a right to believe not only prevailed among the Roman Catholics of these countries, but were allowed and recognised by the authorities of their Church; and would continue, therefore, to form the basis of their system, permanent and undisturbed. For the more complete attainment of this object, I must now proceed to gather together the many threads of the controversy, as it has been left by my numerous opponents. This I shall do, not from any mere call of speculation or logical consistency, but for strong practical reasons.

Dr. Newman's letter to the Duke of Norfolk is of the highest interest as a psychological study. Whatever he writes, whether we agree with him or not, presents to us this great attraction as well as advantage, that we have everywhere the man in the work, that his words are the transparent covering of his nature. If there be obliquity in them, it is purely intellectual obliquity; the work of an intellect sharp enough to cut the diamond, and bright as the diamond which it cuts. How rarely it is found, in the wayward and inscrutable records of our race, that with these instruments of an almost superhuman force and subtlety, robustness of character and energy of will are or can be developed in the same extraordinary proportions, so as to integrate that structure of combined thought and action, which makes life a moral whole! "There are gifts too large and too fearful to be handled freely."* But I turn from an incidental reflection to observe that my duty is to appreciate the letter of Dr. Newman exclusively in relation to my Tract. I thankfully here record, in the first place, the kindliness of his tone. If he has striven to minimise the Decrees of the Vatican, I am certain he has also striven to minimise his censures, and has put words aside before they touched his paper, which must have been in his thoughts, if not upon his pen. I sum up this pleasant portion of my duty with the language of Helen respecting Hector: πατὴρ ὡς ἤπιος αἰεί.†

It is, in my opinion, an entire mistake to suppose that theories like those, of which Rome is the centre, are not operative on the thoughts and actions of men. An army of teachers, the largest and the most compact in the world, is ever sedulously at work to bring them into practice. Within our own time they have most powerfully, as well as most injuriously, altered the spirit and feeling of the Roman Church at large; and it will be strange indeed if, having done so much in the last half-century, they shall effect nothing in the next. I must avow, then, that I do not feel exactly the same security for the future as for the present. Still less do I feel the same security for other lands as for this. Nor can I overlook indications which lead to the belief that, even in this country, and at this time, the proceedings of Vaticanism threaten to be a source of some practical inconvenience. I am confident that if a system so radically bad is to be made or kept innocuous, the first condition for attaining such a result is that its movements should be carefully watched,

---

* Dr. Newman, p. 127. † Iliad, xxiv. 770.

and, above all, that the bases on which they work should be faithfully and unflinchingly exposed. Nor can I quit this portion of the subject without these remarks. The satisfactory views of Archbishop Manning on the present rule of civil allegiance have not prevented him from giving his countenance as a responsible editor* to the lucubrations of a gentleman, who denies liberty of conscience, and asserts the right to persecute when there is the power; a right which, indeed, the Prelate has not himself disclaimed.

Nor must it be forgotten, that the very best of all the declarations we have heard from those who allow themselves to be entangled in the meshes of the Vatican Decrees, are, every one of them, uttered subject to the condition that, upon orders from Rome, if such orders should issue, they shall be qualified, or retracted, or reversed.

"A breath can *un*make them, as a breath has made."

But even apart from all this, do what we may in checking external developments, it is not in our power to neutralise the mischiefs of the wanton aggression of 1870 upon the liberties—too scanty, it is excusable to think—which up to that epoch had been allowed to private Christians in the Roman communion. Even in those parts of Christendom where the Decrees and the present attitude of the Papal See do not produce or aggravate open broils with the civil power, by undermining moral liberty they impair moral responsibility, and silently, in the succession of generations if not even in the lifetime of individuals, tend to emasculate the vigour of the mind.

In the tract on the Vatican Decrees I passed briefly by those portions of my original statement which most

---

* 'Essays,' edited by Archbishop Manning, pp. 401-5, 467.

lay within the province of theology, and dwelt principally on two main propositions.

I. That Rome had reproduced for active service those doctrines of former times, termed by me "rusty tools," which she was fondly thought to have disused.

II. That the Pope now claims, with plenary authority, from every convert and member of his Church, that he "shall place his loyalty and civil duty at the mercy of another:" that other being himself.

These are the assertions, which I now hold myself bound further to sustain and prove.

II. THE RUSTY TOOLS. THE SYLLABUS.

1. *Its Contents.*
2. *Its Authority.*

With regard to the proposition that Rome has refurbished her "rusty" tools, Dr. Newman says it was by these tools that Europe was brought into a civilized condition: and thinks it worth while to ask whether it is my wish that penalties so sharp, and expressions so high, should be of daily use.*

I may be allowed to say, in reply to the remark I have cited, that I have nowhere presumed to pronounce a general censure on the conduct of the Papacy in the middle ages. That is a vast question, reaching far beyond my knowledge or capacity. I believe much is to be justly said in praise, much as justly in blame. But I cannot view the statement that Papal claims and conduct created the civilization of Europe as other than thoroughly unhistorical and one-sided: as resting upon a narrow selection of evidence, upon strong exaggeration of what that evidence imports, and upon an "invincible ignorance" as to all the rest.

Many things may have been suited, or not unsuited, to rude times and indeterminate ideas of political right, the reproduction of which is at the least strange, perhaps even monstrous. We look back with interest and respect upon our early fire-arms as they rest peacefully ranged upon

---

* Dr. Newman, p. 32.

the wall; but we cannot think highly of the judgment which would recommend their use in modern warfare. As for those weapons which had been consigned to obscurity and rust, my answer to Dr. Newman's question is that they should have slept for ever, till perchance some reclaiming plough of the future should disturb them.

> " . . . quum finibus illis
> Agricola, incurvo terram molitus aratro,
> Exesa inveniet scabrâ rubigine pila." *

As to the proof of my accusation, it appeared to me that it might be sufficiently given in a summary but true account† of some important portions of the Encyclica of December 8th, 1864, and especially of the accompanying Syllabus of the same date.

The replies to the five or six pages, in which I dealt with this subject, have so swollen as to reach fifteen or twenty times the bulk. I am sorry that they involve me in the necessity of entering upon a few pages of detail which may be wearisome. But I am bound to vindicate my good faith and care, where a failure in either involves results of real importance. These results fall under the two following heads:—

(1). The Syllabus; what is its language?
(2). The Syllabus; what is its authority?

As to the language, I have justly represented it: as to its authority, my statement is not above, but below the mark.

---

* Virgil, Georgics i. 493.

† Erroneously called by some of my antagonists a translation, and then condemned as a bad translation. But I know of no *recipe* for translating into less than half the bulk of the original.

1. *The Contents of the Syllabus.*

My representation of the language of the Syllabus has been assailed in strong terms. I proceed to defend it: observing, however, that my legitimate object was to state in popular terms the effect of propositions more or less technical and scholastic: and, secondly, that I did not present each and every proposition for a separate disapproval, but directed attention rather to the effect of the document as a whole, in a qualifying passage (p. 13) which no one of my critics has been at the pains to notice.

Nos. 1–3.—The first charge of unjust representation is this.* I have stated that the Pope condemns (p. 25) liberty of the press, and liberty of speech. By reference to the original it is shown, that the right of printing and speaking is not in terms condemned universally; but only the right of each man to print or speak all his thoughts (*suos conceptus quoscunque*), whatever they may be. Hereupon it is justly observed, that in all countries there are laws against blasphemy, or obscenity, or sedition, or all three. It is argued, then, that men are not allowed the right to speak or print *all* their thoughts, and that such an extreme right only is what the Pope has condemned.

It appears to me that this is, to use a mild phrase, mere trifling with the subject. We are asked to believe that what the Pope intended to condemn was a state of things, which never has existed in any country of the world. Now, he says he is condemning one of the commonly prevailing errors of the time, familiarly known

---

* 'The Month,' December 1874, p. 494. Coleridge, 'Abomination of Desolation,' p. 20. Bishop Ullathorne, 'Pastoral Letter,' p. 16. Monk of St. Augustine's, p. 15. Dr. Newman, pp. 59, 72, in some part.

to the bishops whom he addresses.* What bishop knows of a State which by law allows a perfectly free course to blasphemy, filthiness, and sedition? The world knows quite well what is meant by free speech and a free press. It does mean, generally, perhaps it may be said universally, the right of declaring all opinions whatsoever. The limit of freedom is not the justness of the opinion, but it is this, that it shall be opinion in good faith, and not mere grossness, passion, or appeal to violence. The law of England at this moment, allowing all opinions whatever, provided they are treated by way of rational discourse, most closely corresponds to what the Pope has condemned. His condemnation is illustrated by his own practice as Governor in the Roman States, where no opinion could be spoken or printed but such as he approved. Once, indeed, he permitted a free discussion on Saint Peter's presence and prelacy in the city; but he repented quickly, and forbade the repetition of it. We might even cite his practice as Pope in 1870, where everything was done to keep the proceedings of the Council secret from the Church which it professed to represent, and even practically secret from its members, except those who were of the governing cabal. But there can be no better mode of exhibiting his real meaning than by referring to his account of the Austrian law. *Ilâc lege omnis omnium opinionum et librariæ artis libertas, omnis tum fidei, tum conscientiæ ac doctrinæ, libertas statuitur.*† To the kind of condemnation given, I shall again

---

* "Probè noscitis hoc tempore non paucos reperiri, qui," &c.— 'Encycl.,' December 8, 1864.

† From the Pope's Allocution of June 22, 1868: "By this law is established universal liberty of all opinions and of the press, and, as of belief, so of conscience and of teaching." See Vering,

refer; but the matter of it is nothing abstract or imaginary, it is actual freedom of thinking, speaking, and printing, as it is practised in a great civilized and Christian empire. I repel, then, the charge against me as no better than a verbal subterfuge; and I again affirm that in his Syllabus, as in his acts, the Pope has condemned liberty of speech and liberty of the press.

No. 5.—I have stated that the Pope condemns " those who assign to the State the power of defining the civil rights (*jura*) and province of the Church." Hereupon it is boldly stated that " the word civil is a pure interpolation."* This statement Dr. Newman's undertaking tempts him to quote, but his sagacity and scholarship save him from adopting. Anticipating some cavil such as this, I took care (which is not noticed) to place the word *jura* in my text. I now affirm that my translation is correct. *Jus* means, not right at large, but a specific form of right, and in this case civil right, to which meaning indeed the word constantly leans. It refers to right which is social, relative, extrinsic. *Jus hominum situm est in generis humani societate* (Cic. Tusc. ii. 26). If a theological definition is desired, take that of Dens: *Accipitur potissimum pro jure prout est in altero, cui debet satisfieri ad æqualitatem; de jure sic sumpto hic agitur.*† It is not of the internal constitution of the Church and the rights of its members *inter se* that the proposition treats; nor yet of its ecclesiastical standing in reference to other bodies; but of its rights in the face of the State; that is to say, of

---

Archiv für Katholisches Kirchenrecht.' Mainz, 1868, p. 171, Band xx.
* 'The Abomination of Desolation,' p. 21. Dr. Newman, p. 87.
† 'Tractatus de jure et justitiâ,' No. 6.

its civil rights. My account therefore was accurate; and Mr. Coleridge's criticism superfluous.

I must, however, admit that Vaticanism has a way of escape. For perhaps it does not admit that the Church enjoys any civil rights: but considers as her own, and therefore spiritual in their source, such rights as we consider accidental and derivative, even where not abusive.

On this subject I will refer to a high authority. The Jesuit Schrader was, I believe, one of those employed in drawing up the Syllabus. He has published a work, with a Papal Approbation attached to it, in which he converts the condemnatory negations of the Syllabus into the corresponding affirmatives. For Article XXX. he gives the following proposition:—

"The immunities of the Church, and of ecclesiastical persons, have not their origin in civil right."

He adds the remark: "but are rooted in the Church's own right, given to her from God." *

No. 7.—I have said those persons are condemned by the Syllabus, who hold that in countries called Catholic the free exercise of other religions may laudably be allowed. Dr. Newman truly observes,† that it is the free exercise of religion by immigrants or foreigners which is meant (hominibus *illuc immigrantibus*), and that I have omitted the words. I omitted them, for my case was strong enough without them. But they seem to strengthen my case. For the claim to a free exercise of religion on behalf of immigrants or foreigners is a stronger one than on behalf of natives, and has been so recognised in Italy and in

---

* 'Der Papst und die Modernen Ideen.' Von P. Clemens Schrader, S.J. Heft ii. 65.
† Dr. Newman, p. 86.

Rome itself. I think I am right in saying that difference of tongue has generally been recognised by Church law as mitigating the objections to the toleration of dissidence. And it is this stronger claim, not the weaker one, which is condemned. So that if there be a fault, it is the fault of under-, not of over-statement.

Again I support myself by the high authority of Schrader the Jesuit. The following is his Article LXXVII. It draws no distinction of countries:—

"In our view it is still useful that the Catholic religion should be maintained as the only State religion to the exclusion of every other."*

In the appended remark he observes, that *on this account* the Pope, in 1856, condemned the then recent Spanish law which tolerated other forms of worship.†

No. 8.—I am charged, again,‡ with mistranslating under my eighth head. The condemnation in the Syllabus is, as I conceived, capable of being construed to apply to the entire proposition as it is there given, or to a part of it only. In brief it is this: "The Episcopate has a certain power not inherent, but conferred by the State, which may therefore be withdrawn at the pleasure of the State." The condemnation might be aimed at the assertion that such a power exists, or at the assertion that it is withdrawable at pleasure. In the latter sense, the condemnation is unwise and questionable as a general proposition: in the former sense it is outrageous beyond all bounds; and I am boldly accused of mistranslating‡ because I chose the milder imputation of the two, and understood the censure to apply only to withdrawal *ad libitum*. I learn now that, in the

---

* Schrader, p. 80.
† *Infra*.
‡ Mr. Coleridge, 'Abomination of Desolation,' p. 21.

opinion of this antagonist at least, the State was not the source of (for example) the power of coinage, which was at one time exercised by the Bishops of Durham. So that the upshot is: either my construction is right, or my charge is milder than it should have been.

Nos. 13, 14.—A grave charge is made against me respecting the matrimonial propositions: because I have cited the Pope as condemning those who affirm that the matrimonial contract is binding whether there is or is not (according to the Roman doctrine) a Sacrament; and have not at the same time stated that English marriages are held by Rome to be Sacramental, and therefore valid.*

No charge, serious or slight, could be more entirely futile. But it is serious and not slight; and those who prompt the examination must abide the recoil. I begin thus:—

1. I am censured for not having given distinctions between one country and another, which the Pope himself has not given.

2. And which are also thought unnecessary by authorised expounders of the Syllabus for the faithful.†

I have before me the Exposition,‡ with the text, of the Encyclica and Syllabus, published at Cologne in 1874, with the approval of authority (*mit oberkirchlicher Approbation*). In p. 45 it is distinctly taught that with marriage the State has nothing to do; that it may safely rely upon the Church; that civil marriage, in the eyes of the Church, is only concubinage; and that the State, by the use of worldly compulsion, prevents the two concubinary

---

* Monk of St. Augustine's, p. 15. 'Abomination,' p. 22.

† Appendix B.

‡ '*Die Encyclica, der Syllabus, und die wichtigsten darin angeführten Actenstücke, nebst einer ausführlichen Einleitung.*' Köln, 1874.

parties from repenting and abandoning their guilty relation to one another. Exactly the same is the doctrine of the Pope himself, in his Speeches published at Rome; where civil marriage is declared to be, for Christians, nothing more than a mere concubinage, and a filthy concubinage (*sozzo concubinato*).* These extraordinary declarations are not due to the fondness of the Pontiff for speaking *impromptu*. In his letter of September 19th, 1852, to King Victor Emmanuel, he declares that matrimony carrying the sacrament is alone lawful for Christians, and that a law of civil marriage, which goes to divide them for practical purposes, constitutes a concubinage in the guise of legitimate marriage.† So that, in truth, in all countries within the scope of these denunciations, the parties to a civil marriage are declared to be living in an illicit connection, which they are called upon to renounce. This call is addressed to them separately as well as jointly, the wife being summoned to leave her husband, and the husband to abandon his wife; and after this pretended repentance from a state of sin, unless the law of the land and fear of consequences prevail, a new connection, under the name of a marriage, may be formed with the sanction of the Church of Rome. It is not possible, in the limited space here at my command, adequately to exhibit a state of facts, thus created by the highest authorities of the Roman Church, which I shall now not shrink from calling horrible and revolting in itself, and dangerous to the morals of society, the structure of the family, and the peace of life.

---

* 'Discorsi di Pio IX.' Roma, 1872, 1873. Vol. i. p. 193, vol. ii. p. 355.
† 'Recueil des Allocutions de Pie IX.' &c. Paris: Leclerc, 1865, p. 312.

It is true, indeed, that the two hundred thousand non-Roman marriages, which are annually celebrated in England, do not at present fall under the foul epithets of Rome. But why? Not because we marry, as I believe nineteen-twentieths of us marry, under the sanctions of religion; for our marriages are, in the eye of the Pope, purely civil marriages; but only for the technical, accidental, and precarious reason, that the disciplinary decrees of Trent are not canonically in force in this country. There is nothing, unless it be motives of mere policy, to prevent the Pope from giving them force here when he pleases. If, and when that is done, every marriage thereafter concluded in the English Church will, according to his own words, be a filthy concubinage.

The decrees have force already in many parts of Germany, and in many entire countries of Europe. Within these limits, every civil marriage, and every religious marriage not contracted before a Roman *parochus*, as the Council of Trent requires, is but the formation of a guilty connection, which each of the parties severally is charged by the Church of Rome to dissolve, under pain of being held to be in mortal sin.

In 1602, when the Decree of Trent had been in force for thirty-eight years, it was applied by the *Congregatio Concilii*, with the approval of Pope Clement VIII., to non-Roman marriages, by a declaration that heretics were bound to conform (which was impossible) to the rules of the Council, in default of which their marriages, whether religious or civil, were null and void.*

---

* "Hæreticos quoque, ubi Decretum dicti capitis est publicatum, teneri talem formam observare, et propterea ipsorum etiam matrimonia, absque formâ Concilii quamvis coram ministro hæretico vel magistratu loci contracta, nulla atque irrita esse."—Vering, Archiv, xvii. 461, *seq. See* Sicherer, 'Eherecht in Bayern,' Munich, 1875, p. 12, n.

To this portentous rule exceptions have been made, especially by Benedict XIV. in the case of Holland. Indeed, he questioned its propriety; and Pius VII., in a communication to the Primate Dalberg, formerly Archbishop of Mentz, referred with approval to the language of Benedict XIV. Many theologians have held an opinion adverse to it, and clergy have been allowed to act at times upon that opinion, but only under cover of a policy of dissimulation, a name by which the Court of Rome itself has not been ashamed to describe its own conduct.* But when the abrogation of the rule for non-Roman marriages has been prayed for, even by Bishops, and bodies of Bishops, the prayer has failed.† It has been kept alive; and transactions positively dreadful have taken place under its authority, and under other provisions calculated for the same end. Perrone, who may be called the favourite theologian of the Curia, points out that it works for the benefit of heretics, as on their conversion it has often given them an opportunity of contracting a new marriage; during the lifetime, that is to say, of the former wife.‡

The upshot, then, seems to be this: that Rome, while stigmatising marriages not Tridentine as concubinages in the manner we have seen, reserves a power, under the name or plea of special circumstances, to acknowledge them or not, as policy may recommend. This is but

---

* Sicherer, ibid., p. 37, n. 56, 58.
† Sicherer, ibid., p. 66, n.
‡ "Si quid ex hâc doctrinâ et praxi provenit, vertitur demum in bonum ipsorum acatholicorum, si quando contingat eos in Ecclesiæ Catholicæ sinum redire, dum ipsis indulgetur, ita poscentibus rerum adjunctis, vel ob mutua dissidia, vel ob separationem ab invicem, aliaque ejusmodi, novas inire nuptias, uti ex non paucis resolutionibus liquet: aut proprium instaurare conjugium, si ambo convertantur conjuges." 'De Matrim. Christ.,' ii. 245, ed. Rome, 1856.

the old story. All problems, which menace the Roman Chair with difficulties it dare not face, are to be solved, not by the laying down of principles, good or bad, strict or lax, in an intelligible manner, but by reserving all cases as matters of discretion to the breast of the *Curia*, which will decide from time to time, according to its pleasure, whether there has been a sacrament or not, and whether we are married folks, or persons living in guilty commerce, and rearing our children under a false pretext of legitimacy.

This, then, is the statement I now make. It has been drawn from me by the exuberant zeal and precipitate accusations of the school of Loyola.

No. 18.—Finally, it is contended that I misrepresent Rome in stating that it condemns the call to reconcile itself with progress, liberalism, and modern civilization.

It is boldly stated that the Pope condemns not these, but only what is bad in these.* And thus it is that, to avert public displeasure, words are put into the Pope's mouth, which he has not used, and which are at variance with the whole spirit of the document that he has sent forth to alarm, as Dr. Newman too well sees, the educated mind of Europe.† It appears to be claimed for Popes, that they shall be supreme over the laws of language. But mankind protests against a system which palters in a double sense with its own solemn declarations; imposing them on the weak, glorying in them before those who are favourably prepossessed, and then contracting their sense *ad libitum*, even to the point of nullity, by arbitrary interpolation, to appease the scandalised understanding of

---

* 'The Month,' as *sup.* p. 496. Bishop Ullathorne, 'Expostulation Unravelled,' p. 69.
† Dr. Newman, p. 90.

Christian nations. Without doubt progress, liberalism, modern civilization, are terms more or less ambiguous; but they are, under a sound general rule, determinable by the context. Now, the contexts of the Syllabus and Encyclica are perfectly unambiguous; they perfectly explain what the Pope means by the words. He means to condemn all that we consider fair limitation of the claims of priestly power; to repudiate the title of man to general freedom of thought, and of speech in all its varied forms of utterance; the title of a nation to resist those, who treat the sovereignty over it as a property, and who would enforce on the people—for example, of the Papal States—a government independently of or against its will; in a word, the true and only sure titles of freedom in all its branches, inward and outward, mental, moral and political, as they are ordinarily understood in the judgment of this age and country.

I have gone, I believe, through every particular impeachment of my account of the language of the Syllabus and the Encyclica. If each and all of these have failed, I presume that I need not dwell upon the general allegations of opponents in respect to those heads where they have not been pleased to enter upon details.*

Now, it is quite idle to escape the force of these charges by reproaches aimed at my unacquaintance with theology, and by recommendations, sarcastic or sincere, that I should obtain some instruction in its elements. To such reproaches I shall peacefully and respectfully bow, so soon as I shall have been convicted of error. But I think I have shown that the only variations from exact truth, to which I can

---

* 'The Month,' as *sup.* p. 497.

plead guilty, are variations in the way of understatements of the case which it was my duty to produce.

2. *The Authority of the Syllabus.*

I have next to inquire what is the authority of the Syllabus?

Had I been inclined to push my case to extremes, I might very well have contended that this document was delivered *ex cathedrâ*. Schulte, whose authority as a Canonist is allowed on all hands to be great, founds his argument on that opinion.* Dr. Ward, who has been thanked† by His Holiness for his defence of the faith, wonders that any one can doubt it.‡ The Pope himself, in his speeches, couples the Syllabus with the Decrees of the Vatican Council, as being jointly the great fundamental teachings of these latter days; and he even describes it as the only anchor of safety for the coming time.§ Bishop Fessler, whose work was published some time after the Council, to tone down alarms, and has had a formal approval from the Pope,‖ holds that the Syllabus is not a document proceeding *ex cathedrâ*. But it touches faith and morals: its condemnations are, and are allowed to be, assertions of their contradictories, into which assertions they have been formally converted by Schrader, a writer of authority, who was officially employed in its compilation. Furthermore, though I was wrong (as Dr. Newman has properly observed¶) in assuming that the Encyclica directly covered all the propositions of the Syllabus, yet

---

* 'Power of the Roman Popes' (Transl. by Sommers. Adelaide, 1871).
† 'Dublin Review,' July, 1870, p. 224.
‡ *Ibid.* July, 1874, p. 9.
§ 'Discorsi di Pio IX.,' vol. i. p. 59.
‖ Fessler, 'True and False Infallibility,' English transl., p. iii.
¶ Newman, p. 82.

this document is addressed by the Pope through Cardinal Antonelli to all the Bishops of the Christian (Papal) world, therefore in his capacity as universal Teacher.

The reasons advanced by Bishop Fessler in the opposite sense appear to be very weak. When the Pope (by conversion of the 23rd Proposition) declares that preceding pontiffs have not exceeded the limits of their power, and have not usurped the rights of princes, Bishop Fessler replies that we are here dealing only with facts of history, not touching faith or morals, so that there is no subject-matter for a dogmatic definition.* But the depositions of sovereigns were often founded on such considerations; as when Gregory VII., in A.D. 1079, charged upon Henry IV. many capital crimes,† and as when Innocent III. deposed Raymond of Toulouse for (among other reasons) not proceeding satisfactorily with the extirpation of the Albigenses.‡ The Christian creed itself is chiefly composed of matters of fact set forth as articles of belief. And apart from this, he who asserts, that the acts of Popes did not go beyond their rights, thereby avers his belief in the claims of right which those acts of deposition involved.

Fessler's other objection is, that the form of the Syllabus does not set forth the intention of the Pope.§ But he appears to have overlooked the perfectly explicit covering letter of Antonelli, which in the Pope's name transmits the Syllabus, in order that the whole body of Latin Bishops might have before their eyes those errors and false doctrines of the age which the Pope had proscribed. Nor does Fessler venture to assert, that the Syllabus is without

---

* Fessler, 'Vraie et fausse Infaillibilité des Papes,' French transl., p. 89.
† Greenwood, 'Cathedra Petri,' iv. 420.
‡ Ibid. v. 546. § Fessler, p. 132.

dogmatic authority. He only says many theologians have doubts upon the question whether it be *ex cathedrâ*: theological science will hereafter have to examine and decide the matter :* in the meantime every Roman Catholic is bound to submit to and obey it. Such is the low or moderate doctrine concerning the Syllabus.† Thus its dogmatic authority is probable : its title to universal obedience is absolute, while among its assertions is that the Church has the right to employ force, and that the Popes have not exceeded their powers or invaded the rights of princes.

Now, when I turn to the seductive pages of **Dr. Newman**, I find myself to be breathing another air, and discussing, it would seem, some other Syllabus. If the Pope were the author of it, he would accept it.‡ But he is not,§ and no one knows who is. Therefore it has no dogmatic force.‖ It is an index to a set of dogmatic Bulls and Allocutions, but it is no more dogmatic itself than any other index, or table of contents.¶ Its value lies in its references, and from them alone can we learn its meaning.

If we had Dr. Newman for Pope, we should be tolerably safe, so merciful and genial would be his rule. But when Dr. Newman, not being Pope, contradicts and nullifies what the Pope declares, whatever we may wish, we cannot renounce the use of our eyes. Fessler, who writes, as Dr. Newman truly says, to curb exaggerations,** and who is approved by the Pope, declares†† that every subject of the Pope, and thus that Dr. Newman, is bound to obey the Syllabus, because it is from the Pope and of the Pope. "Before the Council of the Vatican, every Catholic was

---

* Fessler, pp. 8, 132, 134. † *Ibid.* p. 8.
‡ Newman, p. 20.   § *Ibid.* p. 79.
‖ *Ibid.* p. 81.   ¶ *Ibid.* p. 8.
** *Ibid.* p. 81.   †† Fessler, p. 8 (Fr. trans.).

bound to submit to and obey the Syllabus: the Council of the Vatican has made no difference in that obligation of conscience." He questions its title, indeed, to be held as *ex cathedrâ*, and this is his main contention against Schulte; but he nowhere denies its infallibility, and he distinctly includes it in the range of Christian obedience.

Next, Dr. Newman lays it down that the words of the Syllabus are of no force in themselves, except as far as they correspond with the terms of the briefs to which references are given, and which he admits to be binding. But here Dr. Newman is in flat contradiction to the official letter of Cardinal Antonelli, who states that the Syllabus has been framed, and is sent to the Bishops, by command of the Pope, inasmuch as it is likely that they have by no means all seen the prior instruments, and in order that they may know from the Syllabus itself what it is that has been condemned. Thus then it will be seen that the Syllabus has been authoritatively substituted for the original documents as a guide to the Bishops. And if, as Dr. Newman says, and as I think in some cases is the fact, the propositions of the Syllabus widen the propositions of those documents, it is the wider and not the narrower form that binds, unless Dr. Newman is more in the confidence of Rome than the Secretary of the Vatican Council, and than the regular minister of the Pope.

Again, I am reminded by the 'Dublin Review,' a favoured organ of Roman opinions, that utterances *ex cathedrâ** are not the only form in which Infallibility can speak: and that the Syllabus, whether *ex cathedrâ* or not, since it has been uttered by the Pope, and accepted by the Church diffused, that is to say, by the Bishops diffused, is undoubtedly infallible. This would seem to be the

---

* 'Dublin Review,' Jan. 1875, pp. 177, 310.

opinion of Bishop Ullathorne.* But what is conclusive as to practical effect upon the whole case is this—that while not one among the Roman apologists admits that the Syllabus is or may be erroneous, the obligation to obey it is asserted on all hands, and is founded on the language of an infallible Vatican Decree.

I have been content to argue the case of the Syllabus upon the supposition that, in relation to this country at least, its declarations were purely abstract. The readers, however, of 'Macmillan's Magazine' for February may perceive that even now we are not without a sample of its fruits in a matrimonial case, of which particulars were long ago given in the 'Times' newspaper, and which may possibly again become the object of public notice.

It is therefore absolutely superfluous to follow Dr. Newman through his references to the Briefs and Allocutions marginally noted. The Syllabus is part of that series of acts to which the dogmatisations of 1854 and 1870 also belong; and it bridges over the interval between them. It generalises, and advisedly enlarges, a number of particular condemnations; and, addressing them to all the Bishops, brings the whole of the Latin obedience within its net. The fish, when it is inclosed and beached, may struggle for a while: but it dies, while the fisherman lives, carries it to market, and quietly puts the price into his till.

The result then is:

1. I abide by my account of the contents of the Syllabus.

2. I have understated, not overstated, its authority.

3. It may be *ex cathedrâ*; it seems to have the infallibility of dogma: it unquestionably demands, and is entitled (in the code of Vaticanism) to demand, obedience.

---

* Bishop Ullathorne, 'Expost. Unravelled,' p. 66.

III. THE VATICAN COUNCIL AND THE INFALLIBILITY OF THE POPE.

Breach with History, No. 1.

LIKE the chieftains of the heroic time, Archbishop Manning takes his place with promptitude, and operates in front of the force he leads.

Upon the first appearance of my tract, he instantly gave utterance to the following propositions; nor has he since receded from them:

1. That the Infallibility of the Pope was a doctrine of Divine Faith before the Council of the Vatican was held.

2. That the Vatican Decrees have in no jot or tittle changed either the obligations or the conditions of civil allegiance.

3. That the civil allegiance of Roman Catholics is as undivided as that of other Christians, and neither more nor less limited.

4. That the claim of the Roman Church against obedience to the civil power in certain cases is the same as that made by other religious communions in this country.

These four propositions may be treated as two. The first is so allied with the second, and the third with the fourth, that the two members of each pair respectively must stand or fall together. I can make no objection to the manner in which they raise the question. I shall leave it to others, whom it may more concern, to treat that portion of his work in which, passing by matters that more nearly touched his argument, he has entered at large on the controversy between Rome and the German Empire; nor shall I now discuss his compendium of Italian history, which in no manner touches the question whether the dominion of the Pope ought again to be imposed by foreign arms upon a portion of the Italian people. But of the four propositions I will say that I accept them all, subject to the very simple condition that the word "not" be inserted in the three which are affirmative, and its equivalent struck out from the one which is negative.

Or, to state the case in my own words:

My task will be to make good the two following assertions, which were the principal subjects of my former argument:

1. That upon the authority, for many generations, of those who preceded Archbishop Manning and his coadjutors in their present official position, as well as upon other authority, Papal Infallibility was not "a doctrine of Divine Faith before the Council of the Vatican was held."

And that therefore the Vatican Decrees have changed the obligations and conditions of civil allegiance.

2. That the claim of the Papal Church against obedience to the civil power in certain cases not only goes beyond, but is essentially different from, that made by other religious communions or by their members in this country.

And that, therefore, the civil allegiance of those, who admit the claim, and carry it to its logical consequences, is not for the purposes of the State the same with that of other Christians, but is differently limited.

In his able and lengthened work, Archbishop Manning has found space for a dissertation on the great German quarrel, but has not included, in his proof of the belief in Papal Infallibility before 1870, any reference to the history of the Church over which he presides, or the sister Church in Ireland. This very grave deficiency I shall endeavour to make good, by enlarging and completing the statement briefly given in my tract. That statement was that the English and Irish penal laws against Roman Catholics were repealed on the faith of assurances, which have not been fulfilled.

Had all antagonists been content to reply with the simple ingenuousness of Dr. Newman, it might have been unnecessary to resume this portion of the subject. I make no complaint of the Archbishop; for such a reply would have destroyed his case. Dr. Newman, struggling hard with the difficulties of his task, finds that the statement of Dr. Doyle requires (p. 12) " some pious interpretation :" that in 1826 the clergy both of England and Ireland were trained in Gallican opinions (p. 13), and had modes of thinking " foreign altogether to the minds of the *entourage* of the Holy See :" that the British ministers ought to have applied to Rome (p. 14), to learn the civil duties of British subjects : and that " no pledge from Catholics was of any value, to which Rome was not a party."

This declaration involves all, and more than all, that I had ventured reluctantly to impute. Statesmen of the future, recollect the words, and recollect from whom they came : from the man who by his genius, piety, and learning, towers above all the eminences of the Anglo-papal communion ; who, so declares a Romish organ,* " has been the mind and tongue to shape and express the English Catholic position in the many controversies which have arisen " since 1845, and who has been roused from his repose on this occasion only by the most fervid appeals to him as the man that could best teach his co-religionists how and what to think. The lesson received is this. Although pledges were given, although their validity

---

* 'The Month,' December, 1874, p. 461.

was firmly and even passionately* asserted, although the subject-matter was one of civil allegiance, "no pledge from Catholics was of any value, to which Rome was not a party" (p. 14).

In all seriousness I ask whether there is not involved in these words of Dr. Newman an ominous approximation to my allegation, that the seceder to the Roman Church "places his loyalty and civil duty at the mercy of another"?

But as Archbishop Manning has asserted that the Decrees of the Vatican have "in no jot or tittle" altered civil allegiance,† and that "before the Council was held, the infallibility of the Pope was a doctrine of Divine Faith,"‡ and as he is the official head of the Anglo-Roman body, I must test his assertions by one of those appeals to history, which he has sometimes said are treason to the Church: § as indeed they are, in his sense of the Church, and in his sense of treason. It is only justice to the Archbishop to add, that he does not stand alone. Bishop Ullathorne says, "The Pope always wielded this infallibility, and all men knew this to be the fact." ‖ We shall presently find some men, whose history the Bishop should have been familiar with, and who did not know this to be the fact, but very solemnly assured us they knew the exact contrary.

This is not an affair, as Dr. Newman seems to think, of a particular generation of clergy who had been edu-

---

* Bishop Doyle, 'Essay on the Claims,' p. 38.
† Letter to the 'Times,' Nov. 7, 1874.
‡ Letter to 'New York Herald,' Nov. 10, 1874. Letter to 'Macmillan's Magazine,' Oct. 22.
§ 'Temporal Mission of the Holy Ghost,' p. 226. 'The Vatican Council and its Definitions,' 1870, p. 119.
‖ Bishop Ullathorne, Letter, p. 14.

cated in Gallican opinions. In all times, from the reign of Elizabeth to that of Victoria, the lay Roman Catholics of England, as a body, have been eminently and unreservedly loyal. But they have been as eminently noted for their thorough estrangement from Ultramontane opinions; and their clergy, down to the period of the Emancipation Act, felt with them; though a school addicted to curialism and Jesuitism, thrust among them by the Popes at the commencement of the period, first brought upon them grievous sufferings, then succeeded in attaching a stigma to their name, and now threatens gradually to accomplish a transformation of their opinions, with an eventual change in their spirit, of which it is difficult to foresee the bounds. Not that the men who now hold the ancestral view will, as a rule, exchange it for the view of the Vatican; but that, as in the course of nature they depart, Vaticanists will grow up, and take their places.

The first official head of the Anglo-Roman body in England was the wise and loyal Archpriest Blackwell. He was deposed by the Pope in 1608, "chiefly, it is supposed, for his advocacy of the oath of allegiance,"* which had been devised by King James, in order that he might confer peace and security upon loyal Roman Catholics.† Bellarmine denounced, as heretical, its denial of the power of the Pope to depose the king, and release his subjects from their allegiance. Pope Paul V. condemned the oath by a brief in October, 1606. The unfortunate members of his communion could not believe this brief to be authentic.‡ So a second brief was sent in September, 1607, to confirm and enforce the first. Blackwell gallantly advised his

---

* Butler, 'Historical Memoirs,' iii. 411.
† *Ibid.* i. 303, *seq.*   ‡ *Ibid.* 317.

flock to take the oath in defiance of the brief. Priests confined in Newgate petitioned the Pope to have compassion on them. Forty-eight doctors of the Sorbonne against six, declared that it might be taken with good conscience. And taken it was by many; but taken in despite of the tyrannical injunctions of Paul V., unhappily confirmed by Urban VIII. and by Innocent X.*

When it was proposed, in 1648, to banish Roman Catholics on account of the deposing power, their divines met and renounced the doctrine. This renunciation was condemned at Rome as heretical; but the attitude of France on these questions at the time prevented the publication of the decree.†

When the loyal remonstrance of 1661 had been signed by certain Bishops and others of Ireland, it was condemned at Rome, in July 1662, by the Congregation *de propagandâ*; and in the same month the Papal Nuncio at Brussels, who superintended the concerns of Irish Roman Catholics at the time, denounced it as already condemned by the constitutions of Paul V. and Innocent X.; and specially censured the ecclesiastics who, by signing it, had misled the laity.‡

Well may Butler say, " The claim of the Popes to temporal power, by Divine right, has been one of the most calamitous events in the history of the Church. Its effects since the Reformation, on the English and Irish Catholics, have been dreadful." § And again : " How often did our ancestors experience that ultra-catholicism is one of the worst enemies of catholicity !"‖

---

* Butler, i. 352.

† Caron, ' Remonstrantia Hibernorum.' Ed. 1731, p. 7. Comp. Butler, ' Hist. Memoirs,' ii. 18.

‡ Caron, p. 4. Butler, ii. 401, 402.

§ Butler, i. 192. ‖ *Ibid.* ii. 85; also ii. 20.

The vigour of the mind of Dryden is nowhere more evident than in parts of his poems of controversial theology; and they are important, as exhibiting that view of Roman Catholic tenets, which was presented at the time for the purposes of proselytism. He mentions various opinions as to the seat of infallibility, describing that of the Pope's infallibility, with others, as held by "some doctors," and states what he considers to be the true doctrine of the Latin Church, as follows:—

> " I then affirm, that this unfailing guide
> In Pope and general councils must reside,
> Both lawful, both combined: what one decrees,
> By numerous votes, the other ratifies:
> On this undoubted sense the Church relies."*

When, in 1682, the Gallican Church, by the first of its four Articles, rejected the sophistical distinction of direct and indirect authority, and absolutely denied the power of the Pope in temporals, to this article, says Butler, there was hardly a dissentient voice either clerical or lay. He adds that this principle is "now adopted by the universal Catholic Church."†

Such was the sad condition of the Anglo-Roman body in the seventeenth century. They were ground between the demands of the civil power, stern, but substantially just, on the one hand, and the cruel and outrageous impositions of the Court of Rome on the other. Even for the shameful scenes associated with the name and time of Titus Oates, that Court is largely responsible: and the spirit that governed it in regard to the oath of Allegiance is the very same spirit, which gained its latest triumphs in the Council of the Vatican.

---

* 'The Hind and Panther,' part ii.
† Butler, i. 358, and ii. 20.

I now pass to the period, which followed the Revolution of 1688, especially with reference to the bold assertion that before 1870 the Pope's infallibility was a doctrine of Divine faith.

The Revolution, brought about by invasions of the law and the constitution, with which the Church of Rome was disastrously associated, necessarily partook of a somewhat vindictive character as towards the Anglo-Roman body. Our penal provisions were a mitigated, but also a debased, copy of the Papal enactments against heresy. It was not until 1757, on the appointment of the Duke of Bedford to the Lord-Lieutenancy of Ireland, that the first sign of life was given.* Indeed it was only in 1756 that a new penal law had been proposed in Ireland.† But, in the next year, the Irish Roman Catholic Committee published a Declaration which disavowed the deposing and absolving power, with other odious opinions. Here it was averred that the Pope had "no temporal or civil jurisdiction," "directly or indirectly, within this realm." And it was also averred that it "is not an article of the Catholic faith, neither are we thereby required to believe or profess that the Pope is infallible": in diametrical contradiction to the declaration of Archbishop Manning, that persons of his religion were bound to this belief before the Council of 1870.‡

It may, indeed, be observed that in declaring they are not required to believe the infallibility of the Pope, the subscribers to this document do not say anything to show

---

* Butler, iv. 511. Sir H. Parnell, 'History of the Penal Laws.'
† Madden, 'Historical Notice of the Penal Laws,' p. 8.
‡ I cite the terms of this document from 'The Elector's Guide,' addressed to the freeholders of the county of York. No. 1, p. 44. York, 1826. It is also, I believe, to be found in Parnell's 'History of the Penal Laws,' 1808.

that they did not for themselves hold the tenet. But a brief explanation will show that the distinction in this case is little better than futile. As we have seen, the Declaration set forth that the Pope had no temporal power in England. Now, in the notorious Bull, *Unam Sanctam*, it had been positively declared *ex cathedrâ* that both the temporal and the spiritual sword were at the command of the Church, and that it was the office of the Pope, by a power not human but Divine, to judge and correct the secular authority. The language of the Declaration of 1757 was directly at variance with the language of the Pope, speaking *ex cathedrâ*, and therefore here if anywhere infallible. It could, therefore, only have been consistently used by persons, who for themselves did not accept the tenet. I am aware it will be argued that the infallible part of the Bull is only the last sentence. It is well for those who so teach that Boniface VIII. is not alive to hear them. The last sentence is introduced by the word "Porro," *furthermore*: a strange substitute for "Be it enacted." The true force of that sentence seems to be: "Furthermore we declare that this subjection to the Roman Pontiff, as hereinbefore described, is to be held as necessary for salvation." It is not the substance; but an addition to the substance.

If, however, anything had been wanting in this Declaration, it would have been abundantly supplied by the Protestation of the Roman Catholics of England in 1788–9. In this very important document, which brought about the passing of the great English Relief Act of 1791, besides a repetition of the assurances generally, which had been theretofore conveyed, there are contained statements of the greatest significance.

1. That the subscribers to it "acknowledge no infallibility in the Pope."

2. That their Church has no power that can directly or indirectly injure Protestants, as all she can do is to refuse them her sacraments, which they do not want.

3. That no ecclesiastical power whatever can "directly or indirectly affect or interfere with the independence, sovereignty, laws, constitution, or government," of the realm.

This Protestation was, in the strictest sense, a representative and binding document. It was signed by two hundred and forty-one priests,* including all the Vicars Apostolic : by all the clergy and laity in England of any note ; and in 1789, at a general meeting of the English Catholics in London, it was subscribed by every person present.†

Thus we have on the part of the entire body, of which Archbishop Manning is now the head,‡ a direct, literal, and unconditional rejection of the cardinal tenet which he tells us has always been believed by his Church, and was an article of Divine faith before as well as after 1870. Nor was it merely that the Protestation and the Relief coincided in time. The protesters explicitly set forth that the penal laws against them were founded on the doctrines imputed

---

* Slater's Letters on 'Roman Catholic Tenets,' p. 6.

† Butler, 'Hist. Memoirs,' ii. 118, 126.

‡ Prelates really should remember that they may lead their trustful lay followers into strange predicaments. Thus Mr. Towneley (of Towneley, I believe), in his letter of Nov. 18 to the 'Times,' dwells, I have no doubt with perfect justice, on the loyalty of his ancestors; but, unhappily, goes on to assert that "the Catholic Church has always held and taught the infallibility of the Pope in matters of faith and morals." No: the Roman Catholics of England denied it in their ¡Protestation of 1788-9 ; and on the list of the Committee, which prepared and promoted that Protestation, I find the name of Peregrine Towneley, of Towneley.—*Ibid.* ii. 304.

to them, and they asked and obtained the relief on the express ground that they renounced and condemned the doctrines.*

Some objection seems to have been taken at Rome to a portion (we are not told what) of the terms of the Protestation. The history connected herewith is rather obscurely given in Butler. But the Protestation itself was, while the Bill was before Parliament, deposited in the British Museum, by order of the Anglo-Roman body: " that it may be preserved there as a lasting memorial of their political and moral integrity."† Two of the four Vicars Apostolic, two clergymen, and one layman, withdrew their names from the Protestation on the deposit; all the rest of the signatures remained.

Canon Flanagan's 'History of the Church in England' impugns the representative character of the Committee, and declares that the Court of Rome approved of proceedings taken in opposition to it.‡ But the material fact is the subscription of the Protestation by the clergy and laity at large. On this subject he admits that it was signed by " the greater part of both clergy and laity ";§ and states that an organisation in opposition to the Committee, founded in 1794 by one of the Vicars Apostolic, died a natural death after " a very few years." ‖ The most significant part of the case, however, is perhaps this: that the work of Flanagan, which aims at giving a tinge of the new historical colour to the opinions of the Anglo-Roman body, was not published until 1857, when things had taken an altogether new direction, and when the Emancipation controversies had been long at rest.

---

* Butler, 'Hist. Memoirs,' ii. 119, 125. † *Ibid.* ii. 136–8.
‡ Flanagan, ii. 398. § *Ibid.* ii. 394.
‖ *Ibid.* ii. 407.

The Act of 1791 for England was followed by that of 1793 for Ireland. The Oath inserted in this Act is founded upon the Declaration of 1757, and embodies a large portion of it, including the words:—

"It is not an article of the Catholic Faith, neither am I thereby required to believe or profess, that the Pope is infallible."

I refer to this oath, not because I attach an especial value to that class of security, but because we now come to a Synodical Declaration of the Irish Bishops, which constitutes perhaps the most salient point of the whole of this singular history.

On the 26th of February, 1810, those Bishops declared as follows:—

"That said Oath, and the promises, declarations, abjurations, and protestations therein contained are, *notoriously, to the Roman Catholic Church at large, become a part of the Roman Catholic religion, as taught by us the Bishops, and received and maintained by the Roman Catholic Churches in Ireland; and as such are approved and sanctioned by the other Roman Catholic Churches.*"*

Finally: it will scarcely be denied that Bishop Baines was, to say the least, a very eminent and representative member of the Anglo-Roman body. In 1822, he wrote as follows:—

"Bellarmine, and some other Divines, chiefly Italians, have believed the Pope infallible, when proposing *ex cathedrâ* an article of faith. *But in England or Ireland I do not believe that any Catholic maintains the infallibility of the Pope.*" †

It will now, I think, have sufficiently appeared to the reader who has followed this narration, how mildly, I may say how inadequately, I have set forth in my former tract the pledges which were given by the authorities of the Roman Catholic Church to the Crown and State of the

---

* Slater on 'Roman Catholic Tenets,' pp. 14, 15.
† Defence against Dr. Moysey, p. 230, 1822.

United Kingdom, and by means of which principally they obtained the remission of the penal laws, and admission to full civil equality. We were told in England by the Anglo-Roman Bishops, clergy, and laity, that they rejected the tenet of the Pope's infallibility. We were told in Ireland that they rejected the doctrine of the Pope's temporal power, whether direct or indirect, although the Pope had in the most solemn and formal manner asserted his possession of it. We were also told in Ireland that Papal infallibility was no part of the Roman Catholic faith, and never could be made a part of it: and that the impossibility of incorporating it in their religion was notorious to the Roman Catholic Church at large, and was become part of their religion, and this not only in Ireland, but throughout the world. These are the declarations, which reach in effect from 1661 to 1810; and it is in the light of these declarations that the evidence of Dr. Doyle in 1825, and the declarations of the English and Irish prelates of the Papal communion shortly afterwards, are to be read. Here, then, is an extraordinary fulness and clearness of evidence, reaching over nearly two centuries: given by and on behalf of millions of men: given in documents patent to all the world: perfectly well known to the See and Court of Rome, as we know expressly with respect to nearly the most important of all these assurances, namely, the actual and direct repudiation of infallibility in 1788-9. So that either that See and Court had at the last-named date, and at the date of the Synod of 1810, abandoned the dream of enforcing infallibility on the Church, or else by wilful silence they were guilty of practising upon the British Crown one of the blackest frauds recorded in history.

The difficulties now before us were fully foreseen during

the sittings of the Council of 1870. In the Address prepared by Archbishop Kenrick, of St. Louis, but not delivered, because a stop was put to the debate, I find these words:—

"Quomodo fides sic gubernio Anglicano data conciliari possit cum definitione papalis infallibilitatis . . . ipsi viderint qui ex Episcopis Hiberniensibus, sicut ego ipse, illud juramentum præstiterint."*

"In what way the pledge thus given to the English Government can be reconciled with the definition of Papal infallibility let those of the Irish Bishops consider, who, like myself, have taken the oath in question."

The oath was, I presume, that of 1793. However, in Friedberg's 'Sammlung der Actenstücke zum Concil,' p. 151 (Tübingen, 1872), I find it stated, I hope untruly, that the 'Civiltà Cattolica,' the prime favourite of Vaticanism, in Series viii. vol. i. p. 730, announced, among those who had submitted to the Definition, the name of Archbishop Kenrick.

Let it not, however, be for a moment supposed that I mean to charge upon those who gave the assurances of 1661, of 1757, of 1783, of 1793, of 1810, of 1825–6, the guilt of falsehood. I have not a doubt that what they said, they one and all believed. It is for Archbishop Manning and his confederates, not for me, to explain how these things have come about; or it is for Archbishop MacHale, who joined as a Bishop in the assurances of 1826, and who then stood in the shadow and recent recollection of the Synod of 1810, but who now is understood to have become a party, by promulgation, to the Decree of the Pope's infallibility. There are but two alternatives to choose between: on the one side, that which I reject, the hypothesis of sheer perjury and falsehood;

* Friedrich, 'Doc. ad Illust. Conc. Vat.,' i. 219.

on the other, that policy of "violence and change in faith" which I charged, and stirred so much wrath by charging, in my former tract. I believed, and I still believe it to be the true, as well as the milder, explanation. It is for those who reject it to explain their preference for the other solution of this most curious problem of history.*

And now what shall we say to that colouring power of imagination with which Dr. Newman† tints the wide landscape of these most intractable facts, when he says it is a pity the Bishops could not have anticipated the likelihood that in 1870 the Council of the Vatican would attach to the Christian creed the Article of the Pope's infallibility? A pity it may be; but it surely is not a wonder: because they told us, as a fact notorious to themselves and to the whole Roman Catholic world, that the passing of such a decree was impossible.‡ Let us reserve our faculty of wondering for the letter of an Anglo-Roman, or if he prefers it, Romano-Anglian Bishop, who in a published circular presumes to term "scandalous" the letter of an English gentleman, because in that letter he had declared he still held the belief which, in 1788-9, the whole body of the Roman Catholics of England assured Mr. Pitt that they held;§ and let us learn which of the resources of theological skill will avail to bring together these innovations and the *semper eadem* of which I am, I fear, but writing the lamentable epitaph.

"Non bene conveniunt, nec in unâ sede morantur."

---

* See Appendices D and E.
† Dr. Newman, p. 17.   ‡ See Appendix D.
§ Letter of Mr. Petre to the 'Times' of Nov. 15, 1874; of Bishop Vaughan, Jan. 2, 1875.   ‖ Ov. Metamorph.

This question has been raised by me primarily as a British question; and I hope that, so far as this country is concerned, I have now done something to throw light upon the question whether Papal infallibility was or was not matter of Divine Faith before 1870; and consequently on the question whether the Vatican Decrees have "in no jot or tittle" altered the conditions of civil allegiance in connection with this infallibility.*

The declaration of the Irish prelates in 1810 was a full assurance to us that what they asserted for their country was also asserted for the whole Romish world.

But as evidence has been produced which goes directly into antiquity, and arguments have been made to show how innocuous is the new-fangled form of religion, I proceed to deal with such evidence and argument, in regard to my twofold contention against the Decrees—

1. In respect to infallibility.
2. In respect to obedience.

---

* For a practical indication of the effect produced by the Roman Catholic disclaimers, now denounced as "scandalous," see Appendix E.

IV. THE VATICAN COUNCIL AND THE INFALLIBILITY OF THE POPE, CONTINUED.

Breach with History, No. 2.

In a single instance, I have to express my regret for a statement made with culpable inadvertence. It is in p. 28, where I have stated that the Popes had kept up their claim to dogmatic infallibility with comparatively little intermission " for well-nigh one thousand years." I cannot even account for so loose an assertion, except by the fact that the point lay out of the main line of my argument, and thus the slip of the pen once made escaped correction. Of the claim to a supremacy virtually absolute, which I combined with the other claim, the statement is true; for this may be carried back, perhaps, to the ninth century and the appearance of the false decretals. That was the point, which entered so largely into the great conflicts of the Middle Ages. It is the point which I have treated as the more momentous; and the importance of the tenet of infallibility in faith and morals seems to me to arise chiefly from its aptitude for combination with the other. As matter of fact, the stability, and great authority, of the Roman Church in controversies of faith were acknowledged generally from an early period. But the heresy of Honorius, to say nothing of other Popes, became, from his condemnation by a General Council and by a long series of Popes as well as by other Councils, a matter so notorious, that it could not fade from the view even of the darkest age; and the possibility of an heretical Pope grew to be an idea perfectly familiar to the general mind of Christendom. Hence in the Bull, *Cum ex Apostolatûs*

Officio, Paul IV. declares (1559), that if a heretic is chosen as Pope, all his acts shall be void *ab initio*. All Christians are absolved from their obedience to him, and enjoined to have recourse to the temporal power.* So likewise, in the Decretum of Gratian itself it is provided, that the Pope can only be brought to trial in case he is found to deviate from the faith.†

It is an opinion held by great authorities, that no pontiff before Leo X. attempted to set up the infallibility of Popes as a dogma. Of the citations in its favour which are arrayed by Archbishop Manning in his *Privilegium Petri*,‡ I do not perceive any earlier than the thirteenth century, which appear so much as to bear upon the question. There is no Conciliary declaration, as I need scarcely add, of the doctrine. This being so, the point is not of primary importance. The claim is one thing, its adoption by the Church, and the interlacing of it with a like adoption of the claim to obedience, are another. I do not deny to the opinion of Papal infallibility an active, though a chequered and intermittent, life exceeding six centuries.

Since, then, I admit that for so long a time the influences now triumphant in the Roman Church have been directed towards the end they have at last attained, and seeing that my statement as to the liberty which prevailed before 1870 has been impugned, I am bound to offer some proof of that statement. I will proceed, in this instance as in others, by showing that my allegation

---

* Schulte, 'Power of the Popes,' iv. 30.

† "Hujus culpas istic redarguere præsumit mortalium nullus, quia cunctos ipse judicaturus a nemine est judicandus, *nisi deprehendatur a fide devius*."—Decr. i. Dist. xl. c. vi.

‡ 'Petri Privilegium,' ii. 70–91.

is much within the truth : that not only had the Latin Church forborne to adopt the tenet of Papal infallibility, but that she was rather bound by consistency with her own principles, as recorded in history, to repel and repudiate that tenet. I refer to the events of the great epoch marked by the Council of Constance. And the proof of the state of facts with regard to that epoch will also be proof of my more general allegation that the Church of Rome does not keep good faith with history, as it is handed down to her, and marked out for her, by her own annals. I avoided this discussion in the former tract, because it is necessarily tinctured with theology : but the denial is a challenge, which I cannot refuse to take up.

It is alleged that certain of my assertions may be left to confute one another. I will show that they are perfectly consistent with one another.

The first of them charged on Vaticanism that it had disinterred and brought into action the extravagant claims of Papal authority, which were advanced by Popes at the climax of their power, but which never entered into the faith even of the Latin Church.

The second, that it had added two if not three new articles to the Christian Creed; the two articles of the Immaculate Conception, and of Papal Infallibility; with what is at least a new law of Christian obligation, the absolute duty of all Christians and all Councils to obey the Pope in his decrees and commands, even where fallible, over the whole domain of faith, morals, and the government and discipline of the Church. This law is now for the first time, I believe, laid down by the joint and infallible authority of Pope and council. Dr. Newman[*]

---

[*] Dr. Newman, pp. 45, 53.

wonders that I should call the law absolute. I call it absolute, because it is without exception, and without limitation.

To revive obsolete claims to authority, and to innovate in matter of belief, are things perfectly compatible: we have seen them disastrously combined. In such innovation is involved, as I will now show, a daring breach with history.

While one portion of the Roman theologians have held the infallibility of the Pope, many others have taught that an Ecumenical Council together with a Pope constitutes *per se* an infallible authority in faith and morals. I believe it to be also true that it was, down to that disastrous date, compatible with Roman orthodoxy to hold that not even a Pope and a Council united could give the final seal of certainty to a definition, and that for this end there was further necessary the sanction, by acceptance, of the Church diffused. This last opinion, however, seems to have gone quite out of fashion; and I now address myself to the position in argument of those who hold that in the decree of a Council, approved by the Pope, the character of infallibility resides.

Both the Council of Constance and the Council of the Vatican were in the Roman sense Œcumenical: and it is this class of councils alone that is meant, where infallibility is treated of. I shall endeavour to be brief, and to use the simplest language.

The Council of the Vatican decreed (chap. iii.) that the Pope had from Christ immediate power over the universal Church (par. ii.).

That all were bound to obey him, of whatever rite and dignity, collectively as well as individually (*cujuscunque ritûs et dignitatis . . . tam seorsum singuli, quam simul omnes.* Ibid.)

That this duty of obedience extended to all matters of

faith, of morals, and of the discipline and government of the Church (*ibid.*, and par. iv.).

That in all ecclesiastical causes he is judge, without appeal, or possibility of reversal (par. iv.).

That the definitions of the Pope in faith and morals, delivered *ex cathedrâ*, are irreformable, *ex sese, non autem ex consensu Ecclesiæ*, and are invested with the infallibility granted by Christ in the said subject matter to the Church (ch. iv.).

Now let us turn to the Council of Constance.

This Council, supported by the following Council of Basle before its translation to Ferrara, had decreed in explicit terms that it had from Christ immediate power over the universal Church, of which it was the representative.

That all were bound to obey it, of whatever state and dignity, even if Papal, in all matters pertaining to faith, or to the extirpation of the subsisting schism, or to the reformation of the Church in its head and its members.[*]

In conformity herewith, the Council of Constance cited, as being itself a superior authority, three Popes to its bar. Gregory XII. anticipated his sentence by resignation. Benedict XIII. was deposed, as was John XXIII., for divers crimes and offences, but not for heresy. Having thus made void the Papal Chair, the Council made the provisions, under which Pope Martin V. was elected.

It is not my object to attempt a general appreciation of the Council of Constance. There is much against it to be said from many points of view, if there be more for it. But I point out that, for the matter now in hand, the questions of fact are clear, and that its decrees are in flat and diametrical contradiction to those of the Vatican.

---

[*] Labbe, 'Concilia,' xii. 22, ed. Paris, 1672.

This of itself would not constitute any difficulty for Roman theology, and would give no proof of its breach with history. It is admitted on all or nearly all hands that a Council, however great its authority may be, is not of itself infallible. What really involves a fatal breach with history is, when a body, which professes to appeal to it, having proclaimed a certain organ to be infallible, then proceeds to ascribe to it to-day an utterance contradictory to its utterance of yesterday; and, thus depriving it not only of all certainty, but of all confidence, lays its honour prostrate in the dust. This can only be brought home to the Roman Church, if two of her Councils, contradicting one another in the subject matter of faith or morals, have each respectively been confirmed by the Pope, and have thus obtained, in Roman eyes, the stamp of infallibility. Now this is what I charge in the present instance.

It is not disputed, but loudly asseverated, by Vaticanists, that the Council of the Vatican has been approved and confirmed by the Pope.

But an allegation has been set up that the Council of Constance did not receive that confirmation in respect to the Decree of the Fifth Session which asserted its power, given by Christ, over the Pope. Bishop Ullathorne says:—

"Although the mode of proceeding in that Council was really informal, inasmuch as its members voted by nations, a portion of its doctrinal decrees obtained force through the dogmatic Constitution of Martin V."*

Here it is plainly implied that the Decree of the Fifth Session was not confirmed. And I have read in some Ultramontane production of the last three months an exulting observation, that the Decrees of the Fourth and Fifth Sessions were not confirmed by the Pope, and that

---

* 'Expostulation Unravelled,' p. 42.

thus, I presume like the smitten fig-tree, they have remained a dead letter. Let us examine this allegation; but not that other statement of Archbishop Manning that the proceeding was null from the nullity of the assembly, the irregularity of the voting, and the heterodoxy of the matter.* The Pope's confirmation covers and disposes of all these arbitrary pleas. Whether it was given or not, is to be tried by the evidence of authoritative documents.

In the record of the Council of Constance we are told that, in its Forty-fifth Session, the Pope declared not that he confirmed a part of its doctrinal decrees, but " that he would hold and inviolably observe, and never counteract in any manner, each and all of the things which the Council had in full assembly determined, concluded, and decreed in matters of faith (*in materiis fidei*)." † And he approves and ratifies accordingly.

Embracing all the decrees described in its scope, this declaration is in tone as much an adhesion, as a confirmation by independent or superior authority. But let that pass. Evidently it gives all that the Pope had in his power to give.

The only remaining question is, whether the Decree of the Fifth Session was, or was not, a decree of faith?

Now upon this question there are at least two independent lines of argument, each of which respectively and separately, is fatal to the Ultramontane contention: this contention being that, for want of the confirmation of Pope Martin V., that Decree fell to the ground.

First; Pope Martin V. derived his whole power to

---

* 'Petri Privilegium,' ii. 95.
† Labbe, 'Concilia,' xii. 258. See Appendix F for the most important passages.

confirm from his election to the Papal Chair by the Council. And the Council was competent to elect, because the See was vacant. And the See was vacant, because of the depositions of two rival Popes, and the resignation of the third; for if the See was truly vacant before, there had been no Pope since the schism in 1378, which is not supposed by either side. But the power of the Council to vacate the See was in virtue of the principle asserted by the Decree of the Fifth Session. We arrive then at the following dilemma. Either that Decree had full validity by the confirmation of the Pope, or Martin the Fifth was not a Pope; the Cardinals made or confirmed by him were not Cardinals, and could not elect validly his successor, Eugenius IV.; so that the Papal succession has failed since an early date in the fifteenth century, or more than four hundred and fifty years ago.

Therefore the Decree of the Fifth Session must, upon Roman principles, have been included in the *materiæ fidei* determined by the Council, and, accordingly, in the confirmation by Pope Martin V.

But again. It has been held by some Roman writers that Pope Martin V. only confirmed the Decrees touching Faith; that the Decree of the Fifth Session did not touch Faith, but only Church-government, and that accordingly it remained unconfirmed.

Now in the Apostles' Creed, and in the Nicene Creed, we all express belief in the Holy Catholic Church. Its institution and existence are therefore strictly matter of faith. How can it be reasonably contended, that the organised body is an article of faith, but that the seat of its vital, sovereign power, by and from which it becomes operative for belief and conduct, belongs to the inferior region of the ever mutable discipline of the Church?

But this is argument only; and we have a more sure criterion at command, which will convict Vaticanism for the present purpose out of its own mouth. Vaticanism has effectually settled this question as against itself. For it has declared that the Papal Infallibility is a dogma of Faith (*divinitus revelatum dogma*, 'Const.' ch. iv.). But if by this definition, the Infallibility of the Pope in definitions of faith belongs to the province of *materiæ fidei* and of *ea quæ pertinent ad fidem*, the negative of the proposition thus affirmed, being in the same subject-matter, belongs to the same province. It therefore seems to follow, by a demonstration perfectly rigorous,—

1. That Pope Martin V. confirmed (or adopted) a Decree, which declares the judgments and proceedings of the Pope, in matters of faith, without exception, to be reformable, and therefore fallible.

2. That Pope Pius IX. confirmed (and proposed) a Decree, which declares certain judgments of the Pope, in matters of faith and morals, to be infallible; and these, with his other judgments in faith, morals, and the discipline and government of the Church, to be irreformable.

3. That the new oracle contradicts the old, and again the Roman Church has broken with history in contradicting itself.

4. That no oracle, which contradicts itself, is an infallible oracle.

5. That a so-called Œcumenical Council of the Roman Church, confirmed or non-confirmed by the Pope, has, upon its own showing, no valid claim to infallible authority.

The gigantic forgeries of the false Decretals, the general contempt of Vaticanism for history, are subjects far too wide for me to touch. But for the present I leave my assertion in this matter to stand upon—

1. The case of the Roman Catholics of the United Kingdom before 1829.

2. The Decrees of the Council of Constance, compared with the Decrees of the Council of the Vatican.

When these assertions are disposed of, it will be time enough to place others in the rank. I will now say a word on the cognate subject of Gallicanism, which has also been brought upon the *tapis*.

It would be unreasonable to expect from Archbishop Manning greater accuracy in his account of a foreign Church, than he has exhibited with regard to the history of the communion over which he energetically presides.

As the most famous and distinct of its manifestations was that exhibited in the Four Articles of 1682, it has pleased the Archbishop to imagine, and imagining to state, that in that year Gallicanism took its rise. Even with the help of this airy supposition, he has to admit that in the Church where all is unity, certainty, and authority, a doctrine contrary to Divine faith, yet proclaimed by the Church of France, was, for want of a General Council, tolerated for one hundred and eighty-eight years. Indeed, he alleges* the errors of the Council of Constance, four hundred and sixty years ago, as a reason for the Council of the Vatican.

" Nor were Catholics free to deny his infallibility before 1870. The denial of his infallibility had indeed never been condemned by a definition, because *since the rise of Gallicanism in 1682 no Œcumenical Council had ever been convoked.*" †

I will not stop to inquire why, if the Pope has all this

---

* 'Petri Privilegium,' ii. 40.
† Letter to 'Macmillan's Magazine,' Oct. 22, 1874.

time been infallible, a Council was necessary for the issuing of a definition; since we are now on matters of history, and the real difficulty would be to know where to dip into the prior history of France without finding matter in utter contradiction to the Archbishop's allegation. An Anglo-Roman writer has told us that in the year 1612 [query 1614?] the assembly of the Gallican Church declared that the power of the Popes related to spiritual matters and eternal life, not to civil concerns and temporal possessions.* In the year 1591, at Mantes and Chartres, the prelates of France in their assembly refused the order of the Pope to quit the king, and on the 21st of September repudiated his Bulls, as being null in substance and in form.† It has always been understood that the French Church played a great part in the Council of Constance: is this also to be read backwards, or effaced from the records? Or, to go a little further back, the Council of Paris in 1393 withdrew its obedience altogether from Benedict XIII., without transferring it to his rival at Rome: restored it upon conditions in 1403; again withdrew it, because the conditions had not been fulfilled, in 1406: and so remained until the Council of Constance and the election of Martin V.‡ And what are we to say to Fleury? who writes:

'Le concile de Constance établit la maxime *de tout temps enseignée en France*, que tout Pape est soumis au jugement de tout concile universel en ce qui concerne la foi." §

---

* Cited in Slater's Letters, p. 23, from Hook's 'Principia,' iii. 577.
† Continuator of Fleury, 'Hist. Eccl.,' xxxvi. 337 (Book 169, ch. 84).
‡ Du Chastenet, 'Nouvelle Histoire du Concile de Constance' (preface); and 'Preuves,' pp. 79, 84, *seq.*, 95, 479 (Paris, 1718).
§ Fleury, 'Nouv. Opusc.,' p. 44, cited in Demaistre, 'Du Pape,' p. 82. See also Fleury, 'Hist. Eccl.' (Book 102, ch. 188).

One of the four articles of 1682 simply reaffirms the decree of Constance : and as Archbishop Manning has been the first, so he will probably be the last person to assert, that Gallicanism took its rise in 1682.

This is not the place to show how largely, if less distinctly, the spirit of what are called the Gallican liberties entered into the ideas and institutions of England, Germany, and even Spain. Neither will I dwell on the manner in which the decrees of Constance ruled for a time not only the minds of a school or party, but the policy of the Western Church at large, were confirmed and repeatedly renewed by the succeeding Council of Basle, and proved their efficacy and sway by the remarkable submission of Eugenius IV. to that Council. But I will cite the single sentence in which Mr. Hallam, writing, alas, nearly sixty years back, has summed up the case of the decrees of Constance.

"These decrees are the great pillars of that moderate theory with respect to the Papal authority, which distinguished the Gallican Church, and is embraced, I presume, by almost all laymen, and the major part of ecclesiastics, on this side the Alps." *

---

* 'Hist. of the Middle Ages,' chap. vii. part 2.

V. THE VATICAN COUNCIL AND OBEDIENCE TO THE POPE.

ARCHBISHOP MANNING has boldly grappled with my proposition that the Third Chapter of the Vatican Decrees had forged new chains for the Christian people, in regard to obedience, by giving its authority to what was previously a claim of the Popes only, and so making it a claim of the Church. He is astonished at the statement: and he offers* what he thinks a sufficient confutation of it, in six citations.

The four last begin with Innocent III., and end with the Council of Trent. Two, from Innocent III. and Sixtus IV., simply claim the *regimen*, or government of the Church, which no one denies them. The Council of Florence speaks of *plena potestas*, and the Council of Trent of *suprema potestas*, as belonging to the Pope. Neither of these assertions touches the point. Full power, and supreme power, in the government of a body, may still be limited by law. No other power can be above them. But it does not follow that they can command from all persons an unconditional obedience, unless themselves empowered by law so to do. We are familiar, under the British monarchy, both with the term supreme, and with its limitation.

The Archbishop, however, quotes a Canon or Chapter of a Roman Council in 863, which anathematises all who despise the Pope's orders with much breadth and amplitude of phrase. If taken without the context, it fully covers the ground taken by the Vatican Council. It anathematises

---

* Archbishop Manning, pp. 12, 13.

all who contemn the decrees of the Roman See in faith, discipline, or correction of manners, or for the remedy or prevention of mischief. Considering that the four previous Canons of this Council, and the whole proceedings, relate entirely to the case of the Divorce of Lothair, it might, perhaps, be argued that the whole constitute only a *privilegium*, or law for the individual case, and that the anathema of the Fifth Canon must be limited to those who set at nought the Pope's proceedings in that case. But the point is of small consequence to my argument.

But then the Roman Council is local; and adds no very potent reinforcement to the sole authority of the Pope. The question then remains how to secure for this local and Papal injunction the sanction of the Universal Church, in the Roman sense of the word. Archbishop Manning, perfectly sensible of what is required of him, writes that "this Canon was recognised in the Eighth General Council, held at Constantinople in 869." He is then more than contented with this array of proofs; and, confining himself, as I am bound to say he does, in all personal matters throughout his work, to the mildest language consistent with the full expression of his ideas, he observes that I am manifestly out of my depth.*

I know not the exact theological value of the term "recognised"; but I conceive it to mean virtual adoption. Such an adoption of such a claim by a General Council, appeared to me a fact of the utmost significance. I referred to many of the historians of the Church: but I found no notice of it in those whom I consulted, including Baronius. From these unproductive references I went onwards to the original documents.

---

* Archbishop Manning, 'Vatican Decrees,' pp. 12, 13.

The Eighth General Council, so-called, comprised only those Bishops of the East who adhered to, and were supported by, the See of Rome and the Patriarch Ignatius, in the great conflict of the ninth century. It would not, therefore, have been surprising if its canons had given some at least equivocal sanction to the high Papal claims. But, on the contrary, they may be read with the greatest interest as showing, at the time immediately bordering on the publication of the false Decretals, how little way those claims had made in the general body of the Church. The system which they describe is the Patriarchal, not the Papal system: the fivefold distribution of the Christian Church under the five great Sees of the Elder and the New Rome, Alexandria, Antioch, and Jerusalem. Of these the Pope of Rome is the first, but as *primus inter pares* (Canons XVII., XXI., Lat.).* The causes of clergy on appeal are to be finally decided by the Patriarch in each Patriarchate (Canon XXVI., Lat.) :† and it is declared that any General Council has authority to deal, but should deal respectfully, with controversies of or touching the Roman Church itself (Canon XXI. Lat., XIII. Gr.)‡ This is one of the Councils which solemnly anathematises Pope Honorius as a heretic.

The reference made by Archbishop Manning is, as he has had the goodness to inform me, to the Second Canon.§ The material words are these:—

"Regarding the most blessed Pope Nicholas as an organ of the Holy Spirit, and likewise his most holy successor Adrian, we accordingly

---

* Labbe (ed. Paris, 1671), vol. x. pp. 1136, 1140.
† *Ibid.* 1143.
‡ *Ibid.* 1140, 1375.
§ *Ibid.* p. 1127 Lat., p. 1367 Gr.; where the reader should be on his guard against the Latin version, and look to the Greek original.

define and enact that all which they have set out and promulgated synodically, from time to time, as well for the defence and well-being of the Church of Constantinople, and of its Chief Priest and most holy Patriarch Ignatius, as likewise for the expulsion and condemnation of Photius, neophyte and intruder, be always observed and kept alike entire and untouched, under (or according to) the heads set forth (*cum expositis capitulis*)." *

There is not in the Canon anything relating to the Popes generally, but only to two particular Popes; nor any reference to what they did personally, but only to what they did synodically; nor to what they did synodically in all matters, but only in the controversy with Photius and the Eastern Bishops adhering to him. There is not one word relating to the Canon of 863, or to the Council which passed it: which was a Council having nothing to do with the Photian controversy, but called for the purpose of supporting Pope Nicholas I. in what is commonly deemed his righteous policy with respect to the important case of the Divorce of Lothair.†

So that the demonstration of the Archbishop falls wholly to the ground: and down to this time my statement remains entire and unhurt. The matter contained in it will remain very important until the Council or the Pope shall amend its decree so as to bring it into conformity with the views of Dr. Newman, and provide a relief to the private conscience by opening in the great gate of Obedience a little wicket-door of exceptions for those who are minded to disobey.

Had the Decrees of 1870 been in force in the sixteenth and seventeenth centuries, Roman Catholic peers could not have done what, until the reign of Charles II., they did; could not have made their way to the House of Lords

---

* See the original in Appendix G.
† Labbe, x. 766 *sqq.*

by taking the oath of allegiance, despite the Pope's command. But that is not all. The Pope *ex cathedrâ* had bidden the Roman Catholics of England in the eighteenth century, and in the sixteenth, and from the fourteenth, to believe in the Deposing power as an article of faith. But they rejected it: and no unquestioned law of their Church forbade them to reject it. Are they not forbidden now? The Pope in the sixteenth century bade the Roman Catholics of England assist the invasion of the Spanish Armada. They disobeyed him. The highest law of their Church left them free to disobey. Are they as free now? That they will assert this freedom for themselves I do not question, nay, I sanguinely believe. From every standing-point, except that of Vaticanism, their title to it is perfect. With Vaticanism to supply their premiss, how are they to conclude? Dr. Newman says there are exceptions to this precept of obedience. But this is just what the Council has not said. The Church by the Council imposes Aye. The private conscience reserves to itself the title to say No. I must confess that in this apology there is to me a strong, undeniable, smack of Protestantism. To reconcile Dr. Newman's conclusion with the premisses of the Vatican will surely require all, if not more than all, "the vigilance, acuteness, and subtlety of the *Schola Theologorum* in its acutest member."[*]

The days of such proceedings, it is stated, are gone by: and I believe that, in regard to our country, they have passed away beyond recall. But that is not the present question. The present question is whether the right to perform such acts has been effectually disavowed. With this question I now proceed to deal.

---

[*] Dr. Newman, p. 121.

VI. REVIVED CLAIMS OF THE PAPAL CHAIR.

1. *The Deposing Power.*
2. *The Use of Force.*

It will perhaps have been observed by others, as it has been by me, that from the charges against my account of the Syllabus are notably absent two of its most important and instructive heads. I accuse the Syllabus of teaching the right of the Church to use force, and of maintaining the Deposing power.

When my tract was published, I had little idea of the extent to which, and (as to some of them) the hardihood with which, those who should have confuted my charges would themselves supply evidence to sustain them.

Bishop Clifford, indeed, sustains the deposing power on the ground that it was accorded to the Pope by the nations. It was simply a case like that of the Geneva Arbitrators.[*] Dr. Newman[†] defends it, but only upon conditions. The circumstances must be rare and critical. The proceeding must be judicial. It must appeal to the moral law. Lastly, there must be an united consent of various nations. In fine, Dr. Newman accepts the deposing power only under the conditions which, as he thinks, the Pope himself lays down.

These allegations quiet my fears; but they strain my faith; and, purporting to be historical, they shock my judgment. For they are,to speak plainly, without foundation. The Arbitrators at Geneva settled a dispute,

---

[*] 'Pastoral Letter,' p. 12.
[†] Dr. Newman, pp. 36, 37.

which, as they recited in formal terms, the two parties to it had empowered and invited them to settle. The point of consent is the only weighty one among the four conditions of Dr. Newman, and is the sole point raised by Bishop Clifford. Did then Paul III., as arbitrator in the case of Henry VIII., pursue a like procedure? The first words of his Bull are, "The condemnation and excommunication of Henry VIII., King of England:" not an auspicious beginning. There is nothing at all about arbitration, or consent of any body, but a solemn and fierce recital of power received from God, not from the nations, or from one nation, or from any fraction of a nation; power "over the nations and over the kingdoms, to pluck up and to destroy, to build up and to plant, as chief over all kings of the whole earth, and all peoples possessing rule." Exactly similar is the "arbitration" of Pius V. between himself and Elizabeth, to the "arbitration" of Paul III. between himself and Henry VIII.

Archbishop Manning, indeed,* has thrown in a statement the utility of which it is hard to understand, that Queen Elizabeth "was baptized a Catholic." She was baptized after Appeals to Rome had been abolished, and two years after the Clergy had owned in the King that title of Headship, which Mary abolished, and which never has been revived. But Archbishop Manning knows quite well that the Papal claims of right extend to all baptized persons whatever, and Queen Victoria could have no exemption unless it could be shown that she was unbaptized.

The doctrine of the consent of nations is a pure imagi-

---

* Archbishop Manning, p. 89. See the Anathemas of the Council of Trent against those who deny that heretics, as being baptized persons, are bound to obedience to the Church. I hope the Archbishop has not incautiously incurred them.

nation. The general truth of the matter is, that the Popes of the middle ages, like some other persons and professions, throve upon the discords of their neighbours. Other powers were only somewhere: the Pope, in the West, was everywhere. Of the two parties to a quarrel, it was worth the while of each to bid for the assistance of the Pope against his enemy; and he that bid the highest, not merely in dry acknowledgment of the Papal prerogatives, but also commonly in the solid tribute of Peter's pence, or patronages, or other tangible advantages, most commonly got the support of the Pope. This is a brief and rude outline; but it is history, and the other is fiction.

But does Dr. Newman stand better at this point? He only grants the deposing power in the shape in which the Pope asks it; and he says the Pope only asks it on the conditions of which one is "an united consent of various nations."* In the Speech of the Pope, however, which he cites, there is nothing corresponding to this account. The Pope says distinctly, "of this right the *Fountain* is (not the Infallibility, but) the Pontifical Authority." The people of the middle ages—what did they do? made him an arbitrator or judge? No: but recognised in him that which—what? he was? no: but—"he IS; the Supreme Judge of Christendom." The right was not created, but "assisted, as was DUE to it, by the public law and common consent of the nations." If this is not enough, I will complete the demonstration. An early report of the Speech † from the Roman newspapers winds up the statement by describing the Deposing Power as—

"A right which the Popes, *invited by the call of the nations, had to exercise*, when the general good demanded it."

---

* Dr. Newman, p. 37.
† 'Tablet,' Nov. 21, 1874, Letter of C. S. D.

But in the authorised and final report * given in the Collection of the Speeches of Pius IX., this passage is corrected, and runs thus :—

"A right which the Popes *exercised in virtue of their authority* when the general good demanded it." †

Thus Bishop Clifford and Dr. Newman are entirely at issue with the Pope respecting the deposing power. Will they not have to reconsider what they are to say, and what they are to believe? That power, it must be borne in mind, appears to have one of the firmest possible Pontifical foundations, in the Bull *Unam Sanctam*, which is admitted on all hands to be a declaration *ex cathedrâ*.

But it is not to the more moderate views of the Bishop and Dr. Newman that we are to resort for information on the ruling fashions of Roman doctrine. Among the really orthodox defenders of Vaticanism, who have supplied the large majority of Reproofs and Replies, I do not recollect to have found one single disavowal of the deposing power. Perhaps the nearest approach to it from any writer of this school is supplied by Monsignor Capel, who remarks that the Pope's office of arbiter is at an end, or "at least *in abeyance*." ‡ There are, indeed, enough of disavowals wholly valueless. For example, disavowals of the universal monarchy; by which it appears to be meant that the Popes never claimed, in temporals, such a monarchical power as is now accorded to them in spirituals, namely a

---

* 'Discorsi di Pio IX.' vol. i. p. 203.
† 'Tablet' original (for which I am not responsible): "Un diritto, che i Papi, *chiamati dal voto dei popoli, dovettero esercitare* quando il comun bene lo domandava." Authorised original: "Un diritto che i Papi *esercitarono in virtù della loro Autorità*, quando il comun bene lo dimandava."
‡ Monsignor Capel, p. 60.

power absorbing and comprehending every other power whatever. Or again, disavowals of the *directa potestas*. For one, I attach not a feather's weight to the distinction between the direct power and the indirect. Speaking in his own person, Archbishop Manning eschews the gross assertions to which in another work he has lent a sanction,* and seems to think he has mended the position when he tells us that the Church, that is to say the Pope, "has a supreme judicial office, in respect to the moral law, over all nations, and over all persons, both governors and governed." As long as they do right, it is directive and preceptive; when they do wrong, the black cap of the judge is put on, *ratione peccati*, "by reason of sin." That is to say, in plain words, the right and the wrong in the conduct of States and of individuals is now, as it always has been, a matter for the judicial cognisance of the Church; and the entire judicial power of the Church is summed up in the Pope.

"If Christian princes and their laws deviate from the law of God, the Church has authority from God to judge of that deviation, and *by all its powers* to enforce the correction of that departure from justice."†

I must accord to the Archbishop the praise of manliness. If we are henceforward in any doubt as to his opinions, it is by our own fault. I sorrowfully believe, moreover, that he does no more than express the general opinion of the teachers who form the ruling body in his Church at large, and of the present Anglo-Romish clergy almost without exception. In the episcopal manifesto of Bishop Ullathorne I see nothing to qualify the doctrine. In the Pastoral Letter of Bishop Vaughan the comfort we obtain is this—"it will never, as we believe, be exercised again;" and "it is a question purely speculative. It is

---

* 'Essays,' edited by Archbishop Manning. London.
† Archbishop Manning, 'Vatican Decrees,' pp. 49-51.

no matter of Catholic faith, and is properly relegated to the schools."* Bishop Vaughan does not appear to bear in mind that this is exactly what we were told, not by his predecessors of 1789, who denied Infallibility outright: not by the Synod of 1810, who affirmed it to be impossible that Infallibility ever could become an article of faith; but even in the "bated breath" of later times with respect to Infallibility itself, which, a little while after, was called back from the schools and the speculative region, and uplifted into the list of the Christian *credenda*; and of which we are now told that it has been believed always, and by all, only its boundaries have been a little better marked.

In the train of the Bishops (I except Bishop Clifford) come priests, monks, nay, laymen: Vaticanism in all its ranks and orders. And among these champions, not one adopts the language even of Bishop Doyle, much less of 1810, much less of 1789. The "Monk of St. Augustine's" is not ashamed to say that Bishop Doyle, who was put forward in his day as the champion and representative man of the body, "held opinions openly at variance with those of the great mass."†

2. *Title to the use of Force.*

Equally clear, and equally unsatisfactory, are the Ultramontane declarations with respect to the title of the Church to employ force. Dr. Newman holds out a hand to brethren in distress by showing that a theological authority who inclines to the milder side, limits the kind of force, which the Church has of herself a right to employ.

---

* 'Pastoral Letter,' pp. 33, 34.

† See 'The Month,' Jan. 1875, pp. 82–4. Monk of St. Augustine's, p. 27, *seq.* Rev. J. Curry's 'Disquisition,' pp. 35, 41. Lord R. Montagu, 'Expostulation in extremis,' p. 51.

"The lighter punishments, though temporal and corporal, such as shutting up in a monastery, prison, flogging, and others of the same kind, short of effusion of blood, the Church, *jure suo*, can inflict."* And again: the Church does not claim the use of force generally, but only *that* use of force which Professor Nuytz denied.

We can from this source better understand the meaning of Archbishop Manning, when he states,† that the Church has authority from God to correct departures from justice by the use of "all its powers." The favourite mode of conveying this portion of truth—a portion so modest that it loves not to be seen—is by stating that the Church is a "perfect society." "The Church is a society complete and perfect in and by itself, and amply sufficing not only to bring men to salvation and everlasting bliss, but also to establish and perfectly regulate social life among them."‡ The Church has been created, says Bishop Vaughan, a "perfect society or kingdom," "with full authority in the triple order, as needful for a perfect kingdom, legislative, judicial, and coercive."§ His Metropolitan treats the subject at some length; assures us that the members of his communion would not make use of force even if they were able, but nowhere disclaims the right.‖ Indeed he cannot: he dares not. The inexorable Syllabus binds him to maintain it, as Ixion was bound to his wheel.

The subject, however, is one of the burning class; and it appears to terrify even Archbishop Manning. He refers us to the famous brief or letter of Innocent III., headed *Novit*, in his Appendix, where he states that the text is

---

* Cardinal Soglia, as cited by Dr. Newman, pp. 89, 90.
† 'Vatican Decrees,' p. 43.
‡ Martin, S.J., 'De Matrimonio, Notiones Præviæ,' ci.
§ 'Pastoral Letter,' p. 13. ‖ See Appendix II.

given in full.* In the document, as it is there given, will be found the Pope's assertion, that it is his part to pass judgment on sovereigns in respect of sin (*ratione peccati*), and that he can coerce them by ecclesiastical constraint (*districtionem*). But the text of the brief is, according to my copy of the Decretals, not given in full; and the copyist has done the Pope scanty justice. He seems to have omitted what is the clearest and most important passage of the whole, since it distinctly shows that what is contemplated is the use of force.

"The Apostle also admonishes us to rebuke disturbers, and elsewhere he says: 'reprove, intreat, rebuke with all patience and doctrine.' Now that we are *able, and also bound to coerce*, is plain from this, that the Lord says to the Prophet, who was one of the priests of Anathoth: 'Behold, I have appointed thee over the nations and the kings, that thou mayest tear up, and pull down, and scatter, and build, and plant.'"†

With regard to Dr. Newman's limitation of the Proposition, I must cite an authority certainly higher in the Papal sense. The Jesuit Schrader has published, with a Papal approbation attached, a list of the affirmative propositions answering to the negative condemnations of the Syllabus. I extract his Article 24 :—‡

"The Church has the power to apply external coercion (*äusseren Zwang anzuwenden*): she has also a temporal authority direct and indirect."

The remark is appended, "Not souls alone are subject to her authority."

All, then, that I stated in the Expostulation, on the

---

* Archbishop Manning, p. 62 n.

† 'Corpus Juris Canonici Decret. Greg. IX.,' II. I. 13. I cite from Richter's ed. (Leipsic, 1839). It has the pretensions, and I believe the character, of a critical and careful edition. I do not however presume to determine the textual question.

‡ Schrader, as above, p. 64.

Deposing Power, and on the claims of the Roman Church to employ force, is more than made good.

It was, I suppose, to put what Burnet would call a face of propriety on these and such like tenets, that one of the combatants opposed to me in the present controversy has revived an ingenious illustration of that clever and able writer, the late Cardinal Wiseman. He held that certain doctrines present to us an unseemly appearance, because we stand outside the Papal Church, even as the most beautiful window of stained glass in a church offers to those without only a confused congeries of paint and colours, while it is, to an eye viewing it from within, all glory and all beauty. But what does this amount to? It is simply to say, that when we look at the object in the free air and full light of day which God has given us, its structure is repulsive and its arrangement chaotic; but, if we will part with a great portion of that light, by passing within the walls of a building made by the hand of man, then, indeed, it will be better able to bear our scrutiny. It is an ill recommendation of a commodity, to point out that it looks the best where the light is scantiest.

VII. WARRANT OF ALLEGIANCE ACCORDING TO THE VATICAN.

1. *Its alleged Superiority.*
2. *Its real Flaws.*
3. *Alleged Non-interference of the Popes for Two Hundred Years.*

NOT satisfied with claiming to give guarantees for allegiance equal to those of their fellow-citizens, the champions of the Vatican have boldly taken a position in advance. They hold that they are in a condition to offer better warranty than ours, and this because they are guided by an infallible Pope, instead of an erratic private judgment; and because the Pope himself is exceedingly emphatic, even in the Syllabus, on the duties of subjects towards their rulers. Finally, all this is backed and riveted by an appeal to conduct. "The life and conduct of the Church for eighteen centuries are an ample guarantee for her love of peace and justice."* I would rather not discuss this "ample guarantee." Perhaps the Bishop's appeal might shake one who believed: I am certain it would not quiet one who doubted.

The inculcation of civil obedience under the sanction of religion is, so far as I am aware, the principle and practice of all Christian communities. We must therefore look a little farther into the matter in order to detect the distinctive character, in this respect, of the Vatican.

1. Unquestionably the Pope, and all Popes, are full and

---

* Bishop Vaughan, p. 23.

emphatic on the duties of subjects to rulers; but of what subjects to what rulers? It is the Church of England which has ever been the extravagantly loyal Church; I mean which has, in other days, exaggerated the doctrine of civil obedience, and made it an instrument of much political mischief. Passive obedience, non-resistance, and Divine right, with all of good or evil they involve, were specifically her ideas. In the theology now dominant in the Church of Rome, the theology which has so long had its nest in the Roman Court, these ideas prevail, but with a rider to them: obedience is to be given, Divine right is to belong, to those Princes and Governments which adopt the views of Rome, or which promote her interests: to those Princes and Governments which do right, Rome being the measure of right. I have no doubt that many outside the charmed circle praise in perfect good faith the superior bouquet and body of the wine of Roman Catholic loyalty. But those within, can they make such assertions? This is not easy to believe. The great art, nowhere else so well understood or so largely practised, is, in these matters, to seem to assert without asserting. This has been well-known at least for near five centuries, since the time of Gerson, whose name for Vaticanism is *Adulatio*. "*Sentiens autem Adulatio quandoque nimis se cognosci, studet quasi modiciore sermone depressiùs uti, ut credibilior appareat.*"*
I must say that, if Vaticanists have on this occasion paraded the superior quality of the article they vend as loyalty, they have also supplied us with the means of testing the assertion; because one and all of them assert the corrective power of the Pope over Christian Sovereigns

---

* 'De Potest. Eccl.,' Consideratio XII. Works, ii. 246, ed. Hague, 1728.

and Governments. I do not dispute that their commodity is good, in this country, for every-day tear and wear. But as to its ultimate groundwork and principle, on which in other places, and other circumstances, it might fall back, of this I will now cite a description from one of the very highest authorities; from an epistle of a most able and conspicuous Pontiff, to whom reference has already been made, I mean Nicholas the First.

When that Pontiff was prosecuting with iron will the cause against the divorce of Lothair from Theutberga, he was opposed by some Bishops within the dominions of the Emperor. Adventitius, Bishop of Metz, pleaded the duty of obeying his sovereign. Nicholas in reply described his view of that matter in a passage truly classical, which I translate from the Latin, as it is given in Baronius.

"You allege, that you subject yourself to Kings and Princes, because the Apostle says 'Whether to the king, as in authority.' Well and good. Examine, however, whether the Kings and Princes, to whom you say that you submit, are truly Kings and Princes. Examine whether they govern well, first themselves, then the people under them. For if one be evil to himself, how shall he be good to others? Examine whether they conduct themselves rightly as Princes; for otherwise they are rather to be deemed tyrants, than taken for Kings, and we should resist them, and mount up against them, rather than be under them. Otherwise, if we submit to such, and do not put ourselves over them, we must of necessity encourage them in their vices. Therefore be subject 'to the King, as in authority, in his virtues that is to say, not his faults; as the Apostle says, for the sake of God, not against God.'" *

I cite the passage, not to pass a censure in the case, but for its straightforward exposition of the doctrine, now openly and widely preferred, though not so lucidly expounded, by the teaching body of the Romish Church.

---

* Baronius, A.D. 863, c. lxx.

Plainly enough, in point of right, the title of the temporal Sovereign is valid or null according to the view which may be taken by the Pope of the nature of his conduct. "No just prince," says Archbishop Manning, can be deposed by any power on earth; but whether a prince is just or not, is a matter for the Pope to judge of.*

We are told, indeed, that it is not now the custom for the Pope to depose princes: not even Victor Emmanuel.† True: he does no more than exhort the crowds who wait upon him in the Vatican to seek for the restoration of those Italian sovereigns whom the people have driven out. But no man is entitled to take credit for not doing that which he has no power to do. And one of the many irregularities in the mode of argument pursued by Vaticanism is, that such credit is constantly taken for not attempting the impossible. It is as if Louis XVI., when a prisoner in the Temple, had vaunted his own clemency in not putting the head of Robespierre under the guillotine.

But there are other kinds of interference and aggression, just as intolerable in principle as the exercise, or pretended exercise, of the deposing power. Have they been given up? We shall presently see.‡

2. *Its real Flaws.*

Cooks and controversialists seem to have this in common, that they nicely appreciate the standard of knowledge in those whose appetites they supply. The cook is tempted to send up ill-dressed dishes to masters who have slight skill in or care for cookery; and the

* Archbishop Manning, p. 46.
† Bishop Vaughan, 'Pastoral,' p. 34.
‡ *Infra*, p. 88.

controversialist occasionally shows his contempt for the intelligence of his readers by the quality of the arguments or statements which he presents for their acceptance. But this, if it is to be done with safety, should be done in measure; and I must protest that Vaticanism really went beyond all measure when it was bold enough to contend that its claims in respect to the civil power are the same as those which are made by the Christian communions generally of modern times. The sole difference, we are told, is that in one case the Pope, in the other the individual, determines the instances when obedience is to be refused; and as the Pope is much wiser than the individual, the difference in the Roman view is all in favour of the order of civil society.

The reader will, I hope, pay close attention to this portion of the subject. The whole argument greatly depends upon it. Before repealing the penal laws, before granting political equality, the statesmen of this country certainly took a very different view. They thought the Roman Catholic, as an individual citizen, was trustworthy. They were not afraid of relying even upon the local Church. What they were anxious to ascertain, and what, as far as men can through language learn the thought and heart of man, they did ascertain, was this; whether the Roman Catholic citizen, and whether the local Church, were free to act, or were subjected to an extraneous authority. This superior wisdom of the Pope of Rome was the very thing of which they had had ample experience in the middle ages; which our Princes and Parliaments long before the reign of Henry VIII. and the birth of Anna Boleyn, had wrought hard to control, and which the Bishops of the sixteenth century, including Tunstal and Stokesley, Gardiner and Bonner, used their best learning to exclude. Those who in 1875 propound the doctrine, which no single century of the middle ages would have admitted, must indeed have a mean opinion of any intellects which their language could cajole.

As a rule, the real independence of States and nations depends upon the exclusion of foreign influence proper from their civil affairs. Wherever the spirit of freedom, even if ever so faintly, breathes, it resents and reacts against any intrusion of another people or Power into the circle of its interior concerns, as alike dangerous and disgraceful. As water finds its level, so, in a certain tolerable manner, the various social forces of a country, if left to themselves, settle down into equilibrium. In the normal posture of things, the State ought to control, and can control, its subjects sufficiently for civil order and peace; and the normal is also the ordinary case, in this respect, through the various countries of the civilised world. But the essential condition of this ability, on which all depends, is that the forces, which the State is to govern, shall be forces having their seat within its own territorial limits. The power of the State is essentially a local power.

But the *Triregno* of the Pope, figured by the Tiara, touches heaven, earth, and Purgatory (*Discorsi*, i. 133). We now deal only with the earthly province. As against the local sway of the State, the power of the Pope is ubiquitous; and the whole of it can be applied at any point within the dominions of any State, although the far larger part of it does not arise within its borders, but constitutes, in the strictest sense, a foreign force. The very first condition of State-rule is thus vitally compromised.

The power, with which the State has thus to deal, is one dwelling beyond its limits, and yet beyond the reach of its arm. All the subjects of the State are responsible to the

State: they must obey, or they must take the consequences. But for the Pope there are no consequences: he is not responsible.

But it may be said, and it is true, that the State will not be much the better for the power it possesses of sending all its subjects to prison for disobedience. And here we come upon the next disagreeable distinction in the case of the Roman Church. She alone arrogates to herself the right to speak to the State, not as a subject but as a superior; not as pleading the right of a conscience staggered by the fear of sin, but as a vast Incorporation, setting up a rival law against the State in the State's own domain, and claiming for it, with a higher sanction, the title to similar coercive means of enforcement.

No doubt, mere submission to consequences is, for the State, an inadequate compensation for the mischief of disobedience. The State has duties which are essential to its existence, and which require active instruments. Passive resistance, widely enough extended, would become general anarchy. With the varying and uncombined influences of individual judgment and conscience, the State can safely take its chance. But here is a Power that claims authority to order the millions; and to rule the rulers of the millions, whenever, in its judgment, those rulers may do wrong.

The first distinction then is, that the Pope is himself foreign and not responsible to the law; the second, that the larger part of his power is derived from foreign sources; the third, that he claims to act, and acts, not by individuals, but on masses; the fourth, that he claims to teach them, so often as he pleases, what to do at each point of their contact with the laws of their country.

Even all this might be borne, and might be comparatively harmless but for that at which I have already glanced. He alone of all ecclesiastical powers presumes not only to limit the domain of the State, but to meet the State in its own domain. The Presbyterian Church of Scotland showed a resolution never exceeded, before the secession of 1843, in resisting the civil power; but it offered the resistance of submission. It spoke for the body, and its ministers in things concerning it: but did not presume to command the private conscience. Its modest language would be far from filling the *os rotundum* of a Roman Pontiff. Nay, the words of the Apostle do not suffice for him. St. Peter himself was not nearly so great as his Successor. He was content with the modest excuse of the individual: "We ought to obey God rather than man." * Rome has improved upon St. Peter : 'Your laws and ordinances we proscribe and condemn, and declare them to be absolutely, both hereafter and from the first, null, void, and of no effect.' That is to say, the Pope takes into his own hand the power which he thinks the State to have misused. Not merely does he aid or direct the conscience of those who object, but he even overrules the conscience of those who approve. Above all, he pretends to annul the law itself.

Such is the fifth point of essential distinction between these monstrous claims, and the modest though in their proper place invincible exigencies of the private conscience. But one void still remains unfilled; one plea not yet unmasked. Shall it be said, this is all true, but it is all spiritual, and therefore harmless? An idle answer at the best, for the origin of spiritual power is and ought to be a real one, and ought not therefore to be used against the civil order: but worse than idle, because

---

* Acts v. 29.

totally untrue, inasmuch as we are now told in the plainest terms (negatively in the Syllabus, affirmatively in Schrader's approved conversion of it),* that the Church is invested with a temporal power direct and indirect, and has authority to employ external coercion.

Am I not right in saying, that after all this to teach the identity of the claims of Vaticanism with those of other forms of Christianity in the great and grave case of conscience against the civil power, is simply to manifest a too thinly veiled contempt for the understanding of the British community, for whose palate and digestion such diet has been offered?

The exact state of the case, as I believe, is this. The right to override all the States of the world and to cancel their acts, within limits assignable from time to time to, but not by those States, and the title to do battle with them, as soon as it may be practicable and expedient, with their own proper weapon and last sanction of exterior force, has been sedulously brought more and more into view of late years. The centre of the operation has lain in the Society of Jesuits; I am loath to call them by the sacred name, which ought never to be placed in the painful associations of controversy. In 1870, the fulness of time was come. The *matter* of the things to be believed and obeyed had been sufficiently developed. But inasmuch as great masses of the Roman Catholic body before that time refused either to believe or to obey, in that year the bold stroke was struck, and it was decided to bring mischievous abstractions if possible into the order of still more mischievous realities. The infallible, that is virtually the Divine, title to command, and the absolute, that is the

---

* Schrader, as above, p. 64.

unconditional duty to obey, were promulgated to an astonished world.

3. *Alleged non-interference of the Popes for Two Hundred Years.*

It has been alleged on this occasion by a British Peer, who I have no doubt has been cruelly misinformed, that the Popes have not invaded the province of the civil power during the last two hundred years.

I will not travel over so long a period, but am content even with the last twenty.

1. In his Allocution of the 22nd January, 1855, Pius IX. declared to be absolutely null and void all acts of the Government of Piedmont which he held to be in prejudice of the rights of Religion, the Church, and the Roman See, and particularly a law proposed for the suppression of the monastic orders as moral entities, that is to say as civil corporations.

2. On the 26th of July in the same year, Pius IX. sent forth another Allocution, in which he recited various acts of the Government of Spain, including the establishment of toleration for non-Roman worship, and the secularisation of ecclesiastical property; and, by his own apostolical authority, he declared all the laws hereto relating to be abrogated, totally null, and of no effect.

3. On the 22nd of June, 1862, in another Allocution, Pius IX. recited the provisions of an Austrian law of the previous December, which established freedom of opinion, of the press, of belief, of conscience, of science, of education, and of religious profession, and which regulated matrimonial jurisdiction and other matters. The whole of these "abominable" laws "have been and shall be totally void, and without all force whatsoever."

In all these cases reference is made, in general terms, to Concordats, of which the Pope alleges the violation; but he never bases his annulment of the laws upon this allegation. And Schrader, in his work on the Syllabus, founds the cancellation of the Spanish law, in the matter of toleration, not on the Concordat, but on the original inherent right of the Pope to enforce the 77th Article of the Syllabus, respecting the exclusive establishment of the Roman religion.*

To provide, however, against all attempts to take refuge in this specialty, I will now give instances where no question of Concordat enters at all into the case.

1. In an Allocution of July 27, 1855, when the law for the suppression of monastic orders and appropriation of their properties had been passed in the kingdom of Sardinia, on the simple ground of his Apostolic authority, the Pope annuls this law, and all other laws injurious to the Church, and excommunicates all who had a hand in them.

2. In an Allocution of December 15, 1856, the Pope recites the interruption of negotiations for a Concordat with Mexico, and the various acts of that Government against religion, such as the abolition of the ecclesiastical *forum*, the secularisation of Church property, and the civil permission to members of monastic establishments to withdraw from them. All of these laws are declared absolutely null and void.

3. On the 17th of September, 1863, in an Encyclical Letter the Pope enumerates like proceedings on the part of the Government of New Granada. Among the wrongs committed, we find the establishment of freedom of worship (*cujusque acatholici cultûs libertas sancita*). These and all

---

* Schrader, p. 80.

other acts against the Church, utterly unjust and impious, the Pope, by his Apostolic authority, declares to be wholly null and void in the future and in the past.*

No more, I hope, will be heard of the allegation that for two hundred years the Popes have not attempted to interfere with the Civil Powers of the world.

But if it be requisite to carry proof a step farther, this may readily be done. In his 'Petri Privilegium,' iii. 19, n., Archbishop Manning quotes the Bull *In Cœnâ Domini* as if it were still in force. Bishop Clifford, in his Pastoral Letter (p. 9), laid it down that though all human actions were moral actions, there were many of them which belonged to the temporal power, and with which the Pope could not interfere. Among these he mentioned the assessment and payment of taxes. But is it not the fact that this Bull excommunicates "all who impose new taxes, not already provided for by law, without the Pope's leave?" and all who impose, without the said leave, special and express, any taxes, new or old, upon clergymen, churches, or monasteries? †

I may be told that Archbishop Manning is not a safe authority in these matters, that the Bull *In Cœnâ Domini* was withdrawn after the assembling of the Council, and the constitution *Apostolicæ Sedis* ‡ substituted for it, in

---

* All these citations, down to 1865, will be found in 'Recueil des Allocutions Consistoriales,' &c. (Paris, 1865, Adrien Leclere et Cie). See also 'Europäische Geschichtskalender,' 1868, p. 249; Von Schulte, 'Powers of the Roman Popes,' iv. 43; Schrader, as above, Heft ii. p. 80; 'Vering, 'Katholisches Kirchenrecht' (Mainz, 1868), Band xx. pp. 170, 1, N. F. Band xiv.

† O'Keeffe, 'Ultramontanism,' pp. 215, 219. The reference is to sections v., xviii.

‡ See Quirinus, p. 105; and see 'Constit. Apostolicæ Sedis' in Friedberg's 'Acta et Decreta Conc. Vat.,' p. 77 (Friburg, 1871).

which this reference to taxes is omitted. But if this be so, is it not an astonishing fact, with reference to the spirit of Curialism, that down to the year 1870 these preposterous claims of aggression should have been upheld and from time to time proclaimed? Indeed the new Constitution itself, dated October, 1869, the latest specimen of reform and concession, without making any reservation whatever on behalf of the laws of the several countries, excommunicates (among others)—

1. All who imprison or prosecute (*hostiliter insequentes*) Archbishops or Bishops.

2. All who directly or indirectly interfere with any ecclesiastical jurisdiction.

3. All who lay hold upon or sequester goods of ecclesiastics held in right of their churches or benefices.

4. All who impede or deter the officers of the Holy Office of the Inquisition in the execution of their duties.

5. All who secularise, or become owners of, Church property, without the permission of the Pope.

VIII. ON THE INTRINSIC NATURE AND CONDITIONS OF THE PAPAL INFALLIBILITY DECREED IN THE VATICAN COUNCIL.

I HAVE now, I think, dealt sufficiently, though at greater length than I could have wished, with the two allegations, first, that the Decrees of 1870 made no difference in the liabilities of Roman Catholics with regard to their civil allegiance; secondly, that the rules of their Church allow them to pay an allegiance no more divided than that of other citizens, and that the claims of Ultramontanism, as against the Civil Power, 'are the very same with those which are advanced by Christian communions and persons generally.

I had an unfeigned anxiety to avoid all discussion of the Decree of Infallibility on its own, the religious, ground; but as matters have gone so far, it may perhaps be allowed me now to say a few words upon the nature of the extraordinary tenet, which the Bishops of one half the Christian world have now placed upon a level with the Apostles' Creed.

The name of Popery, which was formerly imposed *ad invidiam* by heated antagonists, and justly resented by Roman Catholics,* appears now to be perhaps the only name which describes, at once with point and with accuracy, the religion promulgated from the Vatican in 1870. The change made was immense. Bishop Thirlwall, one of the ablest English writers of our time, and one imbued almost beyond any other with what the Germans eulogise as the historic mind, said in his Charge of 1872, that the

---

* 'Petri Privilegium,' part ii. pp. 71-91.

promulgation of the new Dogma, which had occurred since his last meeting with his clergy, was "an event far more important than the great change in the balance of power, which we have witnessed during the same interval."*
The effect of it, described with literal rigour, was in the last resort to place the entire Christian religion in the breast of the Pope, and to suspend it on his will. This is a startling statement; but as it invites, so will it bear, examination. I put it forth not as rhetoric, sarcasm, or invective; but as fact, made good by history.

It is obvious to reply that, if the Christian religion is in the heart of the Pope, so the law of England is in the heart of the Legislature. The case of the Pope and the case of the Legislature are the same in this: that neither the one nor the other is subject to any limitation whatever, except such as he or it respectively shall choose to allow. Here the resemblance begins and ends. The nation is ruled by a Legislature, of which by far the most powerful branch is freely chosen, from time to time, by the community itself by the greater part of the heads of families in the country; and all the proceedings of its Parliament are not only carried on in the face of day, but made known from day to day, almost from hour to hour, in every town and village, and almost in every household of the land. They are governed by rules framed to secure both ample time for consideration, and the utmost freedom, or, it may be, even licence of debate; and all that is said and done is subjected to an immediate sharp and incessant criticism: with the assurance on the part of the critics, that they will have not only favour from their friends, but impunity from their enemies. Erase every one of these propositions,

---

* 'Charge of the Bishop of St. David's,' 1872, p. 2.

and replace it by its contradictory; you will then have a perfect description of the present Government of the Roman Church. The ancient principles of popular election and control, for which room was found in the Apostolic Church under its inspired teachers, and which still subsist in the Christian East, have, by the constant aggressions of Curialism, been in the main effaced, or, where not effaced, reduced to the last stage of practical inanition. We see before us the Pope, the Bishops, the priesthood, and the people. The priests are absolute over the people; the Bishops over both; the Pope over all. Each inferior may appeal against his superior; but he appeals to a tribunal which is secret, which is irresponsible, which he has no share, direct or indirect, in constituting, and no means, however remote, of controlling; and which, during all the long centuries of its existence, but especially during the latest of them, has had for its cardinal rule this—that all its judgments should be given in the sense most calculated to build up priestly power as against the people, episcopal power as against the priests, Papal power as against all three. The mere utterances of the central See are laws; and they override at will all other laws: and if they concern faith or morals, or the discipline of the Church, they are entitled, from all persons without exception, singly or collectively, to an obedience without qualification. Over these utterances—in their preparation as well as after their issue—no man has lawful control. They may be the best, or the worst; the most deliberate, or the most precipitate: as no man can restrain, so no man has knowledge of, what is done or meditated. The prompters are unknown; the consultees are unknown; the procedure is unknown. Not that there are not officers, and rules; but the officers may at will be overridden or superseded;

and the rules at will, and without notice, altered *pro re natâ* and annulled. To secure rights has been, and is, the aim of the Christian civilisation: to destroy them, and to establish the resistless, domineering action of a purely central power, is the aim of the Roman policy. Too much and too long, in other times, was this its tendency: but what was its besetting sin has now become, as far as man can make it, by the crowning triumph of 1870, its undisguised, unchecked rule of action and law of life.

These words, harsh as they may seem, and strange as they must sound, are not the incoherent imaginings of adverse partisanship. The best and greatest of the children of the Roman Church have seen occasion to use the like, with cause less grave than that which now exists, and have pointed to the lust of dominion as the source of these enormous mischiefs:—

> "Dì oggimai, che la Chiesa di Roma
> Per confondere in sè due reggimenti
> Cade nel fango, e sè brutta, e la soma."*

Without doubt there is an answer to all this. Publicity, responsibility, restraint, and all the forms of warranty and safeguard, are wanted for a human institution, but are inapplicable to a "Divine teacher," to an inspired Pontiff, to a "living Christ." The promises of God are sure, and fail not. His promise has been given, and Peter in his Successor shall never fail, never go astray. He needs neither check nor aid, as he will find them for himself. He is an exception to all the rules which determine human action; and his action in this matter is not really human,

---

* Dante, 'Purgatorio,' xvi. 127—9.
> "The Church of Rome,
> Mixing two governments that ill assort,
> Hath missed her footing, fallen into the mire,
> And there herself, and burden, much defiled."—*Cary.*

but Divine. Having, then, the Divine gift of inerrancy, why may he not be invested with the title, and assume the Divine attribute, of omnipotence?

No one can deny that the answer is sufficient, if only it be true. But the weight of such a superstructure requires a firm, broad, well-ascertained foundation. If it can be shown to exist, so far so good. In the due use of the gift of reason with which our nature is endowed, we may look for a blessing from God; but the abandonment of reason is credulity, and the habit of credulity is presumption.

Is there, then, such a foundation disclosed to us by Dr. Newman[*] when he says "the long history of the contest for and against the Pope's infallibility has been but a growing insight through centuries into the meaning of three texts"? First, "Feed my sheep" (John xxi. 15-17); of which Archbishop Kenrick tells us that the very words are disputed, and the meaning forced.[†] Next, "Strengthen thy brethren;" which has no reference whatever to doctrine, but only, if its force extend beyond the immediate occasion, to government; and, finally, "Thou art Peter, and on this rock I will build my Church;" when it is notorious that the large majority of the early expositors declare the rock to be not the person but the previous confession of Saint Peter; and where it is plain that, if his person be really meant, there is no distinction of *ex Cathedrâ* and not *ex Cathedrâ*, but the entire proceedings of his ministry are included without distinction.

---

[*] Dr. Newman, p. 110.

[†] 'Concio habenda at non habita,' i. ii. Friedrich, 'Documenta ad illustrandum,' Conc. Vat. Abth. i. pp. 191, 199. I leave it to those better entitled and better qualified to criticise the purely arbitrary construction attached to the words. Upon inquiry, I find the MSS. give serious grounds of doubt as to the received text.

Into three texts, then, it seems the Church of Rome has at length, in the course of centuries, acquired this deep insight. In the study of these three fragments, how much else has she forgotten! the total ignorance of St. Peter himself respecting his "monarchy;" the exercise of the defining office not by him but by St. James in the Council of Jerusalem; the world-wide commission specially and directly given to St. Paul; the correction of St. Peter by the Apostle of the Gentiles; the independent action of all the Apostles; the twelve foundations of the New Jerusalem, "and in them the names of the twelve Apostles of the Lamb" (Rev. xxi. 14). But let us take a wider ground. Is it not the function of the Church to study the Divine Word as a whole, and to gather into the foci of her teaching the rays that proceed from all its parts? Is not this narrow, sterile, wilful, textualism the favourite resort of sectaries, the general charter of all licence and self-will that lays waste the garden of the Lord? Is it not this that destroys the largeness and fair proportions of the Truth, squeezing here and stretching there, substituting for the reverent jealousy of a faithful guardianship the ambitious aims of a class, and gradually forcing the heavenly pattern into harder and still harder forms of distortion and caricature?

However, it must be observed that the transcendental answer we have been considering, which sets at nought all the analogies of God's Providence in the government of the world, is the only answer of a breadth equal to the case. Other replies, which have been attempted, are perfectly hollow and unreal. For instance, we are told that the Pope cannot alter the already defined doctrines of the Faith. To this I reply, let him alter them as he will, if only he thinks fit to say that he does not alter

H

them, his followers are perfectly and absolutely helpless. For if they allege alteration and innovation, the very same language will be available against them which has been used against the men that have had faith and courage given them to protest against alteration and innovation now. "Most impious are you, in charging on us that which, as you know, we cannot do. We have not altered, we have only defined. What the Church believed implicitly heretofore, she believes implicitly hereafter. Do not appeal to reason; that is rationalism. Do not appeal to Scripture; that is heresy. Do not appeal to history; that is private judgment. Over all these things I am judge, not you. If you tell me that I require you to affirm to-day, under anathema, what yesterday you were allowed or encouraged to deny, my answer is that in and by me alone you have any means of knowing what it is you affirm, or what it is you deny." This is the strain which is consistently held by the bold trumpeters of Vaticanism, and which has been effectual to intimidate the feeble-minded and faint-hearted, who seem to have formed, at the Council of the Vatican, so large a proportion of its opponents; nay, which has convinced them, or has performed in them the inscrutable process, be it what it may, which is the Roman substitute for conviction, that what in the Council itself they denounced as breach of faith, after the Council they are permitted, nay bound, to embrace, nay to enforce.

Let me now refer to another of these fantastic replies.

We are told it would be an entire mistake to confound this Infallibility of the Pope, in the province assigned to it, with absolutism:—

"The Pope is bound by the moral and divine law, by the commandments of God, by the rules of the Gospel, and by every definition in faith and morals that the Church has ever made. No man is more bound by law than the Pope; a fact plainly known to himself, and to every bishop and priest in Christendom." *

Every definition in faith and morals! These are written definitions. What are they but another Scripture? What right of interpreting this other Scripture is granted to the Church at large, more than of the real and greater Scripture? Here is surely, in its perfection, the petition for bread, answered by the gift of a stone. .

Bishop Vaughan does not venture to assert that the Pope is bound by the canon law, the written law of the Church of Rome. The abolition of the French Sees under the Concordat with Napoleon, and the deposition of their legitimate Bishops, even if it were the only instance, has settled that question for ever. Over the written law of his Church the pleasure of the Pope is supreme. And this justifies, for every practical purpose, the assertion that law no longer exists in that Church; in the same very real sense as we should say there was no law in England in the reign of James the Second, while it was subject to a dispensing power. There exists no law, wherever a living ruler, an executive head, claims and exercises, and is allowed to possess, a power of annulling or a power of dispensing with the law. If Bishop Vaughan does not know this, I am sorry to say he does not know the first lesson that every English citizen should learn; he has yet to pass through the lispings of civil childhood. This exemption of the individual, be he who he may, from the restraints of the law is the very thing that in England we term absolutism. By absolutism we mean the superiority of a personal will to law, for the purpose of putting aside or changing law. Now that power is precisely what

* Bishop Vaughan's 'Pastoral Letter,' p. 30.

the Pope possesses. First, because he is infallible in faith and morals, when he speaks *ex cathedrâ*, and he himself is the final judge which of his utterances shall be utterances *ex cathedrâ*. He has only to use the words, " I, *ex cathedrâ*, declare ;" or the words, " I, in the discharge of the office of pastor and teacher of all Christians, by virtue of my supreme Apostolic authority, define as a doctrine regarding faith or morals, to be held by the Universal Church ;"* and all words that may follow, be they what they may, must now and hereafter be as absolutely accepted by every Roman Catholic who takes the Vatican for his teacher, with what in their theological language they call a Divine faith, as must any article of the Apostles' Creed. And what words they are to be that may follow, the Pope by his own will and motion is the sole judge.

It is futile to say, the Pope has the Jesuits and other admirable advisers near him, whom he will always consult. I am bound to add that I am sceptical as to the excellence of these advisers. These are the men who cherish, methodise, transmit, and exaggerate, all the dangerous traditions of the Curia. In them it lives. The ambition and self-seeking of the Court of Rome have here their root. They seem to supply that Roman *malaria*, which Dr. Newman† tells us encircles the base of the rock of St. Peter. But the question is not what the Pope will do; it is what he can do, what he has power to do; whether, in Bishop Vaughan's language, he is bound by law; not whether he is so wise and so well-advised that it is perfectly safe to leave him not bound by law. On this latter question there may be a great conflict of opinions; but it is not the question before us.

---

* 'Vatican Decrees,' chap. iii.
† Dr. Newman, p. 94.

It cannot be pleaded against him, were it ever so clear, that his declaration is contrary to the declaration of some other Popes. For here, as in the case of the Christian Creed, he may tell you—always speaking in the manner supposed—that that other Pope was not speaking *ex cathedrâ*. Or he may tell you that there is no contrariety. If you have read, if you have studied, if you have seen, if you have humbly used every means of getting to the truth, and you return to your point that *contrariety there is*, again his answer is ready: That assertion of yours is simply your private judgment; and your private judgment is just what my infallibility is meant and appointed to put down. My word is the tradition of the Church. It is the nod of Zeus: it is the judgment of the Eternal. There is no escaping it, and no disguising it: the whole Christian religion, according to the modern Church of Rome, is in the breast of one man. The will and arbitrament of one man will for the future decide, through half the Christian world, what religion is to be. It is unnecessary to remind me that this power is limited to faith and morals. We know it is; it does not extend to geometry, or to numbers. Equally is it beside the point to observe that the infallibility alleged has not received a new definition: I have nowhere said it had. It is the old gift: it is newly lodged. Whatever was formerly ascribed either to the Pope, or to the Council, or to the entire governing body of the Church, or to the Church general and diffused, the final sense of the great Christian community, aided by authority, tested by discussion, mellowed and ripened by time—all—no more than all, and no less than all—of what God gave, for guidance, through the power of truth, by the Christian revelation, to the whole redeemed family, the baptized flock of the Saviour in the world; all this is now locked in the breast of one man, opened and distributed at his will, and liable to assume whatever form—whether under the name of identity or other name it matters not—he may think fit to give it.

Idle then it is to tell us, finally, that the Pope is bound " by the moral and divine law, by the commandments of God, by the rules of the Gospel:" and if more verbiage and repetition could be piled up, as Ossa was set upon Olympus, and Pelion upon Ossa, to cover the poverty and irrelevancy of the idea, it would not mend the matter. For of these, one and all, the Pope himself, by himself, is the judge without appeal. If he consults, it is by his will: if he does not consult, no man can call him to account. No man, or assemblage of men, is one whit the less bound to hear and to obey. He is the judge of the moral and Divine law, of the Gospel, and of the commandments; the supreme and only final judge: and he is the judge, with no legislature to correct his errors, with no authoritative rules to guide his proceedings: with no power on earth to question the force, or intercept the effect, of his decisions.

It is indeed said by Dr. Newman, and by others, that this infallibility is not inspiration. On such a statement I have two remarks to make. First, that we have this assurance on the strength only of his own private judgment; secondly, that if bidden by the self-assertion of the Pope, he will be required by his principles to retract it,* and to assert, if occasion should arise, the contrary; thirdly, that he lives under a system of development, through which somebody's private opinion of to-day may become matter of faith for all the to-morrows of the future. What kind and class of private opinions are they that are

---

* Dr. Newman, pp. 99, 131. The Papal newspaper, 'Voce della Verità,' of Jan. 21 complains seriously of parts of Dr. Newman's Reply.

most likely to find favour with the Vatican? History, the history of well-nigh eighteen centuries, supplies the answer, and supplies it with almost the rigour of a mathematical formula. On every contested question, that opinion finds ultimate assent at Rome, which more exalts the power of Rome. Have no Popes claimed this inspiration, which Dr. Newman so reasonably denies? Was it claimed by Clement XI. for the Bull *Unigenitus?* Was it claimed by Gregory the Second in a judgment in which he authorised a man, who had an invalid wife, to quit her and to marry another? Is it or is it not claimed by the present Pope, who says he has a higher title to admonish the governments of Europe than the Prophet Nathan had to admonish David?[*] Shall we be told that these are his utterances only as a private Doctor? But we also learn from Papal divines, and indeed the nature of the case makes it evident, that the non-infallible declarations of the Pope are still declarations of very high authority. Again, is it not the fact that, since 1870, many bishops, German, Italian, French, have ascribed inspiration to the Pope? Opinions dispersed here and there were, in the cases of the Immaculate Conception, and of the Absolute Supremacy and the Infallibility *ex cathedrâ*, gathered up, declared to constitute a *consensus* of the Church, and made the groundwork of new Articles of Faith. Why should not this be done hereafter in the case of Papal inspiration? It is but a mild onward step, in comparison with the strides already made. Those who cried "magnificent," on the last occasion, will cry it again on the next. Dr. Newman and the minimising divines would, perhaps, reply "No: it is impossible." But this was the very

---

[*] 'Discorsi di Pio IX.,' vol. i. p. 366, on March 3, 1872.

assurance which, not a single and half-recognised divine, but the whole synod of Irish prelates gave to the British Government in 1810, and which the Council of the Vatican has authoritatively falsified.

Now, let us look a little more closely at this astonishing gift of Infallibility, and its almost equally astonishing, because arbitrary, limitations. The Pope is only infallible when he speaks *ex cathedrâ*. The gift, we are told, has subsisted for 1800 years. When was the discriminating phrase invented? Was it after Christendom had done without it for one thousand six hundred years, that this limiting formula of such vital moment was discovered? Do we owe its currency and prominence—with so much else of ill omen—to the Jesuits? Before this, if we had not the name, had we the thing?

Dr. Newman, indeed, finds for it a very ancient extraction. He says the Jewish doctors taught *ex cathedrâ*, and our Saviour enjoined that they should be obeyed. Surely there could not be a more calamitous illustration. Observe the terms of the incoherent proposition.

The Scribes and Pharisees sit in the *cathedra* of Moses: "*all* therefore whatsoever they bid you observe, that observe and do."* The Pope sits in the *cathedra* of Peter, not all therefore, but only a very limited part of what he enjoins, you are to accept and follow. Only what he says under four well-defined conditions.† Only, writes Dr. Newman, when he speaks "in matters speculative,"‡ and "bears upon the domain of thought, not directly of action."‡ Let us look again to our four conditions: one of them is that he must address the entire Church. It is singular, to say no more, that St. Peter, in his first

---

* St. Matt. xxiii. 2.   † Newman, p. 115.   ‡ *Ibid.* p. 127.

Epistle, which has always been unquestioned Scripture, does not address the entire Church; but in his Second, which was for a time much questioned, he does. It is much more singular that the early ages are believed to afford no example whatever of a Papal judgment addressed to the entire Church. So that it is easy to say that Honorius did not speak *ex cathedrâ*: for no Pope spoke *ex cathedrâ*. It is even held by some that there was no Bull or other declaration of a Pope corresponding with this condition for one thousand three hundred years; and that the unhappy series began with *Unam Sanctam* of Boniface VIII. But how is it beyond all expression strange that for one thousand three hundred years, or were it but for half one thousand three hundred years, the Church performed her high office, and spread over the nations, without any infallible teaching whatever from the Pope, and then that it should have been reserved for these later ages first to bring into exercise a gift so entirely new, without example in its character, and on the presence or absence of which depends a vital difference in the conditions of Church life?

The declarations of the Pope *ex cathedrâ* are to be the sure guide and mainstay of the Church; and yet she has passed through two-thirds of her existence without once reverting to it! Nor is this all. For in those earlier ages, the fourth century in particular, were raised and settled those tremendous controversies relating to the Godhead, the decision of which was the most arduous work the Church has ever been called to perform in the sphere of thought. This vast work she went through without the infallible utterances of the Pope, nay at three several times in opposition to Papal judgments, now determined to have been heretical. Are more utterances now begun in order to sustain the miserable argument for forcing his

Temporal Sovereignty on a people, whom nothing but the violence of foreign arms will bring or keep beneath it?

Yet one more point of suggestion. There are those who think that the craving after an infallibility which is to speak from human lips, in chapter and verse, upon each question as it arises, is not a sign of the strength and healthiness of faith, but of the diseased avidity of its weakness. Let it, however, be granted, for the sake of argument, that it is a comfort to the infirmity of human nature thus to attain promptly to clear and intelligible solutions of its doubts, instead of waiting on the Divine pleasure, as those who watch for the morning, to receive the supplies required by its intellectual and its moral trials. A recommendation of this kind, however little it may endure the scrutiny of philosophic reflection, may probably have a great power over the imagination and the affections (*affectus*) of mankind. For this, however, it is surely required that by the ordinary faculties of mankind, rationally and honestly used, these infallible decisions should be discernible, and that they should stand severed from the general mass of promiscuous and ambiguous teaching. Even so it was that, when Holy Scripture was appointed to be of final and supreme authority, provision was also made by the wisdom of Providence for the early collection of the New Testament into a single series of Books, so that even we lay persons are allowed to know so far what is Scripture and what is not, without having to resort to the aid of the "scrutinising vigilance, acuteness, and subtlety of the *Schola Theologorum*."* But let not the Papal Christian imagine that he is to have a like advantage in easily understanding

---

* Dr. Newman, p. 121.

what are the Papal Decrees, which for him form part of the unerring revelation of God. It would even be presumptuous in him to have an opinion on the point. The Divine word of Scripture was invested with a power to feed and to refresh. "He shall feed me in a green pasture; and lead me forth beside the waters of comfort."* And, by the blessing and mercy of God, straight and open is the access to them. In no part of the Church of Christ, except the Roman, is it jealously obstructed by ecclesiastical authority; and even there the line of the sacred precinct is at least perfectly defined. But now we are introduced to a new code, dealing with the same high subject-matter, and possessed of the same transcendent prerogative of certain and unchanging truth; but what are the chapters of that code, nobody knows except the *Schola Theologorum*. Is for example the private Christian less humbly desirous to know whether he is or is not to rely absolutely on the declarations of the Syllabus as to the many and great matters which it touches? No one can tell him. Bishop Fessler (approved by the Pope) says so. He admits that he for one does not know. It seems doubtful whether he thought that the Pope himself knew. For instead of asking the Pope, he promises that it shall be made the subject of long inquiry by the *Schola Theologorum*. "*Ce sera tout d'abord à la science théologique que s'imposera le devoir de rechercher les diverses raisons qui militent en faveur des diverses opinions sur cette question.*" † But when the inquiry has ended, and the result has been declared, is he much better off? I doubt

---

* Psalm xxiii. 2.

† 'Vraie et fausse Infaillibilité des Papes,' p. 8. Angl.: "It will at once become the duty of theological science to examine into the various reasons which go to support each of the various opinions on that question."

it. For the declaration need not then be a final one. "Instances," says Dr. Newman, "frequently occur, when it is successfully maintained by some new writer, that the Pope's act does not imply what it has seemed to imply; and questions, which seemed to be closed, are after a course of years reopened."* It does not appear whether there is any limit to this "course of years." But whether there is or is not, one thing is clear: Between the solid ground, the *terra firma* of Infallibility, and the quaking, fluctuating mind of the individual, which seeks to find repose upon it, there is an interval over which he cannot cross. Decrees *ex cathedrâ* are infallible; but determinations what decrees are *ex cathedrâ* are fallible; so that the private person, after he has with all docility handed over his mind and its freedom to the *Schola Theologorum*, can never certainly know, never know with "divine faith," when he is on the rock of infallibility, when on the shifting quicksands of a merely human persuasion.

Dr. Newman† will perhaps now be able to judge the reason which led me to say, "There is no established or accepted definition of the phrase *ex cathedrâ.*" By a definition I understand something calculated to bring the true nature of the thing defined nearer to the rational apprehension of those who seek to understand it; not a volume of words in themselves obscure, only pliable to the professional interest of Curialism, and certainly well calculated to find further employment for its leisure, and fresh means of holding in dependence on its will an unsuspecting laity.

But all that has been said is but a slight sample of the strange aspects and portentous results of the newly discovered *articulus stantis aut cadentis ecclesiæ.*

* Dr. Newman, p. 121. † *Ibid.* p. 107.

CONCLUSION.

I HAVE now, at greater length than I could have wished, but I think with ample proof, justified the following assertions:—

1. That the position of Roman Catholics has been altered by the Decrees of the Vatican on Papal Infallibility, and on obedience to the Pope.

2. That the extreme claims of the Middle Ages have been sanctioned, and have been revived without the warrant or excuse which might in those ages have been shown for them.

3. That the claims asserted by the Pope are such as to place civil allegiance at his mercy.

4. That the State and people of the United Kingdom had a right to rely on the assurances they had received, that Papal Infallibility was not, and could not become, an article of faith in the Roman Church, and that the obedience due to the Pope was limited by laws independent of his will.

I need not any more refer to others of my assertions, more general, or less essential to the main argument.

The appeal of the 'Dublin Review'[*] for union on the basis of common belief in resisting unbelief, which ought to be strong, is unhappily very weak. "Defend," says the Reviewer, "the ark of salvation precious to us both, though you have an interest (so to speak) in only a part of the cargo." But as the Reviewer himself is deck-loading the vessel in such a manner as to threaten her foundering, to stop his very active proceedings is not

---

[*] For Jan. 1875, p. 173.

opposed to, nay, is part of, the duty of caring for the safety of the vessel. But weaker still, if possible, is the appeal which Archbishop Manning has made against my publication, as one which endeavours to create religious divisions among his flock, and instigate them to rise against the authority of the Church. For if the Church of England, of which I am a member, is, as she has never ceased to teach, the ancient, lawful, Catholic Church of this country, it is rather Archbishop Manning than I that may be charged with creating, for the last twenty years and more, religious divisions among our countrymen, and instigating them to rise against that ancient, lawful, and mild authority.

There may be, and probably are, great faults in my manner of conducting this argument. But the claim of Ultramontanism among us seems to amount to this: that there shall be no free, and therefore no effectual, examination of the Vatican Decrees, because they are the words of a Father, and sacred therefore in the eyes of his affectionate children.* It is deliberately held, by grave and serious men, that my construing the Decrees of the Vatican, not arbitrarily, but with argument and proof, in a manner which makes them adverse to civil duty, is an "insult" and an outrage to the Roman Catholic body, which I have nowhere charged with accepting them in that sense. Yet a far greater licence has been assumed by Archbishop Manning, who, without any attempt or proof at all, suggests,† if he does not assert, that the allegiance of the masses of the English people is an inert conformity and a passive compliance, given really for wrath and not for conscience' sake. This opinion is, in my judg-

---

* 'Dublin Review,' Jan. 1875, p. 172.
† Archbishop Manning, pp. 345.

ment, most untrue, most unjust; but to call even this an insult would be an act of folly, betokening, as I think, an unsound and unmanly habit of mind. Again, to call the unseen councillors of the Pope myrmidons, to speak of "aiders and abettors of the Papal chair," to call Rome "headquarters," these and like phrases amount, according to Archbishop Manning,* to "an indulgence of unchastened language rarely to be equalled." I frankly own that this is in my eyes irrational. Not that it is agreeable to me to employ even this far from immoderate liberty of controversial language. I would rather pay an unbroken reverence to all ministers of religion, and especially to one who fills the greatest See of Christendom. But I see this great personage, under ill advice, aiming heavy and, as far as he can make them so, deadly blows at the freedom of mankind, and therein not only at the structure of society, but at the very constitution of our nature, and the high designs of Providence for trying and training it. I cannot under the restraints of courtly phrase convey any adequate idea of such tremendous mischiefs; for, in proportion as the power is venerable, the abuse of it is pernicious. I am driven to the conclusion that this sensitiveness is at the best but morbid. The cause of it may be, that for the last thirty years, in this country at least, Ultramontanism has been very busy in making controversial war upon other people, with singularly little restraint of language; and has had far too little of the truth told to itself. Hence it has lost the habit, almost the idea, of equal laws in discussion. Of that system as a system, especially after the further review of it which it has been my duty to make, I must say that its influence is adverse

---

* Archbishop Manning, p. 177.

to freedom in the State, the family, and the individual; that when weak it is too often crafty, and when strong tyrannical; and that, though in this country no one could fairly deny to its professors the credit of doing what they think is for the glory of God, they exhibit in a notable degree the vast self-deluding forces, which make sport of our common nature. The great instrument to which they look for the promotion of Christianity seems to be an unmeasured exaltation of the clerical class and of its power, as against all that is secular and lay, an exaltation not less unhealthy for that order itself than for society at large. There are those who think, without being mere worshippers of Luther, that he saved the Church of Rome by alarming it, when its Popes, Cardinals, and Prelates were carrying it " down a steep place into the sea ;" and it may be that those who, even if too roughly, challenge the proceedings of the Vatican, are better promoting its interests than such as court its favours, and hang upon its lips.

I am concerned, however, to say that in the quick resentment which has been directed against clearness and strength of language, I seem to perceive not simply a natural sensitiveness, but a great deal of controversial stratagem. The purpose of my pamphlet was to show that the directors of the Roman Church had in the Council of the Vatican committed a gross offence against civil authority, and against civil freedom. The aim of most of those, who have professionally replied to me, seems to have been at all hazards to establish it in the minds of their flocks, that whatever is said against their high clerical superiors is said against them, although they had nothing to do with the Decrees, or with the choice or appointment of the exalted persons, who framed and passed them. But this proposition, if stated calmly as part of an argument, will not bear a moment's examination. Consequently, it has been boldly held that this drawing of distinctions between pastors and the flock, because the one made the Decrees and the other did not, is an insult and an outrage to all alike;* and by this appeal passion is stirred up to darken counsel, and obscure the case.

I am aware that this is no slight matter, and I have acted under a sense of no trivial responsibility. Rarely in the complicated combinations of politics, when holding a high place in the councils of my Sovereign, and when error was commonly visited by some form of sharp and speedy retribution, have I felt that sense as keenly. At any rate, I may and must say that all the words of these Tracts were written as by one who knows that he must answer for them to a Power higher than that of public opinion.

If any motive connected with religion helped to sway me, it was not one of hostility, but the reverse. My hostility, at least, was the sentiment which we feel towards faults which mar the excellencies, which even destroy the hope and the promise of those we are fain to love. Attached to my own religious communion, the Church of my birth and my country, I have never loved it with a merely sectional or insular attachment, but have thankfully regarded it as that portion of the great redeemed Christian family in which my lot had been cast—not by, but for me. In every other portion of that family, whatever its name, whatever its extent, whatever its perfections, or whatever

---

* I withhold the references—they are numerous, although by no means universal. Having said so much of the extreme doctrines of Archbishop Manning, I have pleasure in observing that he does not adopt this language. And also in acknowledging the charitable tone of Cardinal Cullen, who, in his Lenten Pastoral, commends me to the prayers of his people for my enlightenment.

its imperfections. I have sought to feel a kindly interest, varying in its degree according to the likeness it seemed to bear to the heavenly pattern, and according to the capacity it seemed to possess to minister to the health and welfare of the whole.

> "Le frondi, onde s' infronda tutto l' orto
> Del Ortolano Eterno, am' io cotanto
> Quanto da Lui in lor di bene è porto."*

Whether they be Tyrian or Trojan,† Eastern or Western, Reformed or Unreformed, I desire to renounce and repudiate all which needlessly wounds them, which does them less than justice, which overlooks their place in the affections and the care of the Everlasting Father of us all. Common sense seems to me to teach that doctrine, no less than Christianity. Therefore I will say, and I trust to the spirit of Charity to interpret me, I have always entertained a warm desire that the better elements might prevail over the worse in that great Latin communion which we call the Church of Rome, and which comprises one-half, or near one-half, of Christendom: for the Church which gave us Thomas à Kempis, and which produced the scholarlike and statesmanlike mind of Erasmus, the varied and attractive excellencies of Colet, and of More; for the Church of Pascal and Arnauld, of Nicole and Quesnel; for the Church of some now living among us, of whom none would deny that they are as humble, as tender, as self-renouncing, and as self-abased—in a word, as Evangelical as the most 'Evangelical' of Protestants by possibility can be.

---

* Dante, 'Paradiso,' xxvi. 64—6.
"The leaves, wherewith embowered is all the garden
Of the Eternal Gardener, do I love
As much as He has granted them of good."—*Longfellow.*
† Æn. x. 108.

No impartial student of history can, I think, fail to regard with much respect and some sympathy the body of British Christians which, from the middle period of the reign of Elizabeth down to the earlier portion of the present century, adhered with self-denying fidelity, and with a remarkable consistency of temper and belief, to the Latin communion. I lament its formation, and I cannot admit its title-deeds; but justice requires me to appreciate the high qualities which it has exhibited and sadly prolonged under sore disadvantage. It was small, and dispersed through a mass far from friendly. It was cut off from the ancient national hierarchy, and the noble establishments of the national religion: it was severely smitten by the penal laws, and its reasonable aspirations for the measures that would have secured relief were mercilessly thwarted and stifled by those Popes whom they loved too well. Amidst all these cruel difficulties, it retained within itself these high characteristics; it was moderate; it was brave; it was devout; it was learned; it was loyal.

In discussing, however sharply, the Vatican Decrees, I have endeavoured to keep faith; and I think that honour as well as prudence required me, when offering an appeal upon public and civil grounds, to abstain not only from assailing, but even from questioning in any manner or regard, the Roman Catholic religion, such as it stood before 1870 in its general theory, and such as it actually lived and breathed in England during my own early days, half a century ago.

It was to those members of such a body, who still cherish its traditions in consistency as well as in good faith, that I could alone, with any hope of profit, address my appeal. Who are they now? and how many? Has what was most noble in them gone the way of all flesh, together with those clergy of 1826 in England and Ireland, who, as Dr. Newman tells us, had been educated in Gallican opinions?

More than thirty years ago, I expressed to a near friend, slightly younger than myself, and in all gifts standing high even among the highest of his day, the deep alarm I had conceived at the probable consequences of those secessions of educated, able, devout, and in some instances most eminent men to the Church of Rome, which had then begun in series, and which continued for about ten years. I had then an apprehension, which after-experience has confirmed in my mind, though to some it may appear a paradox, that nothing would operate so powerfully upon the England of the nineteenth century as a crowd of these secessions—especially if from Oxford—in stimulating, strengthening, and extending the negative or destructive spirit in religion. My friend replied to me, that at any rate there would, if the case occurred, be some compensation in the powerful effect which any great English infusion could not fail to have, in softening the spirit, and modifying the general attitude, of the Church of Rome itself. The secessions continued, and multiplied. Some years later, the author of this remark himself plunged into the flood of them. How strangely and how sadly has his estimate of their effects been falsified! They are now seen, and felt as well as seen, to have contributed everywhere to the progress and to the highest exaggerations of Vaticanism, and to have altered in that sense both profoundly and extensively, and by a process which gives no sign of having even now reached its last stage, the complexion of the Anglo-Roman communion.

It is hard to recognise the traditions of such a body in the character and action of the Ultramontane policy, or in its influence either upon moderation, or upon learning, or upon loyalty, or upon the general peace.

I have above hazarded an opinion that in this country it may cause inconvenience; and I have had materials ready to hand which would, I think, have enabled me amply to prove this assertion. But to enter into these details might inflame the dispute, and I do not see that it is absolutely necessary. My object has been to produce, if possible, a temper of greater watchfulness; to promote the early and provident fear which, says Mr. Burke, is the mother of necessity; to disturb that lazy way of thought, which acknowledges no danger until it thunders at the doors; to warn my countrymen against the velvet paw, and smooth and soft exterior of a system which is dangerous to the foundations of civil order, and which any one of us may at any time encounter in his daily path. If I am challenged, I must not refuse to say it is not less dangerous, in its ultimate operation on the human mind, to the foundations of that Christian belief, which it loads with false excrescences, and strains even to the bursting.

In some of the works, to which I am now offering my rejoinder, a protest is raised against this discussion in the name of Peace.* I will not speak of the kind of peace which the Roman Propaganda has for the last thirty years been carrying through the private homes of England. But I look out into the world; and I find that now, and in great part since the Vatican Decrees, the Church of Rome, through the Court of Rome and its Head, the Pope, is in direct feud with Portugal, with Spain, with Germany, with Switzerland, with Austria, with Russia, with Brazil, with most of South America: in short, with the far larger

---
* Dr. Capel, p. 48. Archbishop Manning, p. 127.

part of Christendom. The particulars may be found in, nay, they almost fill, the Speeches, Letters, Allocutions, of the Pope himself. So notorious are the facts that, according to Archbishop Manning, they are due to a conspiracy of the Governments. He might as reasonably say they were due to the Council of the Amphictyons. On one point I must strongly insist. In my Expostulation, I laid stress upon the charge of an intention, on the part of Vaticanism, to promote the restoration of the temporal sovereignty of the Pope, on the first favourable opportunity, by foreign arms, and without reference to the wishes of those who were once his people. From Archbishop Manning downwards, not so much as one of those, who have answered me from his standing-ground, has disavowed this project: many of them have openly professed that they adopt it, and glory in it. The meaning of Monsignor Nardi, in his courteous Reply, written almost from beneath the Papal roof, cannot be mistaken (pp. 57–62). Thus my main practical accusation is admitted; and the main motive which prompted me is justified. I am afraid that the cry for peace, in the quarters from which it comes, has been the complaint of the foeman scaling the walls, against the sentry who gives the alarm. That alarm every man is entitled to give, when the very subject, that precipitates the discussion, is the performance of duties towards the Crown and State, to which we are all bound in common, and in which the common interest is so close, that their non-performance by any one is an injury to all the rest.

It may be true that in human things there are great restraining and equalising powers, which work unseen. It may be true that the men of good systems are worse than their principles, and the men of bad systems better than their principles. But, speaking of systems, and not of men, I am convinced that the time has come when religion itself requires a vigorous protest against this kind of religionism.

I am not one of those who find or imagine a hopeless hostility between authority and reason; or who undervalue the vital moment of Christianity to mankind. I believe that religion to be the determining condition of our well or ill-being, and its Church to have been and to be, in its several organisms, by far the greatest institution that the world has ever seen. The poles on which the dispensation rests are truth and freedom. Between this there is a holy, a divine union; and, he that impairs or impugns either, is alike the enemy of both. To tear, or to beguile, away from man the attribute of inward liberty, is not only idle, I would almost say it is impious. When the Christian scheme first went forth, with all its authority, to regenerate the world, it did not discourage, but invited the free action of the human reason and the individual conscience, while it supplied these agents from within with the rules and motives of a humble, which was also a noble, self-restraint. The propagation of the Gospel was committed to an organized society; but in the constitution of that society, as we learn alike from Scripture and from history, the rights of all its orders were well distributed and guaranteed. Of these early provisions for a balance of Church-power, and for securing the laity against sacerdotal domination, the rigid conservatism of the Eastern Church presents us, even down to the present day, with an authentic and living record. But in the Churches subject to the Pope, clerical power, and every doctrine and usage favourable to clerical power, have been developed, and developed, and developed, while all that nurtured freedom, and all that guaranteed it, have been harassed and denounced, cabined and confined, attenuated and starved, with fits and starts of intermitted success and failure, but with a progress on the whole as decisively onward toward its aim, as that which some enthusiasts think they see in the natural movement of humanity at large. At last came the crowning stroke of 1870 : the legal extinction of Right, and the enthronement of Will in its place, throughout the Churches of one-half of Christendom. While freedom and its guarantees are thus attacked on one side, a multitude of busy but undisciplined and incoherent assailants, on the other, are making war, some upon Revelation, some upon dogma, some upon Theism itself. Far be it from me to question the integrity of either party. But as freedom can never be effectually established by the adversaries of that Gospel which has first made it a reality for all orders and degrees of men, so the Gospel never can be effectually defended by a policy, which declines to acknowledge the high place assigned to Liberty in the counsels of Providence, and which, upon the pretext of the abuse that like every other good she suffers, expels her from its system. Among the many noble thoughts of Homer, there is not one more noble or more penetrating than his judgment upon slavery. "On the day," he says, " that makes a bondman of the free,"

"Wide-seeing Zeus takes half the man away."

He thus judges, not because the slavery of his time was cruel, for evidently it was not; but because it was slavery. What he said against servitude in the social order, we may plead against Vaticanism in the spiritual sphere; and no cloud of incense, which zeal, or flattery, or even love, can raise, should hide the disastrous truth from the vision of mankind.

APPENDICES.

APPENDIX A (p. 5).

THE following are the principal Replies from antagonists which I have seen. I have read the whole of them with care; and I have not knowingly omitted in this Rejoinder anything material to the main arguments that they contain. I place them as nearly as I can in chronological order:—

1. 'Reply to Mr. Gladstone.' By A Monk of St. Augustine's, Ramsgate. Nov. 15, 1874. London.
2. 'Expostulation *in extremis*.' By Lord Robert Montagu. London, 1874.
3. 'The Döllingerites, Mr. Gladstone, and the Apostates from the Faith.' By Bishop Ullathorne. Nov. 17, 1874. London.
4. 'The Abomination of Desolation.' By Rev. J. Coleridge, S.J. Nov. 23, 1874. London.
5. Very Rev. Canon Oakeley, Letters of. Nov. 16 and 27, 1874. In the 'Times.'
6. 'Catholic Allegiance.' By Bishop Clifford. Clifton, Nov. 25, 1874.
7. 'Pastoral Letters.' By Bishop Vaughan. Dec. 3, 1874. London. The same, with Appendices, Jan. 1875.
8. Review of Mr. Gladstone's Expostulation, in 'The Month' for Dec. 1874 and Jan. 1875. By Rev. T. B. Parkinson, S.J.
9. 'External Aspects of the Gladstone Controversy.' In 'The Month' of Jan. 1875.
10. 'An Ultramontane's Reply to Mr. Gladstone's Expostulations.' London, 1874.
11. Letter to J. D. Hutchinson, Esq. By Mr. J. Stores Smith, Nov. 29, 1874. In the 'Halifax Courier' of Dec. 5, 1874.
12. 'Letter to the Right Hon. W. E. Gladstone, M.P.' By A Scottish Catholic Layman. London, 1874.
13. 'Reply to the Right Hon. W. E. Gladstone's Political Expostulation.' By Monsignor Capel. London, 1874.
14. 'A Vindication of the Pope and the Catholic Religion.' By Mulhallen Marum, LL.B. Kilkenny, 1874.

15. 'Catholicity, Liberty, Allegiance, a Disquisition on Mr. Gladstone's Expostulation.' By Rev. John Curry, Jan. 1, 1875. London, Dublin, Bradford.
16. 'Mr. Gladstone's Expostulation Unravelled.' By Bishop Ullathorne. London, 1875.
17. 'Sul Tentativo Anticattolico in Inghilterra, e l'Opuscolo del On$^{mo.}$ Sig. Gladstone.' Di Monsignor Francesco Nardi. Roma, 1875.
18. 'A Letter to his Grace the Duke of Norfolk, on occasion of Mr. Gladstone's recent Expostulation.' By John Henry Newman, D.D., of the Oratory. London, 1875.
19. 'The Vatican Decrees in their bearing on Civil Allegiance.' By Henry Edward, Archbishop of Westminster. London, 1875.
20. 'The Dublin Review, Art. VII.' London, Jan. 1875.
21. 'The Union Review,' Art. I. By Mr. A. P. de Lisle. London, February, 1875.

I need not here refer particularly to the significant letters of favourable response which have proceeded from within the Roman Catholic communion, or from those who have been driven out of it by the Vatican Decrees.

APPENDIX B (p. 9).

" I lament not only to read the name, but to trace the arguments of Dr. Von Döllinger in the pamphlet before me."—*Abp. Manning. Letter to the 'Times,' Nov. 7, 1874.*—'*Vatican Decrees,*' p. 4.

Justice to Dr. Von Döllinger requires me to state that he had no concern, direct or indirect, in the production or the publication of the tract, and that he was, until it had gone to press, ignorant of its existence. Had he been a party to it, it could not have failed to be far more worthy of the attention it received.

Bishop Ullathorne goes further, and says of Dr. Von Döllinger that " he never was a theologian."—*Letter*, p. 10.

Then they have made strange mistakes in Germany.

Werner, a writer who I believe is trustworthy, in his ' Geschichte der Katholischen Theologie,' 1866, is led by his subject to survey the actual staff and condition of the Roman Church. He says, p. 470: "Almost for an entire generation, Dr. I. Von Döllinger has been held *the most learned theologian of Catholic Germany;* and he indisputably counts among the greatest intellectual lights that the Catholic Church of the present age has to show."

I cite a still higher authority in Cardinal Schwarzenberg, Archbishop of Prague. On May 25, 1868, he addressed a letter to Cardinal Antonelli, in which he pointed out that the theologians, who had been summoned from Germany to the Council, were all of the same theological school, and that for the treatment of dogmatic matters it was most important that some more profound students, of more rich and universal learning, as well as sound in faith, should be called. He goes on to suggest the names of Hefele, Kuhn, and (with a high eulogy) Von Döllinger.

The strangest of all is yet behind. Cardinal Antonelli, in his reply dated July 15, receives with some favour the suggestion of Cardinal Schwarzenberg, and says that one of the three theologians named would certainly have been invited to the Council, had not the Pope been informed that if invited, he would decline to come. That one was Dr. Von Döllinger.

I cite the original documents, which will be found in Friedrich's 'Documenta ad illustrandum Conc. Vat.,' pp. 277-80.

APPENDIX C (p. 26).

As I have cited Schrader elsewhere, I cite him here also; simply because he translates (into German) upon a different construction of the Seventy-third Article of the Syllabus from that which I had adopted, and makes a disjunctive proposition out of two statements which appear to be in effect identical. In English, his conversion of the article runs as follows:—

"Among Christians no true matrimony can be constituted by virtue of a civil contract; and it is true that either the marriage contract between Christians is a Sacrament, or that the contract is null when the Sacrament is excluded.

"Remark. And, on this very account, is every contract entered into between man and woman, among Christians, without the Sacrament, in virtue of any civil law whatever, nothing else than a shameful and pernicious concubinage, so strongly condemned by the Church; and therefore the marriage-bond can never be separated from the Sacrament."*

The sum of the matter seems to be this. Wherever it has

---

* Schrader, Heft ii. p. 79. Wien, 1865.

pleased the Pope to proclaim the Tridentine Decrees, civil marriage is concubinage. It is the duty of each concubinary (or party to concubinage), with or without the consent of the other party, to quit that guilty state. And as no law of Church or State binds a concubinary to marriage with the other concubinary, he (or she) is free, so far as the Church of Rome can create the freedom, to marry another person.

APPENDIX D (p. 51).

I do not think myself called upon to reply to the statements by which Bishop Vaughan has sought ('Pastoral Letter,' pp. 35–7) to show, that the fear of civil war ultimately turned the scale in the minds of the chief Ministers of 1829, and led them to propose the Bill for Emancipation. First, because the question is not what influences acted at that moment on those particular minds, but how that equilibrium of moral forces in the country had been brought about which made civil war, or something that might be called civil war, a possibility. Secondly, because I am content with the reply provided in the *Concio* of Archbishop Kenrick, c. viii. See Friedrich's 'Documenta ad illustrandum Concilium Vaticanum,' vol. i. p. 219. The statements would, in truth, only be relevant, if they were meant to show that the Roman Catholics of that day were justified in making false statements of their belief in order to obtain civil equality, but that, as those statements did not avail to conciliate the Ministers of 1829, they then materially fell back upon the true ones.

To show, however, how long a time had to pass before the poison could obtain possession of the body, I point, without comment, to the subjoined statement, anonymous, but, so far as I know, uncontradicted, and given with minute particulars, which would have made the exposure of falsehood perfectly easy. It is taken from the 'Cornish Telegraph' of Dec. 9, 1874, and is signed Clericus. It follows a corresponding statement with regard to America, which is completely corroborated by Archbishop Kenrick in his *Concio*: see Friedrich's 'Documenta,' i. 215.

"Of a painful alteration in another popular work, Keenan's 'Controversial Catechism,' (London, Catholic Publishing and Bookselling Company, 53, New Bond Street,) I can speak from two gravely differing copies, both professedly of the same edition, now lying before me. This is so singular a case that I venture to give it in a little detail. Keenan's 'Catechism' has been very extensively used in Great Britain and America. In his preface to the third edition, the author speaks of it as 'having the high approbation of Archbishop Hughes, the Right Rev. Drs. Kyle and Carruthers; as well as the approval of the Right Rev. Dr. Gillis, and the Right Rev. Dr. Murdoch.' These last-named four ecclesiastics were vicars-apostolic of their respective districts in Scotland, and their separate episcopal approbations are prefixed to the 'Catechism;' those of Bishops Carruthers and Kyle are dated, respectively, 10th and 15th April, 1846; those of Bishops Gillis and Murdoch, 14th and 19th November, 1853.

"Thus this work was authenticated by a well-known American archbishop and four British bishops thoroughly familiar with the teaching of their Church, long before Archbishop Manning joined it. Now, at page 112 of one of my copies of the 'new edition, corrected by the author, twenty-fourth thousand,' are the following question and answer:—

Q.—"'Must not Catholics believe the Pope in himself to be infallible?'

"*A.*—'This is a Protestant invention; it is no article of the Catholic faith; no decision of his can oblige, under pain of heresy, unless it be received and enforced by the teaching body,—that is, by the bishops of the Church.'

"It would be satisfactory if Archbishop Manning would explain how his statement to Mr. Bennett squares with this statement of Keenan's, and with that of the 50 *Reasons*.

"But, further, it would be highly satisfactory if Archbishop Manning, or some representative of the 'Catholic Publishing and Bookselling Company' would explain how it came to pass that, on the passing of the Vatican decree, apparently whilst this very edition of Keenan's *Catechism* was passing through the press, the above crucial question and answer were quietly dropped out, though no intimation whatsoever was given that this vital alteration was made in the remainder of the edition. Had a note been appended, intimating that this change had become needful, no objection, of course, could have been made. But no word has been inserted to announce, or explain, this omission of so material a passage; whilst the utmost pains have been taken, and, I must add, with great success, to pass off this gravely altered book as being identical with the rest of the edition. The title-pages of both copies alike profess that it is the 'new edition, corrected by the author,' (who was in his grave before the Vatican Council was dreamed of); both profess to be of the 'twenty-fourth thousand;' both have the same episcopal approbations and prefaces; both are paged alike throughout; so that, from title-page to index, both copies are, apparently, identical. I have very often placed both in the hands of friends, and asked if they could detect any difference,' but have always found they did not. The Roman Catholic booksellers, Messrs. Kelly and Messrs. Gill, in Dublin, from whom I purchased a number of copies in August, 1871, were equally unaware of this change; both believed that the Publishing Company had supplied them with the same book, and both expressed strongly their surprise at finding the change made without notice. Another Dublin Roman Catholic bookseller was very indignant at this imposition, and strongly urged me to expose it. It is no accidental slip of the press; for whilst all the earliest copies of the edition I bought from Messrs. Kelly contained the question and answer, they were omitted in all the later copies of Messrs. Gill's supply. The omission is very neatly, cleverly made by a slight widening of the spaces between the questions and answers on page 112 and the beginning of page 113; so skilfully managed that nobody would be at all likely to notice the difference in these pages of the two copies, unless he carefully looked, as I did, for the express purpose of seeing if both alike contained this question and answer."

APPENDIX E (p. 51).

Extract from 'The Catholic Question;' addressed to the Freeholders of the County of York, on the General Election of 1826, p. 31.

"The Catholic religion has three great æras; first in its commencement to the dark ages; then from the middle centuries down to the Reformation; and lastly from the Reformation to the present day. The Popish religion of the present day has scarcely any resemblance with its middle stage; its powers, its pretensions, its doctrines, its wealth and its object are not the same; it is a phantom, both in theory and practice, to what it once was; and yet the bigots draw all their arguments from the Middle Ages and, passing all the manifest alterations of modern times, set up a cry about the enormities of times long past, and which have been dead and buried these three hundred years. This unjust conduct is just the same as if you were to hang a faithful, tried domestic, who had served you forty years, because he had committed some petty theft when he was a boy. It is the most illiberal and the most unjustifiable mode of arguing, and if applied to the Church of England, would reduce it to a worse case than that of her old rival."

The "bigots," who are here charged by the Liberal electors of Yorkshire with reviving mediæval Romanism, are not Vaticanists, but Protestant bigots, whose sinister predictions the Vaticanists have done, and are doing, their best to verify.

Both by reason of the language of this extract, and of its being taken out of the actual working armoury of one of the great electioneering struggles for the County of York, which then much predominated in importance over every other constituency of the United Kingdom, it is important. It shows by direct evidence how the mitigated professions of the day told, and justly told, on the popular mind of England.

APPENDIX F (p. 59).

I. From the Decree.

"Et primò declarat, quod ipsa in Spiritu Sancto legitimè congregata, concilium generale faciens, et ecclesiam Catholicam repræsentans, potestatem a Christo immediatè habet, cui quilibet cujusque status vel dignitatis, etiam si papalis existat, obedire tenetur *in his quæ pertinent ad fidem* et extirpationem dicti schismatis, et reformationem dictæ ecclesiæ in capite et in membris."— Conc. Const. Sess. v.; Labbe et Cossart, tom. xii. p. 22.

From the account of the Pope's confirmation.

"Quibus sic factis, sanctissimus dominus noster papa dixit, respondendo ad prædicta, quod omnia et singula determinata conclusa et decreta *in materiis fidei* per præsens concilium, conciliariter tenore et inviolabiliter observare volebat, et nunquam contraire quoquo modo. Ipsaque sic conciliariter facta approbat et ratificat, et non aliter, nec alio modo."—Conc. Const. Sess. xlv.; Labbe et Cossart, tom. xii. p. 258.

APPENDIX G (p. 68).

Labbe, Concilia, x. 1127, ed. Paris, 1671, Canon II.

"*Obedite præpositis vestris, et subjacete illis; ipsi enim prævigilant pro animabus vestris, tanquam rationem reddituri:* Paulus magnus Apostolus præcepit. Itaque beatissimum Papam Nicolaum tanquam organum Sancti Spiritus habentes,* necnon et sanctissimum Hadrianum Papam, successorem ejus, definimus atque sancimus, etiam omnia quæ ab eis synodicè per diversa tempora exposita sunt et promulgata, *tam pro defensione ac statu Constantinopolitanorum ecclesiæ, et summi sacerdotis ejus, Ignatii videlicet, sanctissimi Patriarchæ, quam etiam pro Photii, neophyti et invasoris, expulsione ac condemnatione, servari semper et custodiri cum expositis capitulis immutilata pariter et illæsa.*"

The Canon then goes on to enact penalties.

APPENDIX H (p. 76).

It appears to me that Archbishop Manning has completely misapprehended the history of the settlement of Maryland and the establishment of toleration there for all believers in the Holy Trinity. It was a wise measure, for which the two Lords Baltimore, father and son, deserve the highest honour. But the measure was really defensive; and its main and very legitimate purpose plainly was to secure the free exercise of the Roman Catholic religion. Immigration into the colony was by the Charter free: and only by this and other popular provisions could the territory have been extricated from the grasp of its neighbours in Virginia who claimed it as their own. It was apprehended that the Puritans would flood it, as they did: and it seems certain that but for this excellent provision, the handful of Roman Catholic founders would have been unable to hold their ground. The facts are given in Bancroft's 'History of the United States,' vol. i. chap. vii.

I feel it necessary, in concluding this answer, to state that Archbishop Manning has fallen into most serious inaccuracy in his letter of November 10 (p. 6), where he describes my Expostulation as the first event which has overcast a friendship of forty-five years. I allude to the subject with regret, and without entering into details.

[The closing paragraph of Appendix H appeared to Cardinal Manning to convey impressions which he thought it desirable to

---

* In the Greek, *ibid.* p. 1167, ὡς ὄργανον τοῦ ἁγίου Πνεύματος ἔχοντες.

remove. Conformably to his wishes, I substituted for it, in the later impressions of 'Vaticanism,' the following paragraph:—

"One word in conclusion: Archbishop Manning has stated (p. 6*) that a friendship of forty-five years between us had, for the first time, been overcast by the publication of my pamphlet on 'The Vatican Decrees.' The Archbishop, however, has himself mentioned in print on a former occasion, that the intercourse of this friendship was suspended for twelve years after 1851, the date of his secession. I may add, that he appeared to view my words and acts, in relation to the Temporal Power of the Pope, in much the same light as the recent tract. From 1851 onwards, the dictates of conscience on either side were in conflict, and they led to public divergence, without any private variance."]

---

* *I.e.*, of his Reply, which, like my tract, bears the title of "The Vatican Decrees."

SPEECHES

OF

POPE PIUS IX.

[*Republished from the* QUARTERLY REVIEW *for January*, 1875.]

ART. VIII.*—*Discorsi del Sommo Pontefice Pio IX., pronunziati in Vaticano, ai Fedeli di Roma e dell' Orbe, dal principio della sua Prigionia fino al presente.* Vol. I., Roma, Aurelj, 1872; Vol. II., Cuggiani, 1873.

As a general rule, the spirit of a system can nowhere be more fairly, more authentically learned, than from the language of its accredited authorities, especially of its acknowledged Head. The rule applies peculiarly to the case of the Papacy, and of the present Pope, from considerations connected both with the system and with the man. The system aims at passing its operative utterances through the lips of the Supreme Pontiff: and as no holder of the high office has ever more completely thrown his personality into his function, so no lips have ever delivered from the Papal Throne such masses of matter. Pope all over, and from head to foot, he has fed for eight-and-

---

* [At the time when this Article was written and published I was unaware that the Rev. W. Arthur had published, in a small volume entitled 'The Modern Jove,' a searching review of the contents of the first volume of the 'Discorsi,' or I should not have omitted to notice it. In this work Mr. Arthur justly comments on the lack of disposition to estimate these subjects as they deserve (p. 117); an indisposition which I believe to be more characteristic of life and its organs in our metropolis, than in the country at large. "The Ultramontane party in Rome," says Mr. Arthur, "are not accountable for the illusions of English politicians and clergy, for they have of late been very outspoken." He also cites a remarkable exclamation of Mr. O'Connell's, who, on hearing it stated in public that his Church had an infallible head, cried aloud, "No, an infallible body."]

twenty years upon the moral diet which a too sycophantic following supplies, till every fibre of his nature is charged with it, and the simple-minded Bishop and Archbishop Mastai is hardly to be recognized under the Papal mantle.

It can hardly be policy, it must be a necessity of his nature, which prompts his incessant harangues. But they are evidently a true picture of the man; as the man is of the system, except in this that he, to use a homely phrase, blurts out, when he is left to himself, what it delivers in rather more comely phrases, overlaid with art.

Much interest therefore attaches to such a phenomenon as the published Speeches of the Pope; and besides what it teaches in itself, other and singular lessons are to be learned from the strange juxtaposition in which, for more than four years, his action has now been exhibited. Probably in no place and at no period, through the whole history of the world, has there ever been presented to mankind, even in the agony of war or revolution, a more extraordinary spectacle than is now witnessed at Rome. In that city the Italian Government holds a perfectly peaceable, though originally forcible, possession of the residue of the States of the Church; and at the same time the Pope, remaining on his ground, by a perpetual blast of fiery words, appeals to other lands and to future days, and thus makes his wordy, yet not wholly futile, war upon the Italian Government.

The mere extracts and specimens, which have from time to time appeared in the public journals, have stirred a momentary thrill, or sigh, or shrug, according to the temperaments and tendencies of readers. But they have been totally insufficient to convey an idea of the vigour with which this peculiar warfare is carried on; of the absolute, apparently the contemptuous, tolerance with which it is regarded by the Government ruling on the spot; or of the picture which is presented to us by the words and actions of the Pope, taken as a whole, and considered in connection with their possible significance to the future peace of Europe.

Between the 20th of October, 1870, and the 18th of September, 1873, this octogenarian Pontiff (he is now aged, at least, eighty-two), besides bearing all the other cares of ecclesiastical government, and despite intervals of illness, pronounced two hundred and ninety Discourses, which are reported in the eleven hundred pages of the two Volumes now to be introduced to the notice of the reader. They are collected and published for the first time by the Rev. Don Pasquale de Franciscis; and, though they may be deemed highly incendiary documents, they are sold at the bookshop of the Propaganda, and are to be had in the ordinary way of trade, by virtue of that freedom of the press which the Papacy abhors and condemns.

The first question which a judicious reader will put is, whether we have reasonable assurance that this work really reports the Speeches of the Pontiff with accuracy. And on this point there appears to be no room for reasonable doubt. Some few of them are merely given as abstracts, or *sunti*; but by far the larger number *in extenso*, in the first person, with minutely careful notices of the incidents of the occasion, such as the smiles, the sobs, the tears* of the Pontiff on the auditory; the animated

---

* In the estimation of Don Pasquale, all emotion, if within the walls of the Vatican, and on the Papal side, is entitled to respect, and must awaken sympathy, but when he has to describe the tears and sobs which, as he states, accompanied the funeral procession of the ex-Minister Ratazzi (ii. 350), he asks, might not this be a Congress of Crocodiles (*non sembra questo un Congresso di Coccodrilli*)?

gestures of the one, the enthusiastic shoutings of the other, which cause the halls of the Vatican to ring again. In a detailed notice which, instead of introducing the first volume, is rather inconveniently appended to it at the close, the editor gives an account both of the opportunities he has enjoyed and of the loving pains he took in the execution of his task. On nearly every occasion he seems to have been present and employed as a reporter (*raccoglitore*); once his absence is noticed as if an unusual, no less than than unfortunate, circumstance (ii. 284). In a particular instance (ii. 299) he speaks of the Pope himself as personally giving judgment on what might or might not be published (*sarebbe stato pubblicato, se così fosse piaciuto a CIII potea volere altrimenti*). The whole assistance of the Papal press in Rome was freely given him (i. 505). Eyes and ears, he says, far superior to his own, had revised and approved the entire publication (i. 506). The Preface to the Second Volume refers to the enthusiastic reception accorded to the First, and announces the whole work as that which is alone authentic and the most complete (ii. 14, 15). So that our footing plainly is sure enough; and we may reject absolutely the supposition which portions of the book might very well suggest, namely, that we were reading a scandalous Protestant forgery.

Certainly, if the spirit of true adoration will make a good reporter, Don Pasquale ought to be the best in the world. The Speeches he gives to the world are " a treasure," and that treasure is sublime, inspired, divine (i. 1, 2, 3). Not only do we quote these epithets textually, but they, and the like of them, are repeated everywhere, even to satiety, and perhaps something more than satiety. " Receive, then, as from the hands of angels, this Divine Volume of the Angelic Pio Nono " (p. 4); " the most glorious and venerated among all the Popes" (p. 3); "the portentous Father of the nations" (p. 11). This is pretty well, but it is not all. He is "the living Christ" (p. 9); he is the Voice of God. There is but one step more to take, and it is taken. He is (in the face of the Italian Government) Nature, that protests: he IS GOD, THAT CONDEMNS (p. 17).

In a letter dated December 10, 1874, and addressed to a monthly magazine,* Archbishop Manning, with his usual hardihood, says, "for a writer who affirms that the Head of the Catholic Church claims to be the Incarnate and Visible Word of God I have really compassion." Will this bold controversialist spare a little from his fund of pity for the editor of these Speeches, who declares him to be the living Christ, and for the Pope under whose authority this declaration is published and sold?

Truly, some of the consequences of a "free press" are rather startling. And those who are astonished at the strained and preternatural tension, the *surexcitation abnormale*, to borrow a French phrase, the inflamed and inflaming tone of the language ordinarily used by the Pontiff, should carefully bear in mind that the fulsome and revolting strains, of which we have given a sample, exhibits to us the atmosphere which he habitually breathes.

Even those, however, who would most freely criticise, and, indeed, denounce the prevailing strain and too manifest upshot of these Speeches, may find pleasure, while they yield a passing tribute to the persevering tenacity, and, if we may be pardoned such a word, the pluck, which they display. It may be too true that the Pope has brought his misfortunes on his own head. But

---

* 'Macmillan's Magazine' for January 1875.

they are heavy, and they are aggravated by the weight of years : and the strong constitution, indicated by his deep chest and powerful voice, has had to struggle with various infirmities. Yet, by his mental resolution, all " cold obstruction " is kept at arm's length : and he delivers himself from week to week or day to day, sometimes, indeed, more than once in the day, of his copious and highly explosive material, with a really marvellous fluency, versatility, ingenuity, energy, and, in fact, with every good quality, except that, the absence of which, unhappily, spoils all the rest, namely, wisdom. And, odd to say, even the word wisdom (*saviezza*) seems to be almost the only one which in these Speeches does not constantly pass his lips.

Reversing the child's order with his plate at dinner, let us keep to the last that which is the worst, and also the heaviest, part of the task before us : and begin by noticing one or two discourses of the Holy Father to little children, which are full of charm and grace. For even very little children go to him on deputations, and, reciting after the Italian manner, discharge in manufactured verse their anti-revolutionary wrath. An infant of five years old denounces before him the sacrilegious oppressor! (ii. 405.) Another *fanciulletta* declares the Pope to be the King of kings (ii. 465). These interviews were turned by the Pope to edification. He tells the children of their *peccatucci* (ii. 209)—how shall we try to give the graceful *tournure* of the phrase ? " darling little sins :" and certain orphans he again gently touches with the incomparable Italian diminutive on their *difettucci* and their *rabbiette*, and lovingly presents to them the example of their Saviour :—

" Now that the Church commemorates " (it was on Dec. 19) " the birth of Jesus Christ the babe, do you cause Him to be re-born in your hearts. . . . . beg Him to put there something that is good, namely, a good will to study, and to mind your work and all your other duties."

And so he blesses them, and sends them away (ii. 119).

There are other examples not less pleasing, such as a discourse to some Penitents of the Roman Magdalen. After mentioning the case of Rahab, the Pontiff proceeds in a tone both Evangelical and fatherly (ii. 57):—

"You, too, my daughters, carry the red mark; you, too, carry a mark able to deliver you from the assaults that the enemies of your souls will make. This red mark you have put upon you; and its meaning is, the most precious blood of Jesus Christ. Often meditate on this blood, which has merited for you the grace of your salvation and your conversion. At the feet of the crucified Jesus, even as once did the repentant Magdalen, meditate on the love that He has shown you, and you will triumph over all your enemies."

There is, perhaps, not a word of this affectionate and simple address, which would not be acceptable even if it were delivered from a Nonconforming pulpit; so devoid is it of the specialities of the Roman Church. Nor is this the only discourse of which the same might be said (see, for instance, Disc. cxxii.). Nor must we very sharply complain if sometimes we find in these Discourses the religious ideas which we are wont to condemn as Popery. They are, perhaps, less frequent and flagrant than might have been expected. They assume prominence, however, in one passage particularly, where the Pope declares that the prayers of the Mother addressed to her Son have almost the character of commands (*hanno quasi ragion di comando*, ii. 394), and there is traceable in some of the Addresses a curious, sometimes an amusing, idea of the personal claim upon the Blessed Virgin Mary and others of the Saints, which he has established by his acts, especially constituting the Immaculate Conception a part of the Christian faith. "She owes you the finest gem in her coronet," says one deputation (ii. 325). "If," says another, "it be certain that gratitude is more lively in heaven than on earth, let him" (here we are dealing with St. Louis, to whom the Pope had erected a monument), "by way of payment, give you back your crown" (ii. 116). And again, with yet greater naïveté; "and most holy Mary the Immaculate, on whom you conferred so great an honour, surely she will never allow herself to be outdone in generosity?" (ii. 26).

Next after the personal piety and geniality, which not even all the perversions of his policy can extinguish in the Pope, some sympathy remains due to his irrepressible sentiment of fun. To this even social rumour has done justice in some cases. For example, at the time of the Council, when his hospitality was so taxed by the presence of large numbers of very poor bishops as to threaten him with an empty exchequer, he is commonly reported to have said, "*facendomi infallibile, mi faranno fallire:* while declaring me *un-failable*, they will cause me to *fail.*" In these volumes he explains to a group of children the prevailing redundance of demoniacal action in Italy by recounting an observation then recently made to him, "that all the devils had been let out from hell, except a porter, to receive new arrivals." The preface shows he felt the ground to be tender, for he introduced the story by saying (i. 40): "Here I should like to tell you an incident. Yet I am doubtful, as it might excite too much merriment; but come, I will give it you."

This for children; but for bishops also, newly-made bishops, he has his comic anecdote, and in order that it may be suitable, he chooses it from the life of a Saint, though a modern one. Alphonso Liguori, now not only a Saint, but also lately promoted by the Pope to the rank of a Doctor of the Church, in his time, it seems, used to bore the Neapolitan Ministro Tannucci, and consequently sometimes found it hard to get within his doors. One day, having long to wait, the Bishop sat upon the steps and recited his "corona;" and he recounts his weariness in one of his letters, with the comment which shall be given in the original tongue: "*questo benedetto ministro mi fa sputare un' ala di polmone*" (ii. 286).

The Pope's references to Holy Scripture are very frequent; and yet perhaps hardly such as to suggest that he has an accurate or familiar acquaintance with it. They are possibly picked piecemeal out of the services of the Church for the day. It is, for example, to say the least, a most singular method of reference to the difficult subject of the Genealogies of our Lord to say (i. 127), "we read at the commencement of *two* of the Gospels *a* long Genealogy of Him, which comes down from Princes and Kings." Where, again, did the Pontiff learn that the Jews, as a nation, had some celebrity as smiths (*nell' arte fabbrile*, i. 169)? with which imaginary celebrity he oddly enough connects the mention of the antediluvian Tubal-cain in Gen. iv. 22. Nor can anything be more curious than his *exegesis* applied to the Parable of the Sower. He expounds it to a Roman Deputation (i. 335). The wayside represents the impious and unbelievers, and all who are possessed by the devil; those who received the seed among the thorns are those who rob their neighbour and plunder the Church; the stony places represent those who know, but do not act. "And who are the good ground? You. The good ground is that which is found in all good Christians, in all those who belong to the numerous Catholic Clubs." Now the Clubs on the other side are Clubs of Hell (ii. 420 *bis*); sanctity is thus (here and commonly elsewhere) identified with certain politics. Nor does it seem very easy to trace in detail the resemblance between the exposition of the Vicar and that given by the Principal (St. Matt. xiii. 18–23).

Indeed the Papal Exegesis appears somewhat frequently to bear marks of dormitation. Thus, placing King Solomon at a date of twenty-two or twenty-three centuries back (ii. 32), he makes that sovereign the contemporary either of Pericles, or of Alexander the Great. More important, because it is a specimen of the wilful interpretations so prevalent at Rome, is the mode in which he proves his right to be the Teacher-general of all States and all nations, because (ii. 456) Saint Peter was chosen, in the case of Cornelius, to preach the Gospel to the Gentiles.

Many, again, will read with misgiving the Pope's treatment of the text, St. Luke ii. 52; "And Jesus increased in *wisdom* and stature." "This increase was only apparent, for in Him, the Son of God, was" (*i. e.* was already) "the fulness of all wisdom, as of every virtue" (i. 42). To resolve positive statements of Holy Scripture into mere seeming, is not a mode of exposition the most in favour with orthodox Christianity; and, if it is to be applied to statements affecting the Perfect Humanity of our Lord, to what point is it to be carried? The Commentary of Cornelius à Lapide, which will not be viewed with suspicion in Roman quarters, discusses at great length this most interesting text, and, after considering the varied language of the Fathers, proceeds to lay it down that, besides growth in appearance and in the opinion of men, and besides the growth of what we term experience, "tertiò et propriè, esto Christus non creverit sapientiâ et gratiâ habituali, crevit tamen actuali et practicâ; nam robur spiritûs et sapientiam cœlestem in animâ latentem, indies magis et magis exerebat etiam existens puer." Those who desire a more modern statement may with advantage consult a beautiful passage in the commentary of Dean Alford *in loco*.

But what is really sad in the Scriptural references of the Pope is the incessant and violent application which is made of them to political incidents and circumstances, and the too daring appropriation to himself of passages, very exalted indeed, which relate to our Saviour.

As respects the former of these topics, we may take as an example a short speech to a company of ladies engaged in the reclamation of girls who have lived a life of shame: "With the same charity and zeal which you have employed in doing good to these girls, by reclaiming them from sin, be careful to pray the Almighty that your charity may also reach all the enemies of the Church." What would be thought of the taste of any Protestant association of this country which should exhort the managers of the Magdalen never to forget praying God for the conversion of Papists? Tories and Liberals might in this way reciprocally do a stroke of business in politics while exercising their charity and piety. In truth, it might seem to the readers of these volumes as if the putting down of Italian liberalism and nationality (which are for the Pope one and the same thing) had constituted the one great purpose for which the Gospel had been sent into the world. Certainly no one can complain that the Pope's injunctions to pray are not sufficient either in number or in urgency: they are incessant. The Pope gives no countenance whatever to the theory of Professor Tyndall, or to that of Mr. Knight, who, as we understand, so cleverly settles the great Prayer-controversy by "splitting the difference." But of the almost innumerable exhortations to pray in these volumes, at least nineteen in twenty are directed to the establishment of sound Papal politics, and the conversion, or, failing this, the destruction of Liberals, as though they were the people of some new Sodom and Gomorrah, or Tyre and Sidon; to the triumph of the Church, and the restoration of what the Pope, with his peculiar ideas, is pleased to call " peace."

It appears, however, that the comparison, which he draws indirectly between women living by the wages of sin and Liberals, admits of a yet more pungent application in the case of a class who are, in the Pope's eyes, even worse than Liberals. These are the bad Catholics, who have "disdained the light of faith." These will, he says (ii. 31), be judged more severely than women who live in shame, but who are far more likely to repent. "The light of faith" is, we opine, that of the Vatican Council; and the "bad Catholics" appear to be the eminent men who declined to affirm as immemorial truths the novelties and the historical falsehoods it imposed.

One touch remains to be added to this portion of the extraordinary picture. The prisoner not imprisoned, who is weekly visited by crowds or companies of lawbreakers, glorying in impunity, receives from them, and from the sycophants about him, an adulation not only excessive in its degree, but of a kind which, to an unbiassed mind, may seem to border on profanity. To compare him with the Scripture worthies generally is not enough. Claiming, under the new-fangled Roman religion, to possess in his single hands all the governing powers of the Redeemer over his Church, it is also in the sufferings of Christ alone that he and his worshippers, he with some little excuse, they with hardly any, find a fit standard of comparison for what he has to endure. Now as to his own sufferings, we have no doubt he must suffer much, when he looks abroad over the Christian world, and reckons up the results of what the most distinguished of our Roman Catholic laymen, in a lecture to the Roman Catholics of a midland town, recently and justly called the longest and most disastrous Pontificate on record. But the sufferings mentioned incessantly in this book are the sufferings pretended to be inflicted by the Italian Kingdom upon the so-called Prisoner of the Vatican. Let us see how, and with what daring misuse of Holy Scripture, they are illustrated in the authorized work before us. "He and his august consort," says Don Pasquale, speaking of the Count and Countess de Chambord, "were profoundly moved at such great afflictions, which the *Lamb of the Vatican* (*l'Agnello del Vaticano*, ii. 545) has to endure."

On the 23rd of March, 1873 (ii. 291), the Pope draws a picture of the Apostles, repairing to our Lord, and desired by Him to take their rest around him. He proceeds:

"Even now there is a parallel to this; when from different parts of the Catholic world the bishops and missionaries repair to Rome that they may give account of their missions to the present most unworthy Vicar of Jesus Christ, and find within the narrow limits of the Vatican an interval of rest from their labours."

On the 3rd of July, 1871 (i. 131), the Pope reminds his ex-employés of the solemn words used by St. Thomas, when he proposed to accompany his Master to death, "Let us also go, that we may die with him" (John xi. 16). "You," he says, "are they who this morning resemble those faithful followers of Jesus Christ, in your visit to the foot of the Pontifical throne." On the 5th of August.

1871, he is visited by the *Figlie di Maria*; and again, he compares their visit to the act of the Blessed Virgin and her companions, who stood by the Cross of Christ (ii. 212). He adds: " It is not, however, true that on my Calvary I suffer the pains which Jesus Christ suffered on His; and only in a certain sense can it be said that in me there is renewed in figure all that was in fact accomplished on the Divine person of the Redeemer." Even so he quotes the inexpressibly solemn words of our Lord at the moment of His capture (John xviii. 9), " I am the Vicar of Jesus Christ, and I have the right to employ the very words of Jesus Christ. My Father, those whom Thou hast given me I will not lose (*quos dedisti mihi, non perdam*)."*

It is futile to attempt a defence of language such as this by alleging that, according to the beautiful observation of St. Augustine, Christ is relieved in His poor, and that according to the yet loftier teaching of St. Paul, the measure of His sufferings is filled up in His saints. Where St. Paul withheld his foot, Pius IX. does not fear to tread. Where St. Paul gave the catalogue of his sufferings, no less truthful than terrible (2 Cor. xi. 23–27), he did not call them his Calvary, as the Pope calls his voluntary sojourn within the walls of a noble Palace which is open to all the world, and which he can inhabit, leave, re-enter, when and as he pleases. When he recorded the good deeds of Priscilla and Aquila, who for his life had exposed their own (Rom. xvi. 3), he did not compare even these noble sacrifices with the ministries rendered in the

---

* It is strange to observe that the words quoted by the Pope do not correspond with the Vulgate (Ed. Frankfort, 1826, with the approbation of Leo XII.), either in John xviii. 9, where it reads *quos dedisti mihi, non perdidi ex eis quemquam*, or in John xvii. 12, where the words are, *quos dedisti mihi, custodivi*.

Gospels, by her whom the Pope teaches us to deem the holiest of women, to the Son of God himself. His sublimity is ever as simple, natural, and healthy, as the daring and stilted phrases of the modern Vatican are the reverse.

If the Pope sees in his own official character such high personal titles and such nearness to Christ, it can be no wonder that he should raise those titles, which are official, to an extraordinary altitude. He does not, indeed, quite emulate in all points the astounding language of Don Pasquale, who always goes mad in white linen when the Pope goes mad in white satin.* Yet he says (ii. 265), " Keep, my Jesus, through the instrumentality of the successors of the Apostles through the instrumentality of the clergy, this flock, that God has given *to you and to me*."

No wonder then, as he is thus partner with Christ in a separate and transcendent sense, that he should give us as a rule for our Italian politics, whoever is for me, is for God (*chi è con me, è con Dio*). It may be thought that this is the assumption which all Christian men should make. But that is not his opinion. When similar manifestations of piety are hazarded on behalf of the Italian Government, mildly to consecrate their cause, which is after all the cause of a great nation, he executes summary justice (ii. 317) upon such pretences. " Somebody has had the boldness to write, ' God is not on the side of the Pope, but on the side of Italy.' This assertion, *somewhat impudent*, is contrary to the facts. And first of all I shall say, that if

---

* In speaking of the probable condition of Ratazzi in the other world (ii. 342), the Pope says he knows not what his fate may be, and is satisfied with calling him *questo infelice*. Don Pasquale, on the other hand (p. 348), says that the Pope being the Supreme Judge in the Church, was thereby entitled to pronounce a sentence far more definite and terrific on the unhappy Sectarian; but was pleased to hide his judgment under the inscrutable veil of the judgments of God.

M

Italy is with God, then assuredly she is with His Vicar." It is all of a piece. Nothing but the superhuman is good enough for the Pope; and in the next edition of the Roman religion, probably even this will not do. We have already shown where Don Pasquale, an accomplished professor of flunkeyism in things spiritual, calls the Pope outright by the term "inspired." Again, in presenting his volumes to Count de Chambord (ii. 547), he has it thus:

> "Nel gran volume, ove il Divin fecondo
> Spirto, *parlando Pio,* suo verbo detta."

Nor can it be said that the Pope himself, here at least, falls short of his obsequious editor, when we observe the view he takes of his own authority as matched with that of an inspired prophet: even of him whom God "sent unto David" (i. 364), and who professed to tell out to the King the very words which the Lord had given him (2 Sam. vii. 1–14). To the parishioners of two Roman parishes, he as "their Sovereign," explains the misconduct, and false position, not of Italy only, but of the Governments generally: he coolly, after his manner, appropriates to himself the words of our Lord, "He that is not with me, is against me;" and then, apparently under some strange paroxysm of excitement, he proceeds (i. 365):

> "You have, then, my beloved children, the few words which I desired to say to you. But I go farther. My wish is that all governments should know that I am speaking in this strain. I wish that they should know it, inasmuch as I do it for their good. And I have the right to speak, *even more than Nathan the prophet to David the King* (*anche più che Natan profeta al Re Davide*), and a great deal more than Ambrose had to Theodosius."

The comparison with St. Ambrose and his memorable and noble proceedings, is pragmatical enough; but it is entirely eclipsed by the monstrous declaration by the Pope of his superiority to an inspired teacher. We spoke some pages back of sighs or shrugs as the signs of emotion, which the Papal utterances, reported in the public journals, have from time to time suggested. But if Christendom still believes in Christianity, this audacity, of which Exeter Hall will indeed exult to hear, is far beyond either sighs or shrugs: it more fitly may cause a shudder.

This daring assumption, however, is not an accident or a caprice; it is as it were a normal result of the Pope's habitual and morbid self-contemplation, of monstrous flattery perpetually administered, and, yet more, of that ecclesiastical system which is gradually (and, we must hope, without any distinct consciousness) raising the personal glorification of the Pope towards the region of a Divine worship, due from men to one who, in these volumes, is not only the official Vicar, but also, in some undefined way, the personal Representative of God on earth (see *e.g.* i. 430, ii. 165). Not only is his person sacred generally, but we have the sacred hand (i. 397), and the sacred foot (ii. 56, 192, 357), nay even the *most* sacred foot (ii. 330). Well may Dr. Elvenich* say there seems to be meditated a Pope-worship (Papstcult), to stand beside the God-worship. Of the things we are bringing to view, many are so strange that they can hardly at once be believed. In this instance, as in others, the true passes beyond the ordinary limits of the credible.

A subordinate part of this system is to be found in the curious coquetry which the work exhibits to the world, with reference to the assumption of the title "Pius the Great." In dispersed places of the volumes, it is applied;

---

* 'Der unfehlbare Papst.' Breslau, 1874-5.

as well it may be, to a Pope who is termed in them himself a prodigy and a miracle. These precedents carefully gathered, may hereafter form an important element in some *catena* demonstrative of a general *consensus* of mankind. But, moreover, it seems that the Marchese Cavaletti, a leading *Papalino*, made known to the Pope that good Catholics (a phrase which here means flaming Ultramontanes) desired to pay him two new honours. One of them was to adjoin to his name the title of *Il Grande* (ii. 484–87). We may, perhaps, refer to another scene, acted 1800 years ago, not far from the Vatican, and recorded by Shakespeare.

"*Casca.* There was a crown offered him; and, being offered him, he put it by with the back of his hand, thus; and then the people fell a shouting. . . . .
"*Brutus.* Was the crown offered him thrice?
"*Casca.* Aye, marry, was't; and he put it by thrice, every time gentler than other."—*Julius Cæsar*, ii. 2.

So the Pope gives three reasons, as they may be called, for declining, or rather for not accepting; "every reason gentler than other." The first is that our Saviour when called "Good Master," replied "that God alone is good." The second, that "God is great and worthy to be praised." The third admits that three truly great Pontiffs did receive this title, but only when they were dead and gone, and when the judgments of men were therefore more calm and clear. Rather a broad hint for the proper time when it arrives.

But it is time to turn, with whatever reluctance, to the truculent and wrathful aspect, which unhappily prevails over every other in these Discourses.

In order, however, fully to appreciate this portion of the case, it is necessary to bear in mind that the *cadres*, or at least the skeletons and relics, of the old Papal Government over the Roman States are elaborately and carefully maintained;* and it appears to be one of the main purposes of the "alms," collected from the members of the Papal Church all over the world, as doubtless they are aware, to feed ex-customhouse officers, ex-postmasters, and ex-policemen. All these in their turn, and the representatives of several other departments, have from time to time been received by the Pope in solemn deputation, and reap their full share of compliment if not as martyrs yet as confessors of the Church. The police, indeed, who in Italy have had but an unsavoury reputation, and in Rome were notoriously the scum of the earth, have, notwithstanding, been deemed worthy to lead the van (i. 46) on the 20th of January, 1871. The ex-functionaries of the Post Office follow on February 5 (p. 50), and are gravely assured by his Holiness that the Catholic public are everywhere in fond admiration of the conduct of the ex-employés, and that their noble conduct echoes through every portion of the world! With a force of imagination such as this, it never can be difficult to make a case into what one wishes it to be. The Register Office follows, with the Stamp Department, and alas! the Lottery, on the 9th of March (p. 71); and a very conspicuous place is given to the repeated military deputations (i. 69, 87, 99).

We must carefully bear it in mind that none of these appear at the Vatican as friends, as co-religionists, as receivers of the Pontiff's alms, or in any character which

---

* We have seen it stated from a good quarter that no less than three thousand persons, formerly in the Papal employ, now receive some pension or pittance from the Vatican. Doubtless they are expected to be forthcoming on all occasions of great deputations, as they may be wanted, like the *supers* and dummies at the theatres.

could be of doubtful interpretation. They appear as being actually and at the moment his subjects, and his military and civil servants respectively, although only in *disponibilità*, or (so to speak) on furlough; they are headed by the proper leading functionaries, and the Pope receives them as persons come for the purpose of doing homage to their Sovereign (pp. 88, 365). Thickly set among all these appear the deputations of the Roman aristocracy. True, its roll is not complete; for by far the most distinguished member of the body, the able, venerable, and highly cultivated Duke of Sirmoneta is a loyal subject of the Italian Kingdom. As to the residue (so to call them), they are those of whom Edmond About sarcastically said, *Hélas! les pauvres gens! ils n'ont pas même de vices!* They constitute, however, a mainstay of the Papal hope. It was to them he announced (i. 147–8) that Aristocracy and Clergy were the true props of thrones, that plebeian support was naught, and that Jesus Christ loved the aristocracy; and belonged to it. In a somewhat wide construction of the word it must be owned.

But, if we are to accept the statements of this approved Reporter, the popular gatherings were frequent, and not more frequent than remarkable, in the halls of the Vatican. One or two parishes would yield deputations said to consist of 1000 or 1500 persons. But the numbers assembled often, as we shall see, went far beyond this mark. Great masses of persons were, and, we presume, still are encouraged to congregate in the Vatican for the purpose of presenting most seditious and rebellious Addresses, and of hearing highly sympathetic Replies.

We should have supposed it impossible that the language of treason against Italy could go beyond the licence of these volumes. In a few cases, however, our editor informs us that it has been thought right, once under the direct order of the highest personage concerned, to keep back from the press some portion of the language used (ii. 299). What has been published is certainly flagrant up to the highest degree of flagrancy yet known in the annals of the Popedom or the world; though it may be reserved for Pius IX. in this point, as in others, to surpass his predecessors, as they have surpassed the rest of men. The Discourses generally, and all the daring defiances of law which, with the Addresses, they contain, are ordinarily reproduced in the 'Osservatore Romano;' and words spoken in the air, or taken from private manuscripts, are thus at once converted into the grossest offences against public order that a press can commit.*

And all this is borne and allowed by the tyrannical Italian Government, which keeps the Pope a "prisoner," and under which, as the Pope declares, "for good men and for Catholics liberty does not exist" (*questa libertà per gli uomini onesti e pei Cattolici non esiste*, ii. 25).

We have already glanced at the nature of the audiences to which are addressed the speeches we are now about to describe, so far as samples can describe them. We turn to the speeches themselves. "What boldness," says the

[* It is also to be observed that we know from other sources of at least one deputation to the Pope, which has been omitted by Don Pasquale from the record. See the Report of the Council of the League of St. Sebastian for 1872, read at General Meeting January 20, 1873, p. 5: "On June 21st a deputation from the League had the honour of an audience with the Sovereign Pontiff, and presented an address of congratulation and sympathy. The Deputation was introduced by the Hon. and Right Rev. Monsignor Stonor, and was composed of Count de la Poer, M.P., Capt. Coppinger, Mr. Winchester, and Mr. Vansittart. On this occasion, as on the last, the Holy Father bestowed his blessing on the League, and all connected with it."]

Prince Consort, speaking of the King of Prussia in 1847,[*] "in a king to speak extempore!" With his sagacious mind, had he seen what a Pope could do, he would have been tempted to double or treble his notes of admiration.

It is hardly possible to convey to the mind of the reader an adequate idea of the wealth of vituperative power possessed by this really pious Pontiff. But it is certainly expended with that liberality which is so strictly enjoined by the Gospel upon all the rich. The Italian Government and its followers, variously in their various colours, are wolves; perfidious (ii. 83); Pharisees (i. 254, 380); Philistines (ii. 322); thieves (ii. 34, 65); revolutionists (i. 365, and *passim*); Jacobins (ii. 150, 190); sectarians (i. 334); liars (i. 365, ii. 156); hypocrites (i. 341, ii. 179); dropsical (ii. 66); impious (*passim*); children of Satan (ii. 263); of perdition, of sin (i. 375), and corruption (i. 342); enemies of God (i. 283, 332, 380); satellites of Satan in human flesh (ii. 326); monsters of hell, demons incarnate (i. 215, 332, ii. 404); stinking corpses (ii. 47); men issued from the pits of hell (i. 104, 176—these are the conductors of the national press); traitor (i. 198); Judas (*ibid.*); led by the spirit of hell (i. 311); teachers of iniquity (i. 340—these are evangelical ministers in their "diabolical" halls); hell is unchained against him (ii. 387), even its deepest pits (i. 368, ii. 179). Nearly, if not quite, every one of these words is from the Pope's own lips; and the catalogue is not exhaustive. Yet he invites children, and not children only, but even his old postmen and policemen, to keep a watch over their tongue! (*custodendo generosamente la*

---

[*] 'Life of the Prince Consort,' i. 407.

lingua, ii. 125). To call these flowers of speech is too much below the mark: nay, they are of themselves a flower-garden; nay, they are a *Flora,* fit to stock a continent afresh, if every existing species should be extinct. It may be thought that other illustrations may seem, after these, but flat and stale; nevertheless we must resume. What remains will be found worthy of what has preceded.

After what we have shown of the relation which the Pontiff imagines to subsist between himself and the person of Our Lord, it may seem to be a condescension on his part when he compares himself, or complacently allows himself to be compared, to such characters as David, or Tobias, or Job. Perhaps these are introduced to act by way of set-off to the representations of the unfortunate Victor Emmanuel, who in the mouth sometimes of the Pope and sometimes of those who address his delighted ear is Holofernes, as in ii. 143, or Absalom (in conduct, not in attractions), as in ii. 143, or Pilate, Herod, Caiaphas (i. 461), or Goliath (ii. 301), or Attila. But it may be thought our citations thus far have been mere phrases torn from the context; and the height, to which the inflammatory style of speech is capable of soaring, will be more justly understood if we quote one or two passages. Let us begin with vol. ii. p. 77 :

"Woe then to him, and to them, who have been the authors of so great scandal. The soil usurped will be as a volcano, that threatens to devour the usurpers in its flames. The petitions of millions of Catholics cry aloud before God, and are echoed by those of the protecting saints who sit near the throne of the Omnipotent himself. and point out to Him the profanations, the impieties, the acts of injustice, and make their appeal to God's remedies; but to those remedies, which proceed forth from the treasures of His infinite justice."

The Papal thought shall be allowed to develop itself by degrees. Giving his blessing to a deputation of youths, he desires it may accompany them through life, and when they yield their souls to God.

"The soul, too, will the impious yield; but will yield it, as Abraham said to the rich Glutton" (Did he? Not in Luke xvi. 25, 6), "to pass into an eternity of suffering, amidst the din of the blasphemies of the devils, who bear that soul to hell."—i. 430.

But who, it may be asked, are these "impious," whose breath has the stench of a putrid sepulchre (i. 341)? The answer is more easy than agreeable. They are simply the Liberals of Italy. This is the favourite word for them, and a phrase almost exclusively indeed appropriated to their use. One passage in particular fixes the meaning beyond doubt. The Holy Father says (i. 286): "In Rome, not only is it attempted to diffuse impiety all around, but men *even* dare to teach heresy, and to spread unbelief." Now as impiety proper is the last and worst result of heresy or unbelief, it is strange at first sight to find it placed on a lower grade in the scale of sins. But, when we remember that in these volumes it simply means Italian liberalism, the natural order of ideas is perfectly restored.

To a popular audience, from the parish of San Giovanni de' Fiorentini, he says (i. 374):

"At the top of the pyramid is One, who depends on a Council that rules him; the Council is not its own master, but depends on an Assembly that threatens it. The Assembly is not its own master, for it must render an account to a thousand devils who have chosen it, and who drive it along the road of iniquity; and the whole of them together, or at any rate the chief part, are bondmen, are slaves, are children of sin: the Angel of God follows them up, and with bared sword menaces those who pretend to be so much at their ease. The day will come when the destroying Angel will cause to be known the justice of God, and the effect of His mercies."

What and for whom His mercies are will be seen shortly. To certain Clubs Pius IX. says (ii. 421, *bis*) :

" The Cross, appearing in that valley of final judgment, will crush, with the mere view of it, both Deputies and Ministers, *and some one else* (altri) *set higher still;* and all those who have abused the patience of the Eternal. At the sight of that Tree will tremble all the world, and the peoples bowed down to earth will implore the mercy of the divine Redeemer, and will trust in Him; but *certain persons, to whom I have alluded*, and that are now in power for the ruin of Church and people, will utter cries of despair and trouble, inasmuch as there will be no mercy for them."

The door of conversion and return indeed is not yet closed, and frequent prayers are offered for them; but the continued support of Liberalism and Italian nationality can only end in the manner of which the Pope has given so telling a description. Thus for example (i. 224) :

" Ah! even upon these I invoke, yet again, the mercy of the Lord, that He may convert them, and they may live! But I say at the same time, if at all hazards they persist in refusing the light of Divine grace, well, may God at length accomplish that which in His justice He has resolved to do."

A word in summing up this portion of our notice. It was not by words of scorn that Christ began the Sermon on the Mount. It is not by words of scorn that the Pope will revive the flagging and sinking life of Christian belief in Italy, or will put down the spirit of nationality now organised and consolidated, or will convert the world. It would be well if he would take to himself the words of a living English poet :

" For in those days
No knight of Arthur's noblest dealt in scorn ;
But if a man were halt or hunched, in him
By those whom God had made full-limbed and tall
Scorn was allowed as part of his defect,

> And he was answered softly by the King
> And all his table."*

As might be expected, the Addresses to the Pope are not tuned to a lower pitch than his replies. There are hardly any among them which do not contain the language, commonly the most burning language, of treason and of sedition. Manhood, womanhood, childhood, all sing in the same key. Innocence and sedition, as we have already observed, join hands. The little one, who has but just completed a single lustre, announces in the poem she recites (ii. 406) the restoration of the Temporal Power over Italy and the whole world:

> "Poco tempo ancora, o Pio
> Regnerà sul mondo intiero."

The lips are the lips of infancy; but the tune has the true ring of the *Curia*. But there are important distinctions to be observed. Even distant observers may appreciate the wisdom with which the Government of Italy leaves to the Pope a perfect freedom to speak his mind on the laws, the throne, and the constituted order of the country. If such freedom exists we cannot well expect it to be used in any way but one, though the use certainly might have well been restrained to less frequent occasions, and a more civilized range of language. However, let this pass; and let every allowance be made for Papal partisans among those once his subjects. But what are we to say of the sense of public propriety among foreigners, Englishmen we regret to say included in the number, who travel from distant countries, and abuse the immunity thus accorded to offer public and gross

---

* Tennyson's 'Guinevere.'

insult to the Italian Government, under whose protection and hospitality they are living? Perhaps the most inordinate example of this very indecent abuse is in the "most noble Catholic deputation of all nations," which made its appearance in the Vatican on the 7th of March, 1873, and which was headed by Prince Alfred Lichtenstein (ii. 257). In their address they denounce "the most ignoble violation of the law of nations" by the Italian Government, their "execrable crime," their "hypocritical assurances," and so forth. Not content even with this outrage, they proceed to denounce, of their own authority, all ideas of compromise or adjustment, for which the Government of Italy had always been seeking.

"With the enemies that rage against you, Holy Father, and against the religious orders, no reconciliation is possible. War, waged by such enemies, is not terrible: the only thing to be dreaded in this case is peace. (Bravo! bravo! bravo!) No doubt they would be right glad to conclude with you a perfidious compromise; they ardently desire it."

And then with incomparable taste on the part of such Englishmen as were present, towards the King of Italy, the Ally of Her Majesty, "No, no; Peter, alive in your person, will be ever admirable in his heroic resolution against Herod" (ii. 257-9).

After more slang of the same kind—from persons acting thus entirely beyond their right, this language deserves no better name—and a glowing eulogy on the Syllabus and the Encyclical, the addressers give place to the addressed, who assures them that all they have said is true, though some of it severe (*ibid.* 261). Have any of these gentlemen, princes and others, considered what sort of protection their own Governments would be able to afford them if the Italian Government should think fit to take proceedings against them, or to expel them summarily, and rather ignominiously, from its territory, as enemies of the public peace?

It is now time to examine by such lights as we possess what is really the actual state of things in Rome, which furnishes the occasion for the violent and almost furious denunciations of the Pope; and to inquire also what would be the state of things which he desires to have established in its stead.

The condition in which he thinks himself to be is, that he is a prisoner in the Vatican; while outside its walls are ruin, oppression, revolution, confusion, and unrestrained blasphemy and profligacy. And what he desires is simply the restoration of freedom and of peace. It will not be at all difficult to perceive what the Pope signifies by freedom and peace, or by what means they are to be attained: but first a word on the actual condition of Rome. It never had the name, under the Popes, of a very well-ordered city. The Pontiff, however, speaks of it as having been under his dominion holy; whereas now it is a sink of corruption, and devils walk through the streets of it. Now, except upon this authority of one who knows nothing except at second-hand, nothing except as he is prompted by the blindest partisans, it seems totally impossible to discover any evidence that Rome of 1874 is worse than Rome before the occupation, or worse than other large European cities. And this really is a question not of dogmatism or of declamation, but of testimony; and not of the testimony of prejudiced assertion, but of facts and figures. To this test the condition of every city can be brought, with more or less of approach to precision. Except, indeed, under a system like that of the Papal Government; when the press was enslaved, and the stint of public information was such, that even a copy of the Tariff of Customs Duties was not to be had in Rome (as happens to be within our knowledge) for love or money. Now these odious charges that a peculiar immorality and utter disorder prevail in Rome are launched by the Pope with such vagueness, that if they came from a less exalted personage they would at once be called scurrilous and scandalous, and it would be said, here is a common railer who, having no basis of fact for his statements, takes refuge in those cloudy generalities, under colour of which fact and figment are indistinguishable from each other. After taking some pains to make inquiry from impartial sources, we are able to state that the police of the national Rome is superior to that of Papal Rome, that order is well maintained, crime energetically dealt with.

It is known that at the time of the forcible occupation in 1870, a number of bad characters streamed into the city; but by energetic action on the part of the Government, ill-supported, we fear, by the clergy, they were, by degrees, got rid of, and soon ceased to form a noticeable feature in the condition of the place. For ostensible morality the streets will compare favourably with the Boulevards of Paris, and for security they may generally challenge the thoroughfares of London. We cite a few words from a very recent and dispassionate account :—

"The police of Rome is far better than the old Papal police; order is better kept, and outrages in the streets are of rare occurrence. Crime is promptly repressed. . . . . The theatres are not much frequented, and are neither worse nor better than such places elsewhere. The city is clean and well kept. There are not half the number of priests or friars in the streets, and mendicancy is not a tenth part of what it was formerly."

We are entitled, indeed, to waive entering upon any more minute particulars until the charges have been lodged, with some decent attention to presumptions of credibility. But it has been our care to obtain from Rome itself some figures, on which reliance may be placed. They indicate the comparative state of Roman crime in the two last full years of the Papal rule (1868, 1869), and the three full years (1871, 1872, 1873), of the Italian rule:—

	1868.	1869.	1871.	1872.	1873.
Highway robberies	236	123	103	85	26
Thefts	802	714	785	859	698
Crimes of violence	938	886	972	861	603
Total	1976	1723	1860	1805	1327

In 1870, which was a mixed year, and does not assist the comparison, and which was also a year of crisis, the total was 2118, and the crimes of violence (*reati di sangue*) were no less than 1175. It will be observed that these figures confute the statements of the Pope. The two first of the Italian years were affected by the cause to which we have referred; but still their average is lower than that of the last two years in which Rome was still the " holy " city, and in which devils did not walk the streets of it. The average of the three years is 1665 against 1723 in the last Papal year. The year 1873, in which alone we may consider that the special cause of disturbance had ceased to operate, shows a reduction of 391, or more than 22 per cent., on the last year of the Pope. Yet more remarkable is the comparison if we strike out the category of thefts, the least serious of the three in kind. We then obtain the following figures: for the last Papal year, 1869, 1009; for 1873, 634; or a diminution of nearly 40 per cent.

But while the accusations are thus shown to be utterly at variance with the facts, still they are intelligible. The cursing vocabulary, so to call it, which has been given, exhibits their character, though in a wild and wholly reckless manner. Where the passion shown is rather less overbearing, there is more of the daylight of ideas. And the idea everywhere conveyed is briefly this; that a state of violence prevails. There is no liberty for honest men or for Catholics (ii. 25): matters go from bad to worse. What is wanted is that God should liberate His Church, give her the triumph (this is the favourite phrase) which is her due, and re-establish public order (i. 44); it is to escape from this state of violence and oppression, which, in simple truth (*davvero*) is insupportable and impossible for human nature (ii. 54). As for the Pope himself, who does not know, so far as Ultramontane organs all over the world can convey knowledge, that he is a prisoner? Although, it must be confessed, that a new sense of the word has had to be invented, to serve his turn: for, as he himself has explained, his prison is a prison with only moral walls and bars, since he admits there are neither locks nor keepers (i. 298). How, with his sense of humour, how, in making these statements, must he inwardly have smiled the smile of the Haruspex at the gross credulity of his hearers! He cannot go out; and he will not (i. 72). He would be insulted in the streets (i. 298); and here, fortunately, he has a case in point to adduce, for once upon a day it happened that a priest had actually been pelted; and somewhere else (i. 467) it appears that an urchin or two had been heard to shout "*morte ai preti*," down with the priests: though in no instance does he show that, even if a stone was thrown, the public authority had refused or tampered with its duty to afford protection to layman and priest alike.

However, as we have seen, the Pope's allegations of oppression and violence are in terms very grave. But his own lips, and his own volumes, unconsciously supply the confutation; and this in two ways. For first, it is clear, if we accept the statements of this curious and daring work, that the people of Rome are almost wholly on his side against the Government, not on the side of the Government and the nation against him. A careful computation of the editor (ii. 187) reckons, certainly to the full satisfaction of all Ultramontane readers, that seventy-one thousand of the inhabitants of Rome (in a city of some two hundred thousand, old and young, men and women, all told) have given their names to addresses against the suppression of the religious orders (ii. 187), a certain sign of Papalism. But there is yet more conclusive evidence. On January 16, 1873, the whole College of the Parish Priests of Rome presented an address, in which they state that, notwithstanding the influence of intruded foreigners, almost the whole of their former parishioners (*nella quasi totalità*), whom they know by name, still keep the right faith, send their children to the right schools, and remain, subject to but few exceptions, " with the Pope, and for the Pope." " I thank Thee, my God, for the spirit that Thou impartest to this excellent People : I thank Thee for the constancy that Thou givest to the People of Rome " (i. 352, also 229). And yet an urchin, or perhaps two, or even three, cry, " *morte ai preti*," and the Pope dare not go out of the Vatican, although he has seventy-one thousand Romans declared by their signatures, and " almost the entire body of parishioners," except the new-come foreigners, for his fast allies and loyal defenders! It is really idle to talk of dark ages. There never was, until the nineteenth century and the Council of the Vatican, an age so deeply plunged in darkness worthy of Erebus and Styx, as could alone render it a safe enterprise to palm statements like these on the credulity even of the most blear-eyed partisanship.

But then, it may be said, in vain are the people with the Pope; a tyrannical government, supported by hordes of *sbirri* and a brutal soldiery, represses the manifestations of their loyalty by intimidation. But this allegation is cut to pieces, and if possible rendered even more preposterous than the other, by the evidence of the volumes themselves. One exception there appears to have been to the good order of Rome: one single form, in which a kind of anarchy certainly has been permitted. This flagrant exception, however, has been made not against, but in favour of, the Pope. For, strange and almost incredible as it may appear, his partisans are allowed to gather in the face of day, and proceed to the Vatican for the purpose of presenting addresses to the Pontiff known to be almost invariably rife with the most flagrant sedition, and this in numbers not only of a few tens or even hundreds, but even up to 1500, 2000 (i. 242, 258, 353), 2600 (i. 362, 411), 3000 (ii. 92), who shouted all at once, and even (ii. 94) 5000 persons; and again (i. 438), a crowd impossible to count. It may be asked with surprise, has the Pope then at any rate a presentable train of five thousand adherents in Rome? Far be it from us to express an implicit belief in each of our friend Don Pasquale's figures, at the least until they are affirmed by a declaration *ex cathedrâ* or a Conciliary Decree. But in Rome, where the vast body of secular and regular clergy have held so large a proportion of the real property, where all the public establishments were closely associated with the clerical interest and class, where even the numerous functionaries of the civil departments, and where the aristocracy, including families of great wealth, have been, and continue to be, of the Papal party, a long train of dependents must necessarily be found on the same side, and judging from what we have seen and known, we deem it quite possible that in the entire city a minority of Papalini numbering as many as, or even more than, five thousand might be reckoned, though of independent citizens we doubt whether there are five hundred. To these civic adherents would add themselves foreigners, whose zeal or curiosity may have carried them to Rome for the purpose. We have, indeed, learned from an authoritative source that on June 16, 1871, when there were no less than eight Deputations, the Pope received at the Vatican in all about 6200 persons. We find also that the total number of those who waited on him in 1871, on only fourteen separate days (which however certainly included all the occasions of crowded gatherings), were estimated carefully at 13,893; and in 1872, on the same number of occasions, at 17,477. In the two following years the numbers have been much less, namely, 8295 and 9129 respectively. It is quite plain that large crowds—crowds sufficient to give ample ground for interference on the score of order to any Government looking for or willing to use them—again and again have filled the vast halls of the Vatican, as Don Pasquale assures us. That they went there to stir up or prepare (as far as it depended upon them) war, either immediate or eventual, against the Italian Government, is established by every page of these volumes. Going in such numbers, and for such a purpose, it is not disputed that they have gone and returned freely, safely, boastfully, under the protection of the laws they were breaking, and of the Government they reviled.

It may perhaps seem strange that, while the Italian Government is treated as if the Pope were a Power in actual war with it, yet the *Curia* apparently can stoop to communicate with it for certain purposes, which it will be interesting to observe. We have, for instance, in the Appendix (ii. 419) a letter of the Cardinal Vicar to the Minister Lanza, complaining, as the Pope in his Speeches complains, of the immorality of the Roman theatres.

It complains also that the clerical orders are not spared in the exhibitions of the stage. This is a subject on which the *Curia* has always been very much in earnest; and some day it may be necessary to bring before the modern public the almost incredible, but yet indubitable, history of the negotiations and arrangements which were made by the State of Florence with the See of Rome in relation to the Decameron of Boccaccio. But for the present let us take only the point of immorality. The broadest accusations on this subject are lodged by the Cardinal Vicar, without one single point or particular of places, pieces, persons, or times which would have enabled the Italian Government to put their justice to the proof. The Minister, in his reply, could not do more than he has actually done. He declares that the Italian Censorship is remarkable for strictness; and that in Italy, and particularly in Rome, many pieces are prohibited which are permitted in France and in Belgium. And of this there is no denial. With a thorough shabbiness of spirit, the complaint is neither justified nor retracted, but is sent forth to the world with the full knowledge that the good (*i buoni*) will take it as a demonstration that the Italian Government is wholly indifferent to morals (vol. ii. 419–24).

Again, we have a complaint of the non-observance of Sundays and feast-days; but the effort of this kind which most deserves notice is one relating to blasphemy. It appears that the newspaper 'La Capitale' had been publishing piecemeal a Life of our Lord, written in the Unitarian sense. The Cardinal-Vicar represented to the Procurator-General (ii. 520) that this ought to be prosecuted as blasphemous and heretical. It is not stated that he founded himself on the manner of the writer's argument, and therefore it may be presumed that the charge lay against his conclusions only. The Procurator-General replied that the law granted liberty of religious discussion, and that accordingly he could not interfere. The Advocate Caucino of Turin—whose Address to the Pope is almost the only one in the whole work that does not contain direct incentives to sedition (ii. 313)—gave a professional opinion to a contrary effect. He pointed out that the Roman Catholic religion was by the Constitutional Statute the religion of the State, and that other laws actually in force provided punishments for offences against religion. Consequently, as he reasoned, these writings are illegal. Over nine hundred of the Italian lawyers have countersigned this opinion. One of his arguments is, to British eyes, somewhat curious. The laws, he says, declare the person of the Pontiff sacred and inviolable. "But if you take away the Divinity of Jesus Christ, the Pontiff is reduced to a nonentity (il Pontefice non è più *nulla*)." It is difficult to avoid saying, one wishes that were the only consequence.

It would, perhaps, be uncharitable to suggest that this well-arranged endeavour was nothing else than a trap carefully laid for the Italian Government. But it certainly would have served the purpose of a trap. Had the denial of our Lord's Divinity been repressed by law, by reason of its contrariety to the religion of the State, the next step would of course have been to require the Government to proceed in like manner against any one who denied the Infallibility of the Pope. Under the Vatican Decrees this is as essentially and imperatively a part of the Roman Creed as is the great Catholic doctrine of the Divinity of Christ. And the obligation to prohibit the promulgation of the adverse opinion would have been exactly the same. Nor is it easy to suppose that the *Curia* was not sharp enough to anticipate this consequence, and prepare the way for it.

Independently of such a plot, the paltry game of these representations is sufficiently intelligible. It seeks to place the King's Government in a dilemma. Either they enforce restriction in the supposed interest of religion, or they decline to enforce it. In the first case, they diminish the liberties of the people, and provoke discontent; in the second, they afford fresh proof of ungodliness, and fresh matter of complaint to be turned sedulously to account by the political piety of the Vatican. But let us pass on from this small trickery; *paullò majora canamus.*

Considering on the one hand the professedly pacific and unworldly character of the successors of the 'Fisherman,' and on the other the gravity of those moral and social evils which are indeed represented as insupportable (ii. 54), an unbiassed reader would expect to find in these pages constant indications of a desire on the part of the Pope and Court of Rome to effect, by the surrender of extreme claims, some at least tolerable adjustment. There was a time, within the memory of the last twenty years, when Pius IX. might have become the head of an Italian Federation. When that had passed, there was again a time, at which he might have retained, under an European guarantee, the *suzeraineté*, as distinguished from the direct monarchy, of the entire States of the Church. When this, too, had been let slip, and after another contraction of the circle of possibilities, it was still probably open to him to retain the *suzeraineté* of the city of Rome itself, with free access to the sea; it was unquestionably within his choice, at any period down to 1870, to stipulate for the Leonine City, with a like guaranteed liberty of access, and with a permanent engagement that Rome never should become the seat of government or of Royal residence, so that there should not be two suns in one firmament. There was in truth nothing which the Pope might not have had assured to him, by every warranty that the friendliness of all Europe could command, except the luxury of forcing on the people of the Roman States a clerical government which they detested. The Pope preferred the game of 'double or quits.' And he now beholds and experiences the result.

But notwithstanding what he sees and feels, that game is too fascinating to be abandoned. Instead of opening the door to friendly compromise, this is the very thing for the treatment of which the furnace of his wrath is ever seven times heated. "Yes, my sons," he says in a "stupendous" (i. 268) discourse, and himself "resplendent with a grandeur more than human" (269) to an "innumerable multitude of the faithful, Roman and foreign" (266), whom he has already congratulated (283) on their readiness to give all, even *their blood*, for him. "Yes, my sons, draw into ever closer union, nor be arrested even for a moment, by lying reports of an impossible 'reconciliation.' It is futile to talk of reconciliation. The Church can never be reconciled with error,

and the Pope cannot separate himself from the Church
.... No; no reconciliation can ever be possible between Christ and Belial, between light and darkness, between truth and falsehood, between justice and the usurpation."

This passage, by no means isolated, is, it must be admitted, rather "superhuman." The wrath of the aged Pontiff had, in fact, been stirred in a special way by some *abbominevoli immagini*,* some execrable pictures, which were for him most profane. The editor explains to us what they were. Such is the unheard-of audacity of Italian Liberalism, and such its hatred and persecution of the Pope, that (ii. 285) a certain Verzaschi, living in the Corso No. 135, had for several days exhibited to public view a picture, in which the Pope and the King of Italy were—we tremble as we write—embracing one another!

But if the Holy Father is thus decisive on the subject of visible representations which he conceives to be profane, we should greatly value his judgment, were there an

---

* Even from the heart of the Order of Jesuits there sounds a voice of protestation against the insane policy of the Pope. It is that of Curci, a well-known champion, for many long years, of the Papal cause, against Gioberti and others. We learn from a pamphlet published on the part of the Italian Government in reply to a violent and loosely written attack by the Bishop of Orleans (on the merits of which, in other respects, we are not in a condition fully to pronounce), that Padre Curci says it is idle to make a bugbear of conciliation: that much as he laments the departure of the mediæval ways (which perhaps he does not quite understand), they are gone; it is idle to suppose the past can be re-established in the Roman States, either by diplomatic mediation, political re-arrangement, "or even foreign intervention."—'Les Rois Ecclésiastiques de l'Italie,' p. 74. Paris, 1874. It seems, then, that there is at least one way in which a Jesuit can forfeit his title to be heard at Rome, and that is if he speaks good sense.

opportunity of obtaining it, on another commodity of the same class, an Italian work, sold in Rome, and not a production of the hated Liberals. It is stamped 'Diritto di proprietà di Cleofe Ferrari,' with an address in Rome, of which the particulars cannot be clearly deciphered, but it is manifestly authentic.

It is a photograph of $6\frac{1}{2}$ by $4\frac{1}{2}$ inches, and it represents a double scene, one in the heavens above, one on the earth below. Above, and receding from the foreground, is one of those figures of the Eternal Father, which we in England view with repugnance; but that is not the point. On the right hand of that figure stands, towards the foreground, the Blessed Virgin Mary, with the moon under her feet (Rev. xii. 1); on the left-hand, and also towards the front, is Saint Peter, kneeling on one knee; but kneeling to the Virgin, not to God. In the scene below we have an elevated pedestal with a group of figures nearer the eye, and filling the foreground. On the pedestal is Pope Pius IX., in a sitting posture, with his hands clasped, his crown, the Triregno, on his head, and a stream of light falling upon him, from a dove forming part of the upper combination, and representing of course the Holy Spirit. The Pope's head is not turned towards the figure of the Almighty. Round the pedestal are four kneeling figures, apparently representing the four great quarters of the globe, whose corporal adoration is visibly directed towards the Pontiff, and not towards the opened heaven. We omit some other details not so easily understood; and, indeed, the reader will by this time have had a sickening sufficiency of this sort of "abominable images." We commend this most profane piece of adulation to the notice of the Cardinal-Vicar, as it will supply him with a very valuable topic in his next demand upon the Italian

Government to prevent the public exhibition in Rome of what conveys an insult to religion.

The outburst we have quoted against all reconciliation is, as we have said, not an isolated one. Declarations essentially similar may be found in vol. i. 291 (Dec. 7, 1871), 498 (Letter to Cardinal Antonelli), ii. 279 (March 7, 1873, in an address of Bishops, accepted and lauded by the Pope).

Out of these two hundred and ninety Speeches, about two hundred and eighty seem to be addressed to the great political purpose which is now the main aim of all Papal effort—that of the triumph and liberation of the Church in Rome itself, and the re-establishment of peace.

When the Pope speaks of the liberation of the Church, he means merely this, that it is to set its foot on the neck of every other power; and when he speaks of peace in Italy, he means the overthrow of the established order, if, by a reconversion of Italians to his way of thinking, well; but if not, then by the old and favourite Roman expedient, the introduction of foreign arms, invading the land to put down the national sentiment and to re-establish the temporal government of the clerical order.

Everywhere, when he refers to the times which preceded the annexations to Sardinia, and the eventual establishment of the Italian kingdom, he represents them as the happy period of which every good man should desire the return. Even at the moderate suggestions of practical reform which were recommended to Gregory XVI. in the early part of his reign by the Five Great Powers, including the Austria of Metternich, he scoffs; and he appears to think that they brought down upon several of the recommending Sovereigns the judgment due to impiety.

Thus on June 21, 1873, he says (ii. 356): "Let us pray for all; let us pray for Italy, that we may see her set free from her enemies, and restored to her former repose and tranquillity."

Now there can be no doubt what he means by calm and tranquillity. He explains it in a passage (ii. 23) when he has occasion to refer to the opening times and scenes of his ill-omened and ill-ordered reign: "Those times were troublous, just as are the present; but notwithstanding they produced, after no long while, an era of tranquillity and quietude" (ii. 23).

The troubles, for troubles there were, arose from the efforts of a people then without political experience to right themselves under the unskilful handling of a ruler, who prompted movements he had no strength to control, and made promises he had no ability to perform. The tranquillity and quietude were found in the invasion of the State by a French army; in the siege and capture of the city, which its inhabitants and a few Italian sympathisers in vain struggled under Garibaldi to defend; and in an armed occupation which effectually kept down the people for seventeen and a half years; until there came, in 1866, a winter's morning, when at four o'clock the writer of these pages, by help of the struggling gaslights in the gloom, saw the picked regiments of France wheel round the street corners of the queenly city, in their admirable marching trim, on the way to the railway station, and bethought him that in that evacuation there lay the seed of great events.

To those who have not carefully followed the fortunes of Italy and her rulers, it may seem strange that this last and worst extreme of tyranny, the maintenance of a Government, and that a clerical Government, by bayonets, and those foreign bayonets, should be spoken of by any man in his five senses, even though that man be a Pope, in any other terms than those of pain and shame, even if it were at the same time, as a supposed necessity, palliated or defended. But the Pope speaks of it with a coolness, an exultation (ii. 248), a yearning self-complacent desire, which would deserve no other name but that of a brutal inhumanity, were it not that he simply gives utterance to the inveterate tradition of the Roman *Curia*, and the tradition of a political party in Italy, which, as long as it had power, made foreign occupation an everyday occurrence, a standing remedy, a normal state.

In 1815, the Pope was brought back to Rome by foreign arms. But at that time it was by foreign arms that he had been kept out of his dominions. Cardinal Pacca, in his Memoirs, gives us to understand that the Pontiff was received by the people with their good-will. It may have been so. But unhappily, after the great occasion of this restoration, all the mischief was done. Much of local self-government had existed in the Pontifical States before the French Revolution. It was now put down. Of the French institutions and methods, the Pope retained only the worst—the spirit of centralisation, and a police, kept not to repress crime, but to ferret out and proscribe the spirit of liberty. The high sacerdotal party prevailed over the moderate counsels of Gonsalvi. And Farini, in his dispassionate History, gives the following account of the state of things even under Pius VII. :—

"There was no care for the cultivation of the people, no anxiety for public prosperity. Rome was a cesspool of corruption, of exemptions, and of privileges; a clergy, made up of fools and knaves, in power; the laity slaves; the treasury plundered by gangs of tax-farmers and spies; all the business of government consisted in prying into and punishing the notions, the expectations, and the imprudences of the Liberals."*

The result was that, as the Pope's native army was then worthless and even ridiculous, and his foreign mercenaries insufficient in strength, the country was always either actually or virtually occupied by Austrian forces: virtually when not actually, because at those periods when the force had been withdrawn, it was ready, on the first signal of popular movement and Papal distress, to return. So we pass over the interval until the accession of Pius IX., and until the month of July, 1849. Then the Government of France, acting as we believe without the sanction of the public judgment, and in order to reward for the past and purchase for the future the electoral support of the Ultramontane party, assumed the succession to Austria in the discharge of her odious office of repression, and thus left it doubtful to the last whether her splendid services to Italy in 1859 were or were not outweighed by the cruel wrong done for so many years in the violent occupation of Rome. That office has long ago been finally and in good faith renounced by Austria, now the friend of Italy. Let us hope, for the sake of the peace of Europe, that it will never again be assumed by any other Power. It was, however, only the war of 1870 which caused the removal of the French force from Civita Vecchia. That seaport had been re-occupied shortly after the relinquishment of Rome in 1869. In July, 1870, the remonstrances of the Papal Government were met by a neat and telling reply

---

* Farini, 'Hist. of Rome,' Bk. i. chap. i., English translation, vol. i. p. 17.

from France. "The fortunes of the war will be favourable, or they will be adverse. If the former, we can then protect you better than ever; if the latter, we must surely have our men to protect ourselves."

Sad then as it is, and scarcely credible as it may appear, that this great officer of religion, who guides a moiety or thereabouts of Christendom, who

"Looks from his throne of clouds o'er half the world," *

is hopelessly implicated in the double error; first, that he makes the restoration of his temporal power a matter of religious duty and necessity; secondly, that he seeks the accomplishment of that bad end through the outrage of a foreign intervention against the people of Rome, and through the breaking up of the great Italian kingdom.

For indeed it is plain enough, that the assaults of the Pope, though especially directed against that portion of Italy which once formed the States of the Church, are by no means confined to such a narrow range. This approved work describes the Italian Royal Family at the epoch of the occupation of Rome, as the Principi di Piemonte (i. 58): and the Pope assures a deputation from Naples that in his daily prayer he remembers the city, its people, its pastor, and its King; meaning the ex-king Francis II. (i. 118). What he prays is that the longed-for peace may be restored to that "kingdom." And in order that we may know what this peace is, another speech at a later date tells us he prays the Lord that that unfortunate kingdom may return to be that which it was formerly, namely, a kingdom of peace and prosperity (ii. 338). This is the language in which the Pope is not ashamed to speak

---

* Campbell's 'Pleasures of Hope.'

of a Government founded upon the most gross and abominable perjury, cruel and base in all its detail to the last degree, and so lost in the estimation of the people, notwithstanding the existence of its powerful army, that Garibaldi was able in a red shirt to traverse the country as a conqueror, enter the capital, and take peaceable possession of the helm of State.

The kingdoms and states of the world are, in Romish estimation, divided into several classes. Let us put Italy alone in the first and lowest, as a State with which the Pope is undisguisedly at war. Next come the States which pursue a policy adverse to the Ultramontane system; after them, in the upward series, those not very numerous States, with which Rome has no quarrels; next those from which it receives active adhesion or support. And at the head of all comes the Pope's own vanished possession, now represented in his imaginary title to the States of the Church. For whereas the others rule by a *jus humanum*, he ruled by a *jus divinum*; and what is mere revolt, or treason, or rapine elsewhere, has in the Roman States the added guilt of sacrilege. And, indeed, as to revolt or rapine the Pope treats them lightly enough. Nothing can be more curious in this respect than his references to Germany. The territory of the German Emperor was made up by acquisitions yet more recent than those which set up the Italian Kingdom, such as it existed before the war of 1870; and by a like process of putting down divers Governments which were in the Roman sense legitimate, and of absorbing their dominions. But the Pope boasts that he had not been at all squeamish on this score (i. 457), for he had announced to Prince Bismarck that the "Catholics" had been in favour of the German Empire. When, however, the policy of that Empire was developed in a sense adverse to the Roman views, very different ideas as to its basis came into vogue; and the Pope's authorized editor denounces it as the embodied Paganism of Prussia, boldly predicts its early fall (ii. 135, comp. 66), and, speaking of the meeting of three great potentates on a recent occasion, calls them the Emperor of Austria, the Emperor of Russia, and "the new one called of Germany" (*il nuovo detto di Germania*); which, by the way, he is not, for his title is, we believe, the German Emperor. In truth it seems that the legitimacy of every Government is measured by the single rule of its propensity to favour the policy of Rome. And while other Governments generally are here and there admonished, even when they are guilty of no sin of commission, as to the neglect of their duty to restore the Pope (i. 113), there is one which receives his warmest commendations. It is the "glorious" Republic of the Equator, which "amidst the complicity, by silence, of the Powers of Europe" sent its poor, feeble bark (we mean its vocal bark, probably it possesses no other) across the Atlantic to proclaim—

"Auditum admissi risum teneatis, amici?"

the principle of the restoration, by foreign arms, of the Papal throne.

In his desire for the realization of this happy dream, the Pope appears to be wound up to a sensitive irritability of expectation, and accordingly prophecy is liberally scattered over the pages of these volumes. Sometimes he does not know when it will be; sometimes it cannot be long; sometimes he sees the very dawning of the happy day. These varying states of view belong, indeed, to the origin of what is called pious opinion, but to believe that the day will come is matter of duty and faith.

"Yes, this change, yes, this triumph, will have to come; and it is matter of faith (*ed è di fede*). I know not if it will come in my lifetime, the lifetime of this poor Vicar of Jesus Christ. I know that come it will. The rising again must take place, this great impiety must end."—ii. 82.

It is with glee that he inculcates the great duty of prayer, when a hopeful sign comes up on the far horizon: though that sign be no more than some notice given in the Chamber of France. On February 18, 1872, he says:

"At the earliest moment, offer prayer and sacrifice to God for another special object. About this time my affairs are to be the subject of discussion in the National Assembly of a great people; and there are those who will take my part. Let us then pray for this Assembly."

And so forth (i. 352).

Taken by itself, a passage of this kind might be perfectly well understood as contemplating nothing beyond the limits of a simply diplomatic, and even amicable intervention. But then the question arises, why, if diplomacy be in contemplation, are compromises and adjustments so passionately denounced? The answer is, that diplomacy is not in contemplation or in desire, but what is now perfectly well known in Europe as "blood and iron." No careful reader of this authoritative book can doubt that these are the means by which the great Christian Pastor contemplates and asks, aye asks as one who thinks himself entitled to command, the re-establishment of his power in Rome. There is indeed a passage, in which he, addressing his ex-policemen! deprecates an armed reaction, and declares the imputation to be a calumny. And so far as the gallantry of those policemen is concerned, according to all that used to be seen or heard of them, he is quite right. The reaction he desires, in this speech, is good education, respect to the Church and the priests. But this is the local reaction, the reaction *in piccolo*. " As to what remains, God will do as He wills: reactions on the great scale (*reazioni in grande*) cannot be in my hands, but are in His, on whom all depends."

He shows, however, elsewhere and habitually, not only a great activity in seconding the designs of Providence in this matter, but a considerable disposition to take the initiative, if only he could. In words alone, it is true; but he has no power other than of words. Let us hear him address his soldiers, on the 27th of December, 1872. (ii. 141.)

" You, soldiers of honour, attached by affection to this Holy See, constant in the discharge of your duties, come before me, but you still come unarmed; thus proving how evil are the times.

" Oh were I but able to conform to that voice of God, which so many ages back cried to a people: 'Turn your spades, turn your ploughshares and your ploughs, turn all your instruments of husbandry into blades and into swords, turn them into weapons of war, for your enemies approach, and for many arms, and many men with arms, will there be need. Would that the Blessed God would to-day in us repeat these very inspirations! But He is silent: and I His Vicar cannot be otherwise, cannot employ any means but silence.'"

Here we should certainly, with these volumes of loud speech before us, desire to interpolate a sceptical note of interrogation. He proceeds, however, to say, it is not for him to give authority for the manufacture of weapons: and that probably the revolution in Italy will destroy itself. But if that be his idea, why the ferocious passage about blades and swords, which has just been presented to the reader, and the many references to forcible restoration in which he delights? It is probable that the Pontiff relents occasionally, and gives scope to his better mind:

but habitually, and as a rule, he looks forward with eagerness to that restoration by foreign arms in the future, which forms to him, as we have seen, so satisfactory a subject of retrospective contemplation for the period from 1849 to 1866, and again from 1867 to 1870.

Many may desire to know, in concluding this examination, what are the utterances of the Pontiff with respect to the burning questions of the Vatican Decrees. It must be at Rome that the fashions are set in regard to infallibility, to obedience, and to the question of the relation between the Roman See and the Civil Power; and the work under review is perfectly unequivocal on this class of subjects, though less copious than in regard to that cardinal object of Papal desire, the restoration of the Temporal Power.

In times of comparative moderation, not yet forty-five years back, when Montalembert and Lamennais dutifully repaired to Rome to seek guidance from Gregory XVI., that Pontiff, in repudiating their projects through his Minister, paid them a compliment for asking orders from " the infallible mouth of the Successor of Peter." We are often told that the Pope cannot be held to speak *ex cathedrâ* unless he addresses the whole body of Christians, whereas in this case he addressed only two. Now to the outer world, who try these matters by the ordinary rules of the human understanding, it seems to be a very grave inconvenience that the possessor of an admitted Infallibility should formally declare himself infallible in cases where he is allowed in his own title-deeds to be only fallible like the rest of us. One chief mark, however, of declarations *ex cathedrâ* is that they are made to all the Faithful; and we observe in the title of these Discourses that they are addressed *Ai Fedeli di Roma e dell' Orbe.*

In the work of Don Pasquale, the term "infallible" is very frequently applied to the Pope by the deputations. A crowd of three thousand persons shouts Viva il Pontefice Infallibile (i. 372, comp. i. 407); a lawyer, speaking for a company of lawyers (ii. 313), reveres "the great Pope, the superlatively great King, the infallible master of his faith, the most loving father of his soul;" and the like strain prevails elsewhere (*e.g.* ii. 160, 165, 177, 190, 256) in these Addresses, which are always received with approval. Whether advisedly or not, the Pontiff does not (except once, i. 204) apply the term to himself; but is in other places content with alleging his superiority (as has been shown above) to an inspired Prophet, and with commending those who come to hear his words as words proceeding from Jesus Christ (i. 335).

On the matter of Obedience he is perfectly unequivocal. To the Armenians, who have recently resisted his absorbing in himself the national privileges of their Church, he explains (ii. 435) that to him, as the Successor of Saint Peter, and to him alone, is committed by Divine right the Pastorate of the entire Church; plainly there is no other real successor of the Apostles, for Bishops, he says, have their dioceses it is true, but only by a title ecclesiastical, not Divine. To limit this power is heresy, and has ever been so. Not less plain is his sense of his supremacy over the powers of the world. His title and place are to be the Supreme Judge of Christendom (i. p. 204). It is not the office of any Government, but the sublime mission of the Roman Pontificate, to assume the defence of the independence of States (ii. 498); and so far from granting to nations and races any power over the Church, God enjoined upon them the duty of believing, and gave them over to be taught by the Apostles (ii. 452).

Finally, as respects the Syllabus and its mischievous contents, that document is not only upheld, but upheld as the great or only hope of Christian Society. We hear (i. 444) of the advantage secured by the publication of the Syllabus. The Chair of Peter has been teaching, enlightening, and governing, from the foundation of the Church down to the Syllabus and the Decrees of the Vatican (ii. 427, *bis*). The two are manifestly placed on a level. And, grieved as is the Pontiff at the present perversion of mankind, and especially of the young, he is also convinced that the world must come to embrace the Syllabus, which is the only anchor of its salvation (*l'unica ancora di salute*," i. 58-9).

One of the main objects of the Syllabus is to re-establish in the mass all the most extravagant claims which have at any time been lodged by the Church of Rome against the Christian State. Hardly any greater outrage on society, in our judgment, has ever been committed than by Pope Pius IX. in certain declarations (i. 193, and elsewhere) respecting persons married civilly without the Sacrament. For, in condemning them as guilty of concubinage, he releases them from the reciprocal obligations of man and wife. But of all those which we have described as the burning questions, the most familiar to Englishmen is, perhaps, that of the Deposing Power; which, half a century ago, we were assured was dead and buried, and long past the possibility of exhumation or revival. It shall now supply us with our last illustration; for true as is that with reference to the possibilities of life and action, it remains the shadow of a shade; yet we have lived into a time when it is deliberately taught by the

Ultramontane party generally, and not, so far as we know, disavowed by any of them.

Lord Robert Montagu, who was in the last Parliament the High Church and Tory Member for the orthodox county of Huntingdon, and is in this Parliament transformed into an ardent neophyte and champion of the Papal Church, in a recent Lecture before the Catholic Union of Ireland,* took occasion, among other extravagances, to set forth with all honour a passage from a Speech of the Pope, delivered on the 21st of July, 1871, in which he justified and explained the doctrine of the Deposing Power. According to the version he gave of the Italian Discourse, this Power was an "authority, in accordance with public right, which was then vigorous, and with the acquiescence of all Christian nations."

In the 'Tablet' newspaper of November 21 and December 5, 1874, a writer, who signs himself C. S. D., assails Lord Robert Montagu for erroneous translation; and, with undeniable justice, points out that the words, *secondo il diritto pubblico allora vigente*, do not mean " in accordance with public right, which was then vigorous," but " in accordance with the public law " (or right) " then in force." He also quotes words not quoted by Lord Robert, to show that the Popes exercised this power at the call of the Christian nations (*chiamati dal voto dei popoli*); which, as he truly says, give a very different colour to the passage. His citation is, he states, from the *Voce della Verità* of 22nd July, 1871, the day following the Speech, confirmed by the *Civiltà Cattolica* of August 19.

Amidst these grave discrepancies of high authorities,

---

* Dublin: M'Glashan and Gill, 1874, p. 10.

our readers may desire to know what a still higher authority, the Pope himself, really did say; and we have, happily, the means of informing them from the volumes before us, which contain the "sole authentic" report. The Speech was delivered, not on the 21st, but the 20th of July, and will be found at vol. i. p. 203. We need not trouble the reader with a lengthened citation. The passage, as quoted by Lord Robert Montagu, will be found in Mr. Gladstone's " Vatican Decrees," p. 19. The essential point is that, according to C. S. D., the Pope justified the Deposing Power on this specific ground, that they were called to exercise it by the desire, or voice, or demand, of the nations. What will our readers say when we acquaint them that the passage given by C. S. D. in the 'Tablet' is before our eyes as we write, and that the words " called by the voice of the people " (*chiamata dal voto dei popoli*) *are not in it?* Whether they were spoken or not is another question, which we cannot decide. What is material is that, from the fixed, deliberate, and only authentic report, they have been excluded, and that the Pope himself sustains, and therefore claims, the Deposing Power, not on the ground of any demand of the public opinion of the day, but as attaching to his office.

And now, in bidding farewell to Don Pasquale, we offer him our best thanks for his two volumes. Probably this acknowledgment may never meet his eyes. But lest, in the case of its reaching him, it should cause him surprise and self-reproach that he should have extorted praise from England and from Albemarle Street, we will give him " the reason why." We had already and often seen Infallibility in full-dress, in peacock's plumes; Infallibility fenced about with well-set lines of theological phrases, impenetrable by us, the multitude, the uninitiated. But

Don Pasquale has taken us behind the scenes. He has shown us Infallibility in the closet, Infallibility in dishabille, Infallibility able to cut its capers at will, to indulge in its wildest romps with freedom and impunity. And surely we have now made good the assurance with which we began. If ever there was a spectacle, strange beyond all former experience, and charged with many-sided instruction for mankind, here it is. We will conclude by giving our own estimate, in few words, of the central figure and of his situation.

In other days, the days of the great Pontiffs who formidably compete in historic grandeur with Barbarossa, and even with Charlemagne, the tremendous power which they claimed, and which they often contrived to exercise, was weighted with a not less grave and telling responsibility. The bold initiative of Gregories and Alexanders, of Innocents and Bonifaces, hardly indeed could devise bigger and braver words than now issue from the Vatican:

> "Quæ tuto tibi magna volant, dum distinct hostem
> Agger murorum, nec inundant sanguine fossæ." *

But their decisions and announcements did not operate as now through agencies mainly silent, underground, clandestine; the agencies, for example, of affiliated monastic societies, the agency of the consummate scheme of Loyola, the agency, above all, of that baneful system of universal Direction, which unlocks the door of every household, and inserts an opaque sacerdotal medium between the several members of the family, as well as between the several orders of the State. Their warfare was the warfare of a man with men. It recalls those grand words of King David, "Died Abner as a fool

---

* Æn. xi. 382.

dieth? Thy hands were not bound nor thy feet put into fetters: as a man falleth before wicked men, so fellest thou" (2 Sam. iii. 33). When they committed outrage or excess, at least they were liable to suffer for it in a fashion very different from the "Calvary" of Pope Pius IX. They had at their very gates the Barons of Rome, who then, at least, were barons indeed; and the tramp of the mailed hosts of the Hohenstaufens was ever in their ears. But now, when the Pope knows that his income is secured by a heavy mortgage upon the credulity of millions· upon millions, to say nothing of the offers of the Italian Government in reserve, and that his outward conditions of existence are as safe and easy as those of any well-to-do or luxurious gentleman in Paris or in London, his denunciations, apart from all personal responsibility for consequences, lose their dignity in losing much of their manhood and all their danger, and the thunders of the Vatican, though by no means powerless for mischief with a portion of mankind, yet in the generality can neither inspire apprehension nor command respect.

Let us revert for a moment to the month of June, 1846.

A provincial Prelate, of a regular and simple life, endowed with devotional susceptibilities, wholly above the love of money, and with a genial and tender side to his nature, but without any depth of learning, without wide information or experience of the world, without original and masculine vigour of mind, without political insight, without the stern discipline that chastens human vanity, and without mastery over an inflammable temper, is placed, contrary to the general expectation, on the pinnacle, and it is still a lofty pinnacle, of ecclesiastical power. It is but fair towards him to admit, that his predecessors had bequeathed to him a temporal polity as rotten and effete in all its parts as the wide world could show. At the outset of his Pontificate, he attempted to turn popular emotion, and the principles of freedom, to account in the interests of Church power. As to ecclesiastical affairs, he dropped at once into the traditions of the *Curia*. He was and is surrounded by flatterers, who adroitly teach him to speak their words in telling him that he speaks his own, and that they are the most wonderful words ever spoken by man. Having essayed the method of governing by Liberal ideas and promises, and having, by a sad incompetency to control the chargers he had harnessed to his car, become (to say the least) one of the main causes of the European convulsions of 1848, he rushed from the North Pole of politics to the South, and grew to be the partisan of Legitimacy, the champion of the most corrupt and perjured Sovereignties of Italy, that is to say of the whole world. Had he only had the monitions of a free press and of free opinion, valuable to us all, but to Sovereigns absolutely priceless, and the indispensable condition of all their truly useful knowledge, it might have given him a chance; but these he denounces as impiety and madness. As the age grows on one side enlightened, and on another sceptical, he encounters the scepticism with denunciation, and the enlightenment with retrogression. As he rises higher and higher into the regions of transcendental obscurantism, he departs by wider and wider spaces from the living intellect of man; he loses Province after Province, he quarrels with Government after Government, he generates Schism after Schism; and the crowning achievement of the Vatican Council and its decrees is followed, in the mysterious counsels of Providence, by the passing over, for the first time in history, of his temporal dominions to an orderly and national Italian kingdom, and of a German Imperial Crown to the head of a Lutheran King, who is the summit and centre of Continental Protestantism.*

But what then? His clergy are more and more an army, a police, a caste; farther and farther from the Christian Commons, but nearer to one another, and in closer subservience to him. And they have made him "The Infallible;" and they have promised he shall be made "The Great." And, as if to complete the irony of the situation, the owners, or the heirs, of a handful of English titles, formerly unreclaimed, are now enrolled upon the list of his most orthodox, most obsequious followers; although the mass of the British nation repudiates him more eagerly and resolutely than it has done for many generations.

Such is this great, sad, world-historic picture. Sometimes it will happen that, in a great emporium of Art, a shrewd buyer, after hearing the glowing panegyric of a veteran dealer upon some flaming and pretentious product of the brush, will reply, Yes, no doubt, all very true; but it is not a good picture to live with. So with regard to that sketch from the halls of the Vatican, which we have endeavoured faithfully to present, we ask the reader in conclusion, or ask him to ask himself, *Is it a good picture to live with?*

---

* See the remarkable Tract of Franz von Löher: Ueber Deutschlands Weltstellung. München, 1874.

www.ingramcontent.com/pod-product-compliance
Lightning Source LLC
Chambersburg PA
CBHW031953230426
43672CB00010B/2142